Spectrum Guides

African Wildlife Safaris

Kenya Uganda Tanzania

Ethiopia Somalia Malawi Zambia

Rwanda Burundi

Facts On File

New York • Oxford

Spectrum Guides: African Wildlife Safaris

© Camerapix 1989

First published 1989 by
Facts On File, Inc
460 Park Avenue South
New York, NY 10016
USA

Library of Congress
Catalog Card Number 89-35010.
CIP data available on request from the
publisher

ISBN 0-8160-2125-2

This book was designed and produced by
Camerapix Publishers International
P. O. Box 45048,
Nairobi, Kenya

Design: Craig Dodd
Typeset by Hourds Graphic Communication
Ltd. Stoke-on-Trent, England

Printed and Bound in Hong Kong.

EDITORIAL BOARD

Spectrum Guide: African Wildlife, the first of a new series of international *Spectrum Guides* to countries, cultures, flora, and fauna, is the inspiration of **Mohamed Amin** internationally known cameraman, film-maker, and publisher. Together with his Camerapix team, he and **Duncan Willetts** took most of the photographs in it, and, drawing on his wide experience in book production, supervised all aspects of its publication.

The principal editor is **Ian Parker,** an author in his own right. In addition, he has worked in the field of African wildlife for thirty-four years in fourteen countries.

Kenyan **Brian Tetley,** *Spectrum Guides* editorial director, who has written many books and has more than thirty-eight years editorial experience in Europe and Africa, was responsible for editorial production.

Maintaining *Spectrum Guides* in-house style and copy editing was the responsibility of **Barbara Lawrence,** an American freelance editor based in Kenya with wide experience in television production and book publishing.

Design was by London-based **Craig Dodd,** one of Europe's leading graphic designers.

But the credit for the writing and deciding the chapter structure rests largely with Parker, who was ably assisted by one of the most knowledgeable wildlife panels ever to work together on a single project. Each of its members is a leading authority on some aspect of Eastern Africa's natural history — perhaps the most varied, important, and spectacular on earth.

Dr Perez Olindo, Director of Kenya's Wildlife Conservation and Management Department, has more than a quarter of a century's experience in the region's conservation methods and problems.

'Chum' Van Someren, a naturalist of international standing, trained and worked as an entomologist. Reaching normal retirement age, he joined Kenya's National Museum as staff ornithologist. Having retired for the second time, he retains the post of Ornithologist Emeritus at the museum.

John Karmali, a pharmacist by training, has long been internationally recognized as a bird photographer of rare skill, and has been a prominent member of the East African Natural History Society as well as its Chairman.

Alex Mackay, Staff Herpetologist at the National Museum in Nairobi, is a leading authority on eastern Africa's reptiles, amphibians, and fish.

Dr Jesse Hillman, Wildlife Adviser to the Ethiopian Government Wildlife Conservation Organization, has also worked for the New York Zoological Society and as a consultant for an ecological firm in Kenya, Tanzania, and Sudan.

Sheila Hillman, a nurse and midwife, now shares her husband's work in Ethiopia — doing much of the botanical work — and also is involved in education and publicity for Ethiopian Wildlife.

Ato Abdu Mahamued, head of the Utilization and Anti-poaching Section of the Ethiopian Government Wildlife Conservation Organization, has been with the EWCO since 1977. After developing an early interest in ornithology, he also worked as a field ecologist in Gambella and the Deddessa Valley of Illubabor.

Dr Anne Spoerry, a flying doctor and member of the African Medical Research Foundation (AMREF), has practised medicine in Kenya for the past thirty-eight years. Flying her own aircraft to remote areas to help people in need, she is singularly well qualified to advise on medical problems that may occur on safari.

Doreen McColaugh, with degrees in animal sciences, bi-cultural education, and linguistics, enjoyed a teaching career in the United States, Guatemala, Mexico, and Costa Rica before moving to Kenya in 1984. She joined the African Wildlife Foundation in 1985.

Opposite: Flute-mouth or trumpet fish surrounded by cardinal fish and a citron

TABLE OF CONTENTS

Overleaf: Largest of the world's land mammals, the African elephant, weighing up to six tonnes and consuming 250 kilos of fodder a day, is a relatively new species in evolutionary terms. It occupies as wide a range of habitats as its great competitor — man. Following pages: Millions of wildebeest on the annual migration through the Serengeti-Maasai Mara grasslands. Pages 14-15: Giraffe, the world's tallest land animal, has to have a complex system of valves, reservoirs, and canals in its neck veins and arteries to maintain a constant blood pressure in the brain, ensuring balance when running or bending.

PART ONE: THE LAND AND THE BACKGROUND

Above: Sinister and superbly efficient, cold blooded Nile crocodile regulate their body heat by alternately basking and bathing.

Opposite: African sundown frames an Acacia thorn tree.

INTRODUCTION

Wildlife and big game have been synonymous with Eastern Africa since the last decade of the nineteenth century when Europeans entered the region for the first time and were stunned by the variety of wild animals they saw. Returning home to tell and write of what they had seen, it was not long before hunters and naturalists flocked to witness the spectacle for themselves. Many were famous, none more so than Theodore Roosevelt, ex-President of the United States of America.

Later Ernest Hemingway eulogized the region, its big game, and those who made their living conducting sportsmen on hunting safaris. He added immensely to the growing romantic mythology that enveloped the intrepid 'white hunters'. Hollywood spread the myths further. The early wildlife film-makers — Osa and Martin Johnson — publicized Eastern Africa, the region and its animals. By the dawn of the television era it was so well known that photographers turned to it in ever greater numbers for film material. Through the likes of Armand and Michaela Denis, Alan Root, and Simon Trevor, Eastern Africa's savannahs became well-known in living rooms across the world. And the advent of the jet age allowed tourists in their thousands to see the wildlife for themselves, setting the seal on a trend that has grown without let through the century.

There may be wildlife populations elsewhere every bit as spectacular as those in Eastern Africa. The numbers of penguin, seal, and whale in the Antarctic may exceed anything that Eastern Africa has to offer. And, no doubt, the caribou, musk-ox, seal, walrus, and whale ecosystems of northern Canada are equally spectacular. So, too, may the white-eared kob and associated ungulates of the southern Sudan outnumber the Serengeti wildebeest and perform equally impressive mass migrations. Yet all this wildlife is inaccessible and difficult to see. In contrast, it is Eastern Africa's accessibility that has made it so well known. Only a few hours by jet from Europe and North America, its wildlife is instantly on display.

India may boast an impressive faunal array, but it is made up primarily of jungle animals, species of thicket and deep forest that demand time and patience to see.

Eastern Africa is predominantly open savannah. Animals and birds are easily seen from distances which threaten neither watcher nor watched. As natural stages, the open highland plains of Maasailand are unrivalled theatres of the wild. And, although in the tropics, much of Eastern Africa has a temperate, comfortable climate and spectacular scenery.

Indeed, its wildlife is probably better known to the average European or North American than their own native fauna. And, more than any other, it has played a profound role in stimulating public consciousness about conservation and environmental care. If, in retrospect, the twentieth century comes to be known as the century of conservation, history must concede that of all the planet's wild communities, Eastern Africa's played the greater role in drawing man's attention to his place in nature.

What follows is a general description of Eastern Africa's wildlife, notes on evolution and conservation, profiles of the more prominent species' natural history, and advice on where to go to see animals, birds, reptiles, fish, and insects of particular interest.

There is also information on the national park systems and the services visitors can expect, together with general travel information. Aimed at professional guide and visitor alike, it is intended to help all those who wish to enjoy the region's magnificent wildlife to the full.

Although mention of African wildlife normally conjures up visions of grasslands teeming with large mammals — the big game of Africa — there are also a great many animals not so readily seen. Such diversity makes zoology a complex science. Animal life is classified into groups of related types in a basic system:

* Living animals and plants are divided into *Classes*.
* A class is a group of related *Orders*.
* An order is a group of related *Families*.
* A family is a group of related *Genera* (singular = *Genus*)
* A genus is a group of related *Species*.

Overleaf: Sable, one of the largest African antelope, can be found in the great belt of deciduous woodland that spans Africa south of the Equator from the Atlantic to the Indian Ocean.

Above: Lioness return to feed on buffalo kill as vultures wait for pickings.

---

* A species may have several *subspecies* or *races*.

To illustrate the arrangement: all mammals, birds, reptiles, and fish are classes of animal whose distinctions are readily apparent. Within each class there are equally obvious distinctions.

Although ducks and birds of prey are clearly birds, they are extremely different. So they are placed in different orders within the class of birds. And within the birds of prey order there are different families.

Similarly, within each family there are clear distinctions: a golden eagle is starkly different in appearance and behaviour to a goshawk; this is recognized by placing them in different genera. And, within the genus eagle, there are a number of distinctive types, each classified as a species.

Generally, but not always, species do not interbreed, still less can members of different genera breed amongst themselves. Only at the subspecific level can two groups breed with one another.

The best indication of the richness and diversity of wildlife within any area is the number of families, genera, and species it contains.

Specifically, this book covers the fauna of Eastern Africa, nine countries in all: Burundi, Ethiopia, Kenya, Malawi, Rwanda, Somalia, Tanzania, Uganda, and Zambia.

Chapter 1 Why Eastern Africa is so Rich

Eastern Africa contains more than 415 mammal species ranging from the tiny pigmy mouse, *Mus minutoides*, to the world's largest land mammal — the African elephant. It also contains at least 130 species of snakes — of which the majority are harmless but some are not — among them three deadly mambas, 168 lizards and crocodiles, 163 frogs and toads, over one thousand freshwater fish, and equally numerous marine species.

There are nearly 1,500 bird species — from the tiny fire finches, whose bodies are smaller than the top joint of an adult thumb, to the world's largest bird, the African ostrich, which is substantially heavier than man.

And the very large range of vertebrate animals are then dwarfed by the tens of thousands of invertebrates so far recorded in Eastern Africa, a figure certain to be increased as research continues to discover more insect species.

Added to this vast wealth of animal life is an abundance of plants and fungi at least as great again. So many indeed, that they are beyond the scope of this book.

The roots of this wild richness lie in Eastern Africa's geological history. Africa's shape is well enough known to most from school days. It has the profile of a weeping woman facing east: the great West African bulge into the Atlantic is the hair, caught up in a large bun; the Horn of Africa, a quiff of hair that runs down the brow; the nose is the bulge in the coastline of southern Tanzania; and the mouth the Zambezi. Lake Victoria is the eye and Lakes Tanganyika and Malawi the tears that cascade down the face. Despite such flights of fancy, the schoolroom impression of Africa is that of something static.

Yet geologically the continent is highly mobile. Connected only by a narrow desert land bridge at Sinai, it is isolated from the greater land mass of Eurasia. Long, long ago, it was part of a single continent, Gondwanaland, that included southern Asia, Australasia, Africa, and South America.

This broke into many parts, each drifting away from the other, a process that continues. A brief look at any world atlas shows how South America once nestled into Africa's Bight of Biafra. Western Madagascar's shoreline fits neatly into the Mozambique coast. And Arabia's southernmost toe is clearly part of the Ethiopian highlands from which it has come adrift. No single feature shows more clearly than this how Africa is drifting away from Eurasia.

The Great Rift Valley, a vast crack splitting not only Africa from Eurasia but also the Horn of Africa from the continental mainland, is part of this movement. In time, Eastern Africa will form a gigantic island, bigger than Madagascar. The Red Sea represents an advanced stage of this division: it has put a deep saltwater trench between Africa and Arabia, widening by twice an average man's height in an average lifetime of seventy years. This breakup, and the drifting and rifting that followed, explain why many of Africa's faunal and floral components are shared with other continents.

Today it is difficult to think that arid, desert Arabia ever offered much of a route for animals to move between Asia and Africa. But its present, inhospitable, face is new.

In the relatively recent past it was not nearly so hostile. Even after the Red Sea had started to fill with water, the ice ages so lowered the world's sea levels that crossings were far easier than now. Consequently many African animals have Eurasian origins (and the reverse, of course, is true: current theory being that the most significant migrant out of Africa was man himself).

If one root of Eastern Africa's faunal variety lies in that past connection between Africa and the Eurasian land mass, another lies in geological events within Africa itself. Before

Overleaf: Elephant herd feeds on a seasonal flood plain. Following pages: Nowhere is the faulting, downwarping, and uplifting that has produced Africa's rugged scenery more apparent than in the Great Rift Valley. Pages 28-29: In Tanzania's Ngorongoro Crater, a mixture of forested hills, soda lakes, and grass plains forms a wealth of habitats. Pages 30-31: Mount Kenya's shrinking glaciers — a fraction of the size they were in 1900 — indicate the advent of a new dry age in Africa.

Above: Familiar and well-loved, the fish eagle's wild, yelping call is the clichéd sound of Africa.

the Pliocene ten million years ago, Africa was relatively low-lying and flat. Indeed, its landscapes must have been rather boring. In the late Miocene this began to change, and the process, which accelerated through the Pliocene and Pleistocene, continues.

Under the elemental forces of continental drift and tectonic movement, great slabs have been hefted upward into highland plateaux. Volcanoes have burst through the crust's weak spots to form mountains. Fresh, fertile volcanic soils have been laid over an old and weary land.

Nowhere is this more pronounced than in Eastern Africa, where the Rift Valley rent the region from north to south. The outcome is a richness and variety of landscapes, interspersed with plateaux of different levels — the old infertile land cheek by jowl with the new productive soils, snow-capped volcanoes juxtaposed to lowland flats, and deep basins that filled to form extensive inland seas.

Thus Eastern Africa has low-lying, sedi-mentary plains composing most of the Horn of Africa (Somalia) and a narrow band along the Indian Ocean coast (coastal Kenya and Tanzania); volcanic plateaux and soaring mountains (Ethiopia, central Kenya, and northern Tanzania) among which are the continent's two highest points, Kilimanjaro and Mount Kenya; fertile, gently drained tablelands (most of Uganda) and, in the south and south-west, extensive examples of Africa's older landscapes (southern Tanzania and Zambia). Though their leached, infertile soils with granite extrusions may be rich in minerals such as copper and gold, they are poor in sustaining life.

This great physical diversity, Eastern Africa's varied topography and geological chemistry, creates a corresponding variety in habitats. Together with Africa's past connections with Eurasia, they form the foundations for the region's great array of wildlife.

Chapter 2 The Climate Past and Present

If geology and topography are the foundations of Eastern Africa's many habitats, climate determines their form. Though soils may limit what plants grow in any particular area, rainfall and temperatures exert far more influence over the vegetation that does occur. And vegetation is the most important factor in determining where specific animals live.

Lying astride the Equator, Eastern Africa covers the area between latitudes 18° north and south. In view of this, certainly between latitudes 10° north and south, it would be reasonable to expect a humid, tropical climate similar to that of West Africa, South America's Amazon basin, or Malaysia and Indonesia.

The prevailing north-east and south-east monsoon winds blow moisture off the Indian Ocean. But surprisingly the climate is neither humid nor particularly hot. Though there are some very hot places — notably Ethiopia's Red Sea coastal plain and its Danakil Depression, where the Rift Valley debouches into the Red Sea; northern Somalia, and parts of northern Kenya — climates overall are temperate.

Two primary and interacting reasons cause this. The conditions that produce Eastern Africa's rain occur in the zone of low pressure where the northeasterly and southeasterly winds converge: the Tropical Trough or Inter-Tropical Convergence Zone. This follows the sun's annual movements north and south across the Equator between the tropics of Cancer and Capricorn.

Thus when the Tropical Trough sits over them in the northern hemisphere's summer, Ethiopia and northern Somalia receive their annual rain. Conversely, Zambia, Malawi, and southern Tanzania get their rain in the southern summer. And the countries astride or close to the Equator — Uganda, Kenya, southern Somalia, and northern Tanzania — receive two rains each year, the first corresponding to the northern spring as the Trough follows the sun northward, the second in the southern spring as the sun comes south again. In part, these pronounced seasons are responsible for the generally lower than expected humidity.

The second powerful influence upon climate is altitude. Much of Eastern Africa is well above sea level: the higher the land, the cooler and drier the air — despite what might be expected from both latitudes and prevailing winds. Of course, there are many variations. Where mountains and high plateaux force prevailing winds upward into cooler levels, they milk the air of moisture creating heavy rainfall on their windward slopes. But, as elsewhere, the lee of these uplands is invariably drier.

Lake Victoria is a climatic anomaly. Regardless of where the Tropical Trough may be, this huge inland sea creates its own climate, and the lands for 100 kilometres downwind receive rain most days of the year.

Temperatures also influence evaporation — the hotter the atmosphere, the greater its capacity to absorb moisture and vice versa. Where rainfall may be too little to sustain forest at sea level, it may do so at, say, 1,500 metres (5,000 feet). But since plants vary in their temperature needs, those suited to hot lowlands may not cope with cool uplands.

Above: Afro-Alpine "everlasting" flowers, characteristic of Mount Elgon's high, misty, heaths.

Above: Great flock of pelicans gather for a rich harvest of fish in an Eastern Africa lake.

So while forests occur in Eastern Africa at all altitudes up to 3,000 metres (10,000 feet) above sea level, providing there is adequate rainfall, they show marked altitude differences. Generally the higher the altitude, the fewer the plant species. Above 3,000 metres trees are rare. Beyond this level Eastern Africa's mountains are clothed in Afro-Alpine vegetation: coarse tussocky grasses with giant, tree-sized heather, giant lobelias, and giant groundsels — all plants specialized for extreme cold.

Any shift in rainfall, or temperature, changes the relationship between altitude and plant communities. If the average temperature dropped as little as two degrees Celsius, the upper limit of the montane tree lines would drop. So, too, would the lower levels, and there would be an overall spread of the montane forests. If average rainfall increased generally there would be a similar spread of forests — and in both cases the converse would also hold true.

In the past million or so years there have been several climatic changes — the most recent was the last Ice Age 20,000 years ago.

Responding to these climatic shifts, Africa's forests and savannahs have waxed and waned at one another's expense. Not so long ago, West African lowland forests extended right across the continent to the eastern seaboard, bringing with them their plants and animals, and in many places married up with the montane forests.

Later, when conditions changed and the forests retreated, some plant and animal species remained behind, adapting themselves to the montane forests. At other times the arid zones expanded, so much so that at one time the flora and fauna of the Horn of Africa and the Kalahari met. Just like the forests, they introduced new species that were left behind in pockets of low rainfall when wetter conditions returned.

If Eastern Africa's landscapes had been uniform, animals would have come and gone as their habitats responded to climatic change. But the broken and infinitely varied topography produced a wealth of climatic niches and isolated opportunities for small communities to remain; yet another reason for the region's great faunal richness.

Chapter 3 Terrestrial Habitats

Eastern Africa, including Ethiopia, Somalia, Uganda, Kenya, Rwanda, Burundi, Tanzania, Zanzibar, Zambia, and Malawi, is bounded in the north and east by the Red Sea and the Indian Ocean. Its western border is marked by the scarps of the Ethiopian massif, the western arm of the Rift Valley, and lakes Mobutu, Edward, Kivu, and Tanganyika. The valley and the lakes are reinforced by the Ruwenzoris — the 'Mountains of the Moon' — the Virunga volcano chain, and Tanzania's Makari and Mbizi mountains. In the south the Zambezi River, the eastern shore of Lake Malawi, and the Rovuma River form boundaries.

Though these physical features serve as demarcators, ecologically they are incomplete. Between Lake Mobutu and the Ethiopian highlands no barrier separates Eastern Africa from the vast Sudanic flatlands that extend into West Africa. And, in the south-west, there is no distinct physical or zoological break between Zambia, Zaire, or Angola.

Biologists once looked for stable habitats in Africa. They believed that every area had a 'climax' habitat — the mythical point where nature 'balanced'. But it has become more and more apparent that no such condition exists, except in a few extremes — such as the Afro-Alpine zones or swamp forests. Now the evidence is towards constant and considerable ecological change.

In Uganda, open grasslands protected from elephants changed to closed canopy forest in eight years. Similarly dense *Terminalia* woods, which in 1933 appeared to have been 'stable' for a considerable time, have been engulfed by an expanding Budongo rain forest. There are many such instances. Grasslands have become savannahs, savannahs have become bushland and vice versa, and forests have retreated to become savannah.

Change was — and still is — a constant feature in the evolution of African ecosystems.

Given Eastern Africa's geological and climatic diversity, with change so persistent it is

Above: Bushbuck, animals of forest and thicket, are the smallest of the tragelaphine or spiral-horned antelope. In some races males go black with age.

Above: Gerenuk, giraffe-necked gazelle, feeding on Acacia leaves in the dry, scrubby country typical of the Horn of Africa.
Opposite: Giant groundsel, typical plants of Eastern Africa's cold, high-altitude moorlands and heaths above 3,300 metres.

best to describe habitats in general terms only. There are thirteen major categories, with their wildlife distributions described later.

Lowland Rain Forest:

Lowland rain forests require year-round rainfall of at least 1,100 millimetres (45 inches) and occur up to no more than 1,200 metres (4,000 feet) above sea level. In Eastern Africa they occur only on the south-western slopes of the Ethiopian massif, in western Uganda (Budongo, Bugoma, Bwamba, Kabale, Kigezi, and Maramagambo are examples), western Kenya (Kakamega and Kaimosi), as traces along the Kenya-Tanzania coastline, and on the lower eastern slopes of the Usambara Mountains. They form less than one per cent of the region's habitats.

These rain forests have canopies up to sixty metres (200 feet) high, sometimes with secondary and tertiary canopies at the middle and lower levels. Botanically they are the richest habitats; in its 500 or so square kilometres (200 square miles), Uganda's Budongo Forest, for example, contains more than 2,000 plant species.

Lowland Dry Forest:

These are rare forests that occur below 1,200 metres and receive as little as 760 millimetres (thirty inches) of rain annually. The most striking example is the Arabuko-Sokoke forest on the Kenya coast, where trees grow no more than twenty metres (sixty-six feet) in height. Most are considerably smaller.

Swamp Forests:

Swamp forests form a tiny but distinct lowland habitat. Perhaps the largest in Eastern Africa is Sango Bay on the western shore of Lake Victoria. Plants are adapted to having their 'feet' in water. Among these, the most characteristic are the two palms — *Phoenix reclinata* and *Raphia*. Found in many 'gallery' forests — narrow ribbons along river banks — in otherwise unforested country, these draw moisture from the rivers instead of relying upon rainfall.

Montane Forests:

All forests between the 1,200-metre contour and the tree line at 3,000 metres (10,000 feet) are montane in nature. With cooler temperatures and lower evaporation rates, forests exist on rainfall as little as 635 millimetres (twenty-five inches) a year, with long dry spells between. Such 'dry' montane forest occurs near Nairobi, Kenya.

Montane forests show great variety. Those in wet regions are richer in species. And, generally, the higher the forest, the fewer the species. In a few places (the western slopes of the Ethiopian massif, Kabale, Kalinzu-Maramagambo and Kigezi in Uganda, eastern Usambaras in Tanzania) the lowland rain forests merge with montane forests into an unbroken swathe — a feature likely to have once been far more widespread.

More widely distributed in the past, today Eastern Africa's montane forests are overwhelmingly associated with mountains, a result of human settlement. People prefer lower, warmer levels and settle the flatlands and plateaux in preference to high ground and steep slopes.

Montane forests are characteristic of all the larger mountains (Virunga, Elgon, Kenya, Kilimanjaro, Marsabit, Gelai, Oldeani, Meru, Hanang, Rungwe, Cherangani, Mau, Aberdare, Loita, Crater Highland, Pare, Usambara, Nguru, Rubeho, Uluguru, Poroto, Livingstone, Makari, Mbizi, and Ruwenzoris). The largest in Eastern Africa, in the southern highlands of Ethiopia, cover several thousand square kilometres. Relict tufts of forest occur on many lesser hills. But overall they form under two per cent of the total.

Bamboo Zones:

In the higher montane forests, at altitudes dominated by *Podocarpus* or cedar (*Juniperus procera*), extensive alpine bamboo is common up to the edge of the tree line at 3,000 metres. Though technically a grass, bamboo has the physical properties of forest, growing nine metres (thirty feet) high — although individual plants only live for some twenty-five to thirty years before flowering and dying. Bamboo therefore is characterized by patches at different stages of the cycle.

On the western slopes of the Ethiopian massif, outside the montane forests, a smaller species of bamboo behaves in similar manner.

Heath Zones:

Above the tree line, between 3,000 metres (10,000 feet) and 3,500 metres (11,500 feet), Eastern Africa's mountains support giant heath vegetation. Characteristic is heather and *Philippia* up to five metres (sixteen feet) high. Drawing moisture from mists and clouds, even where rainfall is limited it is a sodden habitat and, being cold, loses little to evaporation. Both heather and *Philippia* are festooned with 'old man's beard' and other lichens.

Afro-Alpine Moorland:

Between the heath and the snow line at around 5,000 metres (16,000 feet) lie the most unusual habitats. Tropical in location only, they are in many ways reminiscent of the sub-Arctic tundra. They are subject to the same intense cold at night, but differ from the Arctic in their daytime exposure to intense sunshine.

The most extensive Afro-Alpine zone is found in the Bale Mountains of Ethiopia: more than 1,000 square kilometres (380 square miles) above the 3,700-metre (12,000-foot) mark. Farther north, in Ethiopia's Simien Mountains, there is also a good example of Afro-Alpine moorland.

Three other mountains, all of which have permanent ice-caps and glaciers, share this habitat in full: the Ruwenzoris, Kenya, and Kilimanjaro. A fourth mountain — Elgon, just over 4,200 metres (14,000 feet) high — on the Kenya-Uganda border has most components, but is a shade too low to have other than occasional snow.

The vegetation in these Afro-Alpine habitats is generally wet, tussocky grassland interspersed with curious giant senecios, lobelias, and groundsels.

Opposite: Chimpanzee in Tanzanian forest. Forests hold more species than almost any other habitat on land, but in Africa they are shrinking at between two and six per cent a year.

Overleaf: Impala grazing in scenery characteristic of the highland Maasai plains of southern Kenya and northern Tanzania. Following pages: Zebra flee in dusty panic against the backdrop of majestic Kilimanjaro, Africa's highest mountain.

Woodlands:

Woodland lacks an interlocking, closed canopy. Trees are sufficiently open for grasses and other sun-loving plants to grow beneath. By far the largest woodlands in Eastern Africa are in the 'miombo', *Brachystegia,* belt of southern Tanzania, Zambia, and parts of western Malawi. These grow on the infertile soils of old Africa that existed before the rifting and vulcanism that created much of the region's relatively high fertility and spectacularly varied scenery. Most trees are deciduous and shed their leaves during the long six-month dry season.

This 'miombo' belt is in Eastern Africa's southern, single rainy season zone. In its counterpart in similar latitudes north of the Equator *Isoberlinia* replaces *Brachystegia,* in a band extending right across sub-Saharan Africa, just touching north-west Uganda, west of the Nile.

Less extensive woodlands occur widely. Woodland dominated by *Terminalia* occurs on some of the lower slopes of the western Ethiopian massif and in parts of Uganda. Elsewhere in Eastern Africa there are woodland pockets with a variety of tree species.

Savannah or Wooded Grassland:

Extensive, adopting many forms, this is the

Above: Hostile environment for both plants and animals — hot springs at Kenya's Lake Bogoria on the lava-strewn Rift Valley bottom.

Opposite: Woodlands and grassy glades — favourite haunts of roan antelope.

Overleaf: World's largest bird, the flightless ostrich lays eggs that weigh up to 1.4 kilos — equal to three dozen domestic eggs. On the open plains its sustained speed of fifty kilometres an hour easily outpaces most predators.

Above: Rock hyrax flourish wherever there are cliffs — survivors of a group that once had many species but were ousted by more efficient grazers like the horse and the antelope.

dominant vegetation of Eastern Africa and what the public has come to associate with the region. In some areas the predominant trees may be *Combretae*, in others *Acaciae*. In yet others, as in the Kenya coast hinterland, it may be an African ebony, *Diospyros*. A wide variety of grasses are associated with this most general of habitats, varying with rainfall, soils, altitude, and usage, among a host of influences. Its salient features are trees, grass, and far-distant horizons.

Many savannah plants are adapted to fire. In the wetter savannahs of Uganda, and also in the 'miombo' woodlands where grasses commonly grow two metres (seven feet) high and sometimes to four metres (thirteen feet), extensive fires are yearly events. Set by lightning or people, they fill the dry month air with a dense smoky haze that disconcerts pilots in small aircraft but produces glorious red sunrises and sunsets.

Thicket and Bushland:

Cheek by jowl with savannahs are dense thickets and bushland, where low trees and shrubs shade out grasses. As a result fires cannot take hold and the undergrowth is rich in succulents. Visibility is seldom greater than fifty paces,

often much less. Common on hillsides and in rocky places, such habitats are most extensive around the drier edges of the savannah zones. Thickets are widespread along the landward side of the coastal forest belt, and also occur in central Tanzania, eastern Kenya, and parts of Somalia and Ethiopia.

Semi-desert:

All areas receiving between 127 millimetres (five inches) and 250 millimetres (ten inches) a year fall into this vegetation category. Dominated by short acacia shrubs and *Commiphorae*, this vegetation characterizes the Horn of Africa, of which Somalia is the greater part. Harsh and arid, it is the land of frankincense and myrrh.

Desert:

All areas that receive less than 127 millimetres (five inches) of rain a year, or none at all for several years, qualify as true desert. In this most hostile environment plants lie dormant as seeds, only germinating when conditions are right. Then they grow rapidly in order to ensure survival as the next batch of seeds. Poor wildlife habitats, they are used only briefly during their irregular green flushes. In Eastern Africa the only real deserts are the small Chalbi Desert of northern Kenya and parts of northernmost Somalia.

Grasslands:

Grasslands occur widely in Eastern Africa, in any of the areas occupied by the vegetation categories, other than desert. But most exist through the influences of man or other animals, both wild and domestic. The plains in Kenya's Maasai Mara Game Reserve are a case in point. Seen in 1988, they give the impression of 'natural' grasslands. Yet in the past century this area has changed from grassland, much as it is today, into quite thick woodland and thicket, before reverting back to grassland.

The causes of change were excessive hunting that removed elephants, and then disease that killed grazing animals and drove people away, allowing unimpeded woodland growth. This was followed by an elephant revival which broke down thicket and woodland and allowed fires to complete the process of reversion to grassland. Any radical change in human activity or animal numbers could well see another swing back to woodland and thicket.

Chapter 4 Aquatic Habitats

Fresh Water:

Much of Eastern Africa's northern half is drained by the world's greatest river: the Nile. Pouring in unruly turmoil out of Lake Tana and off the Ethiopian highlands through precipitous gorges, the Blue Nile's silt-laden floods have sustained six thousand years of civilization in the Nile delta. The term 'Blue' is a romantic misnomer. More accurately it should be the 'Brown' Nile.

Also entering the Nile off the southern Ethiopian highlands are the Bara, Gilo, and Akobo which, rising out of still forested highlands — there is little forest left in the Blue Nile's drainage area — are not quite so silt laden.

Flowing west to join the 'White' Nile, they stream across flat lands through vast papyrus filters — the 'sudd'. Cleaning them of any muddy burden, this process is also the origin of the name 'White' applied to the Nile's long southern section. Silt-free, the waters are relatively clear compared to the muddy 'Blue' waters from Lake Tana.

The Omo River flows south off the Ethiopian massif into Lake Turkana (once known as Lake Rudolf). The most northerly of Africa's Great Lakes, it is the only one in the Rift's eastern arm. Sometime in the last 20,000 years it joined the White Nile through a north-westerly outlet across the southern Sudan. Now it has become a vast 6,000-square-kilometre (2,300-square-mile) evaporation pan, 288 kilometres (180 miles) long and up to fifty kilometres (thirty miles) wide, without an

Above: White-faced tree-duck: one of the most widely spread and frequently seen of Africa's waterfowl.

Overleaf: Flocks of lesser flamingos colour Eastern Africa's soda lakes shimmering pink.

outlet. In the south, it is becoming more and more saline and, farthest from the Omo's inflow, is so salty as to be drinkable only *in extremis*.

The lake's level fluctuates seasonally, rising when the Omo floods during Ethiopia's rains and falling throughout the country's dry months.

The southern environs of Lake Turkana are intensely volcanic. Old volcanoes — Mounts Kulal and Nyiru — stand sentinel a short distance from the shore. Closer to, black lava flows, so recent they lack even the scantiest vegetation, run into the water. It is a hot, wild land, seared by daily winds of more than fifty kilometres (thirty miles) an hour, frequently gusting to over 100 kilometres (sixty-three miles) an hour. Blowing over the jade waters, they make the lake dangerous for the unwary and untutored sailor.

The Ruwenzoris, most of Rwanda, much of Burundi, a little of north-westernmost Tanzania, the Kenya highlands west of the Rift's eastern arm, and virtually all of Uganda, drain into the White Nile; the lofty Ruwenzoris via Lakes George and Edward, the Semliki River and Lake Mobutu, before their waters flow north into the 'Albert' section of the White Nile.

Lake Mobutu (formerly Lake Albert), the northernmost of the western Rift's sumps, is truly a 'Great' lake — quite literally an inland sea that dominates the environment about it. The Rift's precipitous walls rise on either side, appearing from the opposite shores as distant blue ranges. But the lake is far too long for one end to be seen from the other.

The other Nile headwaters first collect in Lake Victoria — the world's second-largest freshwater lake. Fed by the Kagera in the west and the Mara, Gucha, Sondu, Yala, Nzoia, and other streams in the east, Victoria is a roughly circular basin some 300 kilometres (190 miles) from north to south and only slightly less from east to west, covering 68,800 square kilometres (26,560 square miles). On this vast surface it is easy to sail beyond sight of land.

Lake Victoria, the only African Great Lake

not in one of the Rift Valley's two arms, lies on a raised table between them. But the land is gradually tilting westward and one day Lake Victoria will empty directly into the western Rift. Even now, it does so indirectly. Its outlet is through the 'Victoria' Nile which flows northward from the Owen Fall's electric turbines for a short section into shallow, papyrus- and water lily-girt Lake Kioga, a mere 100 kilometres (sixty-three miles) long and only twenty kilometres (thirteen miles) wide, before flowing westerly towards the Rift.

When the slow, gentle flow reaches the Karuma Falls, the river changes character and cascades over cataract after cataract, fall after fall, in a roaring maelstrom that ends eighty kilometres (fifty miles) downstream in a spectacular leap over the Rift's last sill. Here, at Murchison Falls, the river thunders through a narrow gorge a mere six metres (nineteen feet) wide. Legend has it that in times of yore a man fleeing for his life actually leapt the chasm. Murchison Falls are the point where, despite its tumultuous, roiling protest, the mighty Nile is finally captured by the Rift Valley in quite the most spectacular event in all its 6,741-kilometre-long course.

Next down the western Rift is Lake Kivu. Blue water surrounded by forested volcanic slopes — in places almost to the water's edge — it is arguably the most beautiful of all African fresh waters. But it serves only as handmaiden to Lake Tanganyika, to which it is connected by the Ruzizi River. Six hundred kilometres (375 miles) long and in places over eighty kilometres (fifty miles) wide, girt by spectacular Rift walls and scenery, 32,900-square-kilometre (12,700-square-mile) Lake Tanganyika is the world's second-deepest lake.

Though it flows into the Zaire River system, Tanganyika has developed in substantial isolation. Silt and detritus sink 1,200 metres (4,000 feet) down into the dark, oxygenless depths beyond the power of wind or upper currents to disturb. Consequently the surface waters are gin clear. Below the 100-fathom mark, where there is little if any life, nothing except tectonic upheaval can move the waters.

Thus they have lain, black and mysterious, for millions of years — quite literally an enormous liquid fossil.

Southernmost of the African Great Lakes is Lake Malawi — 22,490 square kilometres (8,680 square miles). Though connected to the Zambezi drainage through the Shire River, it is all but twin to Lake Tanganyika. Not quite as austere, long, or deep, it nonetheless has the same form. Long and relatively narrow, it, too, fills a deep Rift Valley sump whose bottom lies far below sea level. And, like Lake Tanganyika, Malawi's surface waters are crystal clear.

In addition to the 'Great' lakes, throughout its length the eastern Rift has a series of nineteen shallow lakes. In Ethiopia they are lakes Zway, Langana, Abijatta, Shalla, Awasa, Shamo, and Stephanie; the last transitory. Sometimes after heavy rain it is a large shallow body of water over thirty kilometres (nineteen miles) wide, at other times there is no water at all — just dry, dusty plain. The chain continues in Kenya with lakes Baringo, Bogoria, Nakuru, Elmenteita, Naivasha, and Magadi. In Tanzania there are Natron, Manyara, Eyasi, and Rukwa, and in Malawi the most southerly of all, lakes Chiuta and Chilwa.

Because all are sumps, mostly without outflows, these lakes tend to be saline. This tendency is reinforced by the sodic volcanic soils on which many of them lie, particularly those in Kenya and northern Tanzania. Two of them, Magadi and Natron, are little more than saturated solutions of trona.

Zambia has three unique wetlands: lakes Mweru and Bangweulu and the Kafue Flats. All three are vast, shallow, clear water swamps, seldom more than a metre or two deep, whose levels fluctuate substantially between wet and dry seasons. In many respects they are southern counterparts to the Nile's 'sudd' and 'toich' swamps which occur in similar latitudes north of the Equator, but outside Eastern Africa.

East of the Rift Valley a series of rivers flows off Eastern Africa into the Indian Ocean. Compared to the Nile, Zaire, and Zambezi, they are altogether lesser waterways. The largest are the Rovuma and Rufiji of southern

Opposite: Female waterbuck cools off during the midday heat.

Overleaf: Hippo, which weigh up to four tonnes, can stay submerged for as long as six minutes. Following pages: Reminiscent of the world's tropical ocean shores, Lake Malawi's beaches are typical of Africa's great inland seas. Pages 58-59: Oxbow bend in Kenya's Tana River, red with eroded topsoil as it flows towards the Indian Ocean.

Above: Ubiquitous grey heron, found throughout Africa and Europe — and some remote Indian Ocean islands.

Tanzania; followed by the Pangani, which drains southern Kilimanjaro and Tanzania's Pare and Usambara Mountains; and the Tana, which drains the eastern slopes of Kenya's Aberdare Mountains and Mount Kenya. The Juba and Wabi Shebelle play similar roles in Ethiopia's eastern highlands, flowing through Somalia to the sea.

All rivers that enter the Indian Ocean off Eastern Africa are similar: they have narrow, fringing gallery forests along their lengths, except where man has removed them. Characterized by considerable seasonal fluctuations in depth, all feature extensive white sandbanks through the dry spells. Only in their uppermost reaches, when tumbling from the highlands of their birth, are they turbulent. Once off the mountains they have few falls or barriers, but most are too shallow for navigation except in the smallest craft.

Salt Water:

Off Ethiopia, the Eastern African shoreline is bathed by the Red Sea. For the rest of its length, from northern Somalia to southern Tanzania, it is washed by the Indian Ocean.

Overall, the coastline is uncomplicated and the continental shelf relatively narrow, extending, for the most part, fewer than 160 kilometres (100 miles) offshore.

The oceanography is strongly influenced by the north Equatorial current which flows against the coast after crossing the surface of the Indian Ocean. Travelling thousands of kilometres without upwellings to recharge it with nutrients, this warm stream is relatively infertile and consequently its waters are clear.

Coral reefs stretch along most of the coastline, but with pronounced breaks wherever rivers discharge fresh water. Some rivers are silt laden — particularly Kenya's Tana and Sabaki. While fertilizing the coastal waters, these silt loads (the product of improvident inland agriculture) make the sea turbid and in some places kill the coral reefs.

In the Red Sea, off the Ethiopian coast, the Dhalak archipelago has numerous small coral islets and a more complex reef system than elsewhere on the coastline. The only similar, though less complicated, instance is the Lamu archipelago off northern Kenya and southern Somalia.

PART TWO: THE WILDLIFE

Above: Baboons, inveterate crop-raiders and farm pests, are also hunters, able to catch baby gazelle.

Chapter 5 Primates, Pangolins, and Mermaids

Eastern Africa's fauna reflects its geology, varied landscapes, and past climatic shifts. Animals with strong Eurasian affinities mix with others of purely African origin; some with clear West African or southerly connections occur along the eastern seaboard.

But though this diversity seems to suggest that each species has a special ecological slot — many do occur in limited circumstances, particularly those of the lowland rain forests — the most striking general feature is how widespread most are. They thrive in a variety of habitats and adapt to both dry and wet conditions and a wide range of vegetation, their adaptability no doubt the product of evolving on a continent that has undergone constant and radical change.

It's worth bearing in mind that, almost to a man, Eastern Africa's early white explorers and administrators, many of them competent zoologists or botanists in their own right, were interested in wildlife. By the 1920s, well over ninety per cent of the mammals, birds, rodents, fish, and reptiles had been described for western science. But one area largely unexplored, and still imprecisely known to the West (though obviously well enough known to those who live there), is south-western Ethiopia. Considerable uncertainty about that region's wildlife still exists.

Primates:

Scientists speculate that primates evolved from a small tree shrew-like insectivore more than seventy million years ago. Within forty million years there were four different primate groups of consequence for modern Africa: (1) prosimian galagos and lorises, (2) the guenon or cercopithecine monkeys, with baboons and mangabeys, (3) the colobuses, and (4) the ape and human line.

Prosimians: Eastern Africa today has six, one **potto** (a loris) and five **galagos.** They are all small, omnivorous, tree-dwelling, nocturnal animals, rarely seen unless in a deliberate search. But, as their eyes gleam bright red in reflected torchlight, they are easy enough to find when wanted.

The potto, a curious, lethargic animal that moves with slow and deliberate gait, seems unable or unwilling to jump. But its hand grip is so strong that the animal is a symbol of tenacity among some Africans who share its range. Principally a rain forest species, it is found in most Uganda forests and in Kenya west of the Rift Valley. If there are suitable habitats, it may also occur in westernmost Tanzania, Burundi, and Rwanda.

In contrast to the potto, the five galagos — **pigmy, needle-clawed, Zanzibar, greater,** and **lesser** — are active, fast moving, and noisy. The pigmy and needle-clawed galagos are West African species that overlap into Eastern African forests in western Uganda and possibly Rwanda. The Zanzibar galago occurs not only on that island, as its name implies, but also in Eastern Africa's coastal forests and thickets.

The greater galago ranges widely from the southern tip of Somalia through southern Kenya, into Rwanda, Burundi, all Tanzania, including the islands of Pemba and Zanzibar, Zambia, and Malawi. A forest species, it is found wherever leafed trees are in abundance: in gallery forests, plantations — even suburban gardens. Its presence is betrayed by a loud plaintive call, reminiscent of the cry of a human baby — hence the common name for galagos, **'bush-babies'.**

The lesser galago, the most widespread of the five species, is found almost anywhere below 2,000 metres (6,600 feet) except true forest, desert, and the drier parts of semi-desert. Favoured as a pet, along with the greater galago, they are often caught when they are drunk after raiding the cups that coconut palm tappers leave to collect sap for palm wine.

Guenons: This is the largest monkey family in Africa. Small to medium sized, they vary outwardly but are extraordinarily alike under the skin. In evolutionary terms most species seem closely related. Being overwhelmingly arboreal, the majority only occur

Opposite: Vervets — or green monkeys, as this guenon species is called — are also farm pests.

Above: Chimpanzee in Tanzania's Gombe Stream National Park; a close relative of mankind.

Opposite: Shrewd eyes in a creature that Darwin postulated had evolutionary links with the human race — a theory proven by modern research.

in forest. Not surprisingly, therefore, more species appear in the lowland rain forests of western Uganda than elsewhere.

L'Hoest's and the **Mona** guenons only appear in western Uganda. Another two, the **red-tailed** and **de Brazza's**, occur in Uganda and extend into the isolated forests of western Kenya. The red-tailed has also been reported in north-westernmost Zambia and, relatively recently, de Brazza's was found in the Omo River forest, just north of Lake Turkana (bearing out the belief that these Ethiopian forests deserve closer zoological scrutiny).

The forest-dwelling **blue**, or **Syke's**, monkey ranges from Ethiopia to Malawi and Zambia, from western Uganda to Zanzibar Island, and from sea level to the highest forests. Present in several subspecies, the highland forms, responding to low temperatures, have heavy, shaggy coats, while those of the lowlands have relatively short hair. They also vary widely in colour. In Uganda and western Kenya they have black limbs and an overall grizzled blue-black body coat (hence the name blue monkey). In south-eastern Tanzania the

limbs and tail are blue-black, but the body colour is russet-brown with a prominent white throat collar. Lay observers may be excused for thinking they are entirely different species.

The most widespread guenon of all — the **vervet,** or **green,** monkey — occurs all over Africa south of the Sahara, and outside the forests. It adapted to the woodlands and open country, even inhabiting some of the driest savannahs. Like the Syke's monkey, wide distribution has produced a number of vervet races. It also brings them into contact with farmers. More than any other guenon, the vervet is a pest.

Far back in their evolution another guenon member also left the forests, became genuinely terrestrial and very unguenon-like. The **patas,** or **Hussar,** monkey occupies a band of savannah from Senegal to Somalia, but a southerly finger of its range crosses northern Uganda and runs through central Kenya to the Tanzania border. A large, red-capped monkey, when disturbed it prefers to run on the ground rather than climb a tree.

The **mangabeys,** a small group of medium-

Top: Greater galago, whose loud nocturnal calls gave the family its name of "bush-babies".

Above: Tree hyrax: a nocturnal animal whose presence is more often announced by its call than by sight.

Top: Lesser galago, or bush baby: a widespread nocturnal primate.

Above: Lesser pangolin: a rare ground-dwelling, termite-eating animal.

Above: Baboons occur widely in both savannah and forest.

Above: The appealing 'bush baby', the greater galago, gets its name from its call — sounding like that of an infant in distress.

sized monkeys, are related to the guenons. Again, they are rain forest animals. Two species occur in Eastern Africa — the **black,** which is confined to western Uganda's forests, and the **crested,** which is a Congo-Zaire species. However, a small, isolated relict group of crested mangabeys in Kenya's lower Tana River gallery forests suggests that at one time the West African forests must have been connected to the Indian Ocean shoreline.

Baboons, more distantly related to the guenon stock, specialize in open habitats. They have produced many forms, most now extinct. One, *Simopithecus,* was nearly as large as the modern gorilla. Today only three baboon genera remain: *Mandrillus,* of West Africa, which does not occur in Eastern Africa; *Theropithecus,* which has one species, the **gelada;** and *Papio,* which has two species — the **hamadryas** and the **dog-headed.**

The gelada is endemic to Ethiopia in areas close to the cliffs and gorges of the country's northern plateaux, west of the Rift. The hamadryas is the sacred baboon of old Egypt. Today it is found in the hills, cliffs, and arid 'badlands' of coastal Ethiopia and northern

Somalia. It also occurs in southernmost Arabia, a remnant of the time when Arabia and Africa were one.

Dog-headed baboons occur widely in many local forms. Other than man, they are probably the continent's most successful primate. They range through semi-desert and all intermediate habitats into many — but not all — forests. Omnivorous, they turn to meat-eating with a will. Recorded kills include other monkeys, birds, young antelope and, on rare occasions, human infants.

Intelligent and abundant, living in big packs, they are a serious farm pest everywhere. With all farmers' hands against them, it says a great deal for their competence that they survive as generally as they do. Baboons are also widely used in medical research.

Colobus: Unique among primates in abandoning omnivorism, these monkeys specialize in leaf-eating. Digesting plant material with a high cellulose content calls for fermentation and bacterial assistance. To this end colobus monkeys have complex, sacculated stomachs — very different to the simple stomachs of most primates, including our own.

Above: Abyssinian black-and-white colobus monkeys, widespread in highland forests, differ from most primates in that they have only vestigeal thumbs.

There are two forms: the **red** with one species which has several races, and the **black-and-white** with two species. The red colobus is distributed from Zanzibar Island in the east to Senegal and The Gambia in the west. Predominantly a West African forest species, its range overlaps into Rwanda, Burundi, western Uganda, and north-western Tanzania. East of this, small relict populations occur near Kenya's Tana River delta, Iringa in south-central Tanzania, and on Zanzibar Island. These three groups are remnants of an era when western forests reached the eastern coasts and Zanzibar was still part of the mainland.

Of the two black-and-white colobus species, the **'Abyssinian'** occurs in Ethiopia, highland Kenya, and Uganda. The **pied** is found in isolated populations between the southern Kenya coast and northern Lake Malawi (again, clearly relict groups), but the greater part of its range is in the Zaire basin and West Africa, with a small overlap into western Uganda-Rwanda and the north-western tip of Zambia. Forest animals, both species have handsome black coats and white capes and are among the most striking of primates.

Seemingly more successful than their red cousins, both black-and-white species inhabit forests from sea level to the tree limits at the edge of montane moorlands. Those at high altitudes grow much longer hair and thicker coats than those in the warm lowlands. One is often aware of their presence, long before seeing them, through their loud, croaking call 'horrrr, horrrr, horrrr' which, echoing across the valleys, is a characteristic early morning sound in Eastern Africa's montane forests.

Apes: Two apes survive in Africa — the **gorilla** and the **chimpanzee.** Both are essentially western rain forest animals with marginal overlaps into Eastern Africa. The mountain form of the gorilla holds out in Rwanda and in the south-western tip of Uganda in the higher reaches of the Virunga volcanoes.

Fears for the survival of these largest living primates are well founded. Their habitats are shrinking as humans encroach on their range. Recent research, however, suggests that where western lowland gorillas are concerned the situation is not so critical. There may be more than 50,000.

Above: One form of rock-dwelling hyrax, Bruce's hyrax.

Above: True rock hyrax in Mount Kenya's alpine zone.

Chimpanzees still occur in several Uganda lowland forests and also as small relict populations in forest patches on the eastern shores of Lake Tanganyika. One such group, around Gombe stream, was made famous by the research of Jane Goodall and Hugo Van Lawick.

Hyraxes:

There are three kinds of hyrax in Eastern Africa, all rabbit-sized, brown-furred vegetarians. To the casual observer they look very similar. Two — *Procavia* and *Heterohyrax* — live in crevices among rocks and cliffs and are commonly associated with hills and steep slopes. To make matters more confusing, their ranges overlap. Both climb trees and both are commonly referred to as **rock hyrax.** The third genus — *Dendrohyrax* — is tree dwelling, rightly called **tree hyrax,** but commonly found in trees that grow in rocky places and where they associate closely with rock hyrax.

In distribution *Procavia* occurs in Ethiopia, Somalia, Uganda, Kenya, Rwanda, Burundi, Tanzania, and Malawi, but not Zambia. *Heterohyrax* occurs in all Eastern African countries. *Dendrohyrax* occurs in all except Ethiopia and Somalia (though it is difficult to avoid nagging thoughts that they may occur in Ethiopia's southern forests).

Tour guides often tell visitors that hyraxes are the elephant's closest living relatives. Though it may be true, 'closest' is a relative

term. If they did originate from a common stock, they have been separate for fifty million years or more: longer, that is, than the carnivores have been separated from a common stock with antelope.

Related to elephant or not, the hyrax family was successful until thirty million years ago, producing many forms — one of which was at least as big as a bear. Its decline seems to have come about through inability to compete with the bovid, ruminant ancestors of modern antelope. Hiding in rock crevices and up trees, today's three hyraxes are the specialist survivors of a once far bigger variety.

Pangolins:

Pangolins are unusual mammals — the sort of oddities one might expect to find among Australia's unique fauna. However, they occur in both Africa and tropical Asia and fossil remains have been found in Europe. They are an ancient family with no obvious close relatives. Appearing somewhat reptilian — short limbs, long head and tail, tiny ears and eyes — instead of hair they have a coat of large, overlapping horny scales. In defence they roll up into a ball like an armadillo.

All are insect-eaters, specializing in termites. Their forefeet are equipped with formidable claws — effective tools for breaking open termite nests — but they are toothless and capture their food with an astonishing

70

Above: Typical Syke's monkey of the race found in Kenya's highlands east of the Rift Valley.

tongue. Long and sticky, it is among the most curious of pangolin attributes. Together with its associated muscles it is longer than the animal's head and body together. When withdrawn, the tongue folds, kinked, into the throat. This flicks in and out when the pangolin is eating — the termites sticking to it.

There are four African pangolins, of which three live in Eastern Africa. The giant, which weighs over thirty kilos (sixty-six pounds) is a western species, but occurs in Uganda's wetter savannahs and perhaps also in both western Kenya and western Tanzania. The smaller ground pangolin, up to eighteen kilos (forty pounds), is a savannah species found everywhere but Somalia. The small tree pangolin, weighing three kilos (seven pounds), is another western and lowland species whose range extends into north-western Zambia, Rwanda, Uganda, and the damp Kaimosi forest of western Kenya. It has also been recorded in north-western Tanzania on the shores of Lake Victoria.

Aardvarks:

An important animal—if only because it is the first word of substance in English dictionaries — its name derives from the Afrikaner term meaning 'earth-pig'. This long-nosed eighty-kilo (176-pound) animal, however, is no relation whatever to the pig, but the sole living member of the order *Tubulindentata* — meaning tube-toothed. The animal's teeth are but one of its peculiarities, made up of many fine columns of dentine — the tubes — and lacking enamel.

Aardvarks are ungulates — that is, hoofed animals. But unlike horses or cattle which, through evolution, reduced the number of their toes to one or two, the aardvarks kept a full set of toes, each capped with a massive nail or 'hoof'. These have been adapted to digging to find the subterranean termites, beetle larvae, and other insects that aardvarks eat. Even more impressive is the animal's exceptionally acute sense of smell which enables it to detect insects buried deep underground.

The aardvark's first line of defence is to disappear underground. Using their forelimbs to break the earth and their hind feet to throw it out backwards, the animal literally walks its way underground within minutes. It has an unusual second-line tactic. Very compact, hard-muscled and hard-skinned, should it be

Above: Syke's monkey occurs throughout Eastern Africa's forests in a number of widely differing races — this specimen from Uganda is known as a 'blue' monkey.

Left: Most forest guenons are brightly coloured; few more so than de Brazza's monkey from Uganda and western Kenya.

touched on the back of the neck, the most likely hold that would be taken by a lion or a leopard, it will somersault forward instantaneously — so violently and unexpectedly that it can break any predator's hold or, if it doesn't let go, its neck.

Though common, and distributed throughout Eastern Africa and the continent as a whole, aardvarks are nocturnal and seldom seen in daylight. Their burrows, in which they spend the day, however, are a constant hazard for horse riders and cross-country motorists. Abandoned, they become home to wart hogs, hyaena, jackal, and many other animals.

Although the burrows are usually a single tunnel, sometimes they become deep and complex labyrinths with many entrances. Years ago in Zambia, three men investigating one such warren — a hazardous undertaking which entailed wriggling along on their stomachs — disappeared. After digging for ten days, a rescue party recovered one body, but never found the other two.

Dugongs:

The sirenians, of which the dugongs are members, are thought to have evolved from the same stock that gave rise to elephant and hyraxes more than sixty million years ago. So it would also be accurate to say that they are the nearest living relatives to hyraxes. These harmless marine vegetarians occupy the same ecological niche throughout the tropical Indo-Pacific that the manatees take up in the Atlantic. In classical times they also occurred in the Mediterranean.

The species prefers shallow coral seas with abundant seaweed — *Syringodium*, *Zostera capensis*, *Halodule uninervis*, *Cymodocea ciliata*, and *Halophila*. Eastern Africa's coastline does not have too much of this habitat, and though dugongs are known the whole length of the coastline, the best areas for them are probably in and around the Dhalak archipelago, the Lamu archipelago, Zanzibar, and Mafia Island. They probably occur in greatest number in the shallow seas off northern Australia.

Dugongs have always been hunted for their highly-prized flesh and oil. In recent times, though, the increasing use of nylon shark nets off the Eastern African coast has wastefully killed many.

Worldwide, sailors and fishermen have created myths about sirenians that tell of how they are half woman, half fish. Jonathan Kingdon, the artist and zoologist, wrote:

'There are many legends attached to the dugong. A Lamu story holds that dugongs are the descendants of some women who were lost at sea in ancient days. Classical authors described the siren and gave it the attributes of a seductive girl. This is interesting as to this day fishermen in Zanzibar that have caught a female dugong have to swear that they have not interfered with it. Throughout the ages the exposed nature of the genitals and the two breasts under the flippers seem to have been a sufficient stimulus for sailors' erotic imagination, and with time the stories became elaborated into classical legends.'

Chapter 6 Insectivores, Bats, and Rats

Around 300 species of insectivores, bats, and rats occur in Eastern Africa, most too small to readily observe. Many are nocturnal and in any case, the terrestrial species live in a Lilliputian world among grass stalks or litter on forest floors.

Insectivores:

The term insectivore embraces many, but not all, insect-eating mammals. Aardvarks, which are insectivorous, are classified with the hoofed animals. And the ant-eating aardwolf is classified as a carnivore, as are all the mongooses, even though insects form the bulk of some species' diets. However, all that do qualify as insectivores are small.

Few may have heard of the **potamogale** or **giant otter shrew.** Neither otter nor shrew, the name nonetheless conveys some idea of the animal's appearance. From tip of nose to tip of tail, a large one might be sixty-four centimetres (twenty-five inches) long and weigh one kilo (2.2 pounds). With long flat head, tiny ears, even tinier eyes, and a muzzle bristling with long whiskers, it truly has a 'shrewly' look about it, reinforced by the slender body and short legs.

Yet its long, muscular, and vertically flattened tail is no shrew's appendage, but a highly specialized swimming propeller. And as the potamogale spends a great deal of its time swimming in rivers, catching fish, crabs, and similar aquatic life, it has a superficial resemblance to a small otter.

The potamogale, however, is probably more closely related to the ancient lineage that produced the hedgehog-like **tenrecs** of Madagascar. It is a West African forest zone animal that occurs in western Uganda, Kenya's Kakamega forest, and north-western Zambia.

It has an even less well-known tiny cousin, the **dwarf otter shrew,** which is only thirty-five centimetres (thirteen inches) long, and weighs 135 grams (four ounces). This species looks distinctly shrew-like; small in size and sporting a tail with no apparent purpose — unlike the otter's, which is used as a rudder. It, too, is a rain forest animal which has been found in westernmost Uganda and may occur in Rwanda.

Golden moles, which burrow like the true moles of Europe, eat insects and earthworms in the same manner, and fill a similar ecological niche. But they are not closely related. They look like the moles through evolutionary 'convergence': a similar life style has resulted in a similar shape and habits. Evolving in Southern Africa, they spread into Eastern Africa during a past cold spell that connected the region with more southerly environments. Today one species is found in the cold, high Ruwenzoris, on Mount Elgon, and the higher ground in southernmost Tanzania.

Hedgehogs occur in every Eastern African country and in a range of habitats from dry savannahs to woodlands. Though mainly insect eaters, they do attack and kill small snakes — less than one metre (three and a third feet) long. When they do so, they pull their hood of prickles well down over their noses so that the snake cannot bite through the defensive spines. Curiously, though not totally immune, hedgehogs are forty times more resistant to snake venom than guinea pigs of the same size.

The most active and visible insectivores are the **diurnal elephant shrews.** Thought by some evolutionists to be related to the **tree shrews,** from which primates are held to have evolved, mankind may be related to them at least as closely as hyraxes are to elephant.

The single elephantine feature about elephant shrews are their long flexible noses with which they scent prey. These miniature trunks are not prehensile and cannot pick up objects. **Giant elephant shrews,** *Rhynchocyon,* fifty centimetres (twenty inches) long and weighing 440 grams (one pound), occur on Zanzibar, the Kenya coast, southern Tanzania, western Uganda, and westward into the Zaire basin.

Two other genera occur, *Petrodromus,* with one species occurring in south-eastern Kenya, Tanzania, Rwanda, Burundi, Zambia, and Malawi and *Elephantulus* with two species. One of these, the **spectacled** — from the white ring around the eye — is in all Eastern African countries, the other — the **short-nosed** — being absent from Ethiopia and Somalia.

Eastern Africa's true shrews are imperfectly known to science and their identification bewilders experts, let alone laymen. Suffice it that there are at least six genera contain-

Above: East Africa hedgehog: similar to its European relative, but having four rather than five toes on its forefeet.

Overleaf: Like tiny diamonds, the eyes of clustered rousettine fruit bats sparkle from the roof of a Mount Elgon cave.

ing well over sixty species, many of which look alike. Characteristic of all is a high metabolic rate and a need to eat frequently. They are among the most voracious of mammals.

Bats:

The ignorance about African shrews is greatly exceeded by that concerning bats. Next to rodents they are the must numerous mammals on earth. Worldwide there are more than 170 genera with 800 species. In Eastern Africa there are at least thirty-nine genera containing 122 species. These fall into two major categories: the **fruit bats** which, as their name implies, are basically fruit eaters and the **insect-eating bats,** most of which chase and catch insects.

Because they are aerial and nocturnal, bats are difficult to observe. During daylight they hide in cracks, crevices, and holes. Many are so little known outside scientific circles that they have no English or local vernacular name. Like birds, some species undertake extensive migrations. Knowledge of their distributions is patchy, so whenever serious studies are undertaken, new and startling information is invariably revealed.

Two examples: for decades the insectivorous **woolly bat,** *Kerivoula cuprosa,* was known only from Cameroon in West Africa. In 1955 one was captured in a house on Kenya's Aberdare Mountains, extending the species' known range some 3,600 kilometres (2,250 miles) eastward, and from a lowland forest habitat into a mountain environment.

The second instance concerns the insectivorous bat, *Tadarida condylura* — a relatively well-known species widespread in sub-Saharan Africa. It commonly roosts in house roofs in colonies of several hundred. Prevailing knowledge, however, suggested that its natural habitats may be cracks and hollow

Above: Seychelles fruit bats, similar to the 'flying foxes' of the Far East, are like those found on many Indian Ocean islands, including Pemba.

trees in colonies of no more than ten to twenty individuals.

Yet, in 1983, a colony four million strong was found in some cracked cliffs in central Kenya, the single observation revolutionizing knowledge of the species' previously 'well-known' social behaviour.

There are twelve fruit bat genera, with eighteen species. By bat standards they are large, and even those of medium size can fly considerable distances carrying fruit as big as peaches. All are noisy, most have a variety of calls, large eyes, and exceptionally well-developed vision. Flight is slow and rather owl-like. Apart from one group of three species — the rousettines — fruit bats generally roost in trees.

Some species choose deep shade, but others, such as the **straw-coloured fruit bat,** *Eidolon helvum,* may live in such large colonies that leaf cover is stripped from the trees and all shade lost. Such a colony is a well-known feature of Kampala, Uganda.

The **rousettine fruit bats** are unusual in that they not only have good sight, but also a primitive echo-location system which enables them to enter and roost in deep, dark caves. The **Egyptian rousette bat** is so named because it was found in the Great Pyramid at Gizeh — by a scientist accompanying Napoleon's forces in his invasion of Egypt. However, it also occurs throughout sub-Saharan Africa, India, Indo-China, Indonesia, and northern Australia.

Many fruit bats fly nightly round trips of between forty and sixty kilometres (twenty-five to thirty-eight miles) between roosts and fruiting trees. Their considerable staying power is indicated by one straw-coloured fruit bat arriving on board a ship 200 kilometres (125 miles) out at sea.

Among Africa's bats, the **'flying foxes'** — fruit bats of the genus *Pteropus* — of Pemba and Mafia (but not Zanzibar), off the Tanzania coast, are peculiar. Flying foxes are animals of the tropical Far East, eastern and northern Australia, and the mass of islands between Asia and Australia. They also occur on islands in the western Indian Ocean. Each has its own species: the Seychelles, Mauritius, Reunion,

Madagascar, Aldabra, and the Comoros, as well as Mafia and Pemba.

Why isn't there one on Zanzibar? And, given their apparent success as a group elsewhere, why are there none on the African mainland? How did they get to the islands across the Indian Ocean? These questions plague and intrigue evolutionists. Even if the land masses were closer together in times past, the journey would still have entailed thousands of kilometres over hostile water.

The **hammer bat,** so named from its odd-shaped head, is not only Africa's largest, but truly lives up to its specific Latin name *monstrosus*. No science fiction scenario could improve upon nature's bizarre design. The huge male nose is largely a resonance chamber. In Kingdon's words, 'It could almost be described as a flying loudspeaker or musical box on wings.' The somewhat sinister appearance is reinforced in habits, for this species, alone of the fruit bats, has been known to scavenge meat and attack chickens in the dead of night.

The smallest fruit bat is a specialist: a **nectar bat.** With poorly developed teeth, these harmless little animals live off nectar, pollen, and flowers.. Using long, extendable tongues instead of slender beaks, in pollinating a variety of tree species, among them the baobab, they play a similar ecological role to the diurnal sunbirds.

Eastern Africa's insect-eating bats number twenty-seven genera containing at least 104 species. If any mammal list is incomplete, this is it. Indeed, it is likely that tens of species are still unknown to science. One evening American ornithologist James Chapin collected a bat hawk, a bird of prey that eats bats. When he opened its stomach he discovered two new bat species. It makes the point.

Some insectivorous bats that hunt close to the ground in dense vegetation show flying agility no bird can match. Others fly at mid-level among trees and yet others high in the open air above all obstacles. These high flyers are thin-winged and fast. But, regardless of technique and agility, the insectivorous bats share a common feature. They have replaced sight with sound.

Long before man conceived radar, sonar, or any other form of reflected energy, bats had perfected echo-location. Their eyes are now basically non-functional and, in most species, probably can only determine light from dark.

A blind insectivorous bat can fly and feed with little difficulty; a deaf one is fatally handicapped.

The principle of echo-location is simple enough: the bat emits a sound which bounces off its surroundings. Picking up these echoes, the bat constructs an audial picture of where it is and what lies before or behind it just as precise as any visual image. Thus, not only can the fast-flying mammals locate equally fast-flying insects, but chase them precisely among obstacles. Many can even identify different insect species accurately.

Different bats use different frequencies and techniques. Some project sound through their mouths. Others, more advanced, project it through their nostrils. Some have pursuit systems, rather like fighter aircraft, that search for and lock on to a victim as the bat moves at speed. Others have 'ground radar' that enables them to hang quietly, scanning the air and ground below them, only swooping down to grab a victim once it has been identified as suitable.

Bat signals are emitted in frequency bands from twenty through to 160 kHz, generally inaudible to the average human. Sound pulse durations range from 0.25 to ten milliseconds and may be repeated between five to 200 times a second. The wide variety of facial skin flaps and 'leaves', and the incongruously large ears with complicated folds and hairs, are devices that project sound forward — acting as dampers so that outgoing sound doesn't interfere with incoming echoes — and pick up echoes with the greatest precision. Such phenomena as the Doppler shift are analysed with ease.

The bat sonar world seems to have derived from science fiction. Some insects can detect when a hunting bat has 'locked on' to them and emit jamming signals that interfere with the bat's reception: similar to modern military aircraft jamming devices. For the technically-minded zoologist or the zoologically-minded technician, few things in nature offer so much interesting study as bat research.

Rats:

Rodents, the world's largest mammal group, are well-represented in Eastern Africa. Indeed, no terrestrial part of the region — other than the ice-caps — is without at least one species and many are occupied by several. Most are smaller than the common **black rat** of Eurasia — a species that now occurs everywhere in the world where man lives, with the possible exceptions of the Arctic and Antarctic. Though small, there are millions of them and some species, particularly those of the open grasslands, such as *Arvicanthus*, at times constitute a greater weight — biomass — than the larger herbivores that graze the same areas.

Rodents are of particular concern to man. They may eat as much as forty per cent of Africa's annual grain harvest. Though only a small proportion of Eastern Africa's ninety genera and 135 species may be seriously harmful to crops, farmers understandably consider most as pests.

The largest Eastern African rodents are two species of **porcupine:** the **crested,** which occurs in Ethiopia, Somalia, Uganda, Kenya, and Tanzania, and the **South African,** of Kenya, Tanzania, Rwanda, Burundi, Zambia, and Malawi. To the layman they are difficult to tell apart, both weighing up to twenty-seven kilos (sixty pounds).

They occur in almost all habitats, even semi-desert. Nocturnal and slow-moving, they are vegetarians with a taste for many crops. They also crave old bones and ivory — probably for the minerals they contain — particularly in wet areas. Many an elephant tusk is gnawed by porcupine.

Porcupine spend daylight below ground in a burrow or cave. When foraging after dark they rely for defence on the fearsome quills that arm the tail. Most of the body quills are soft and pliable, but those in the tail are hard with razor-sharp points. Approached by a predator, porcupine rattle these quills in warning and lumber off. If closely pursued they stop so abruptly that the aggressor crashes into the spiked rear end and the stubby tail thrashes about, driving quills into the predator's flesh. These remain like arrows, penetrating deeper whenever the victim moves, to cause painful, festering wounds. Many an unwary lion and leopard has died after a brush with a porcupine. Yet the defence doesn't always work. In the Kalahari, lion often eat porcupine, and must have developed local skills to deal with them.

A third species, the small **tree porcupine,** found in the western forests of Uganda and Kenya, is unlikely to be seen.

Because they are diurnal, **squirrels** are the most obvious rodents. Eastern Africa has at least fifteen tree-dwelling species. However, it is the two ground-dwelling species — the **striped** and the **unstriped** — that catch the eye most. The striped, with a white line along its flank, occurs across the Sahel and Guinea savannahs from Senegal to Ethiopia, Uganda, Kenya, and northernmost Tanzania. The very similar unstriped ground squirrel is a Somalian form that extends into the Ogaden part of Ethiopia, Kenya, and northern Tanzania, overlapping with the striped species.

Related to North America's gophers and prairie dogs and Eurasia's marmots, which they closely resemble, they live in underground burrows and warrens which invariably have a concealed exit. This is good sense, for many small predators prey on them and could corner them underground all too easily. They are commonly seen crossing roads and tracks in the savannah national parks.

Above: Striped ground-squirrel, perhaps the most commonly seen rodent in Eastern Africa.

Chapter 7 Hunters

Nowhere on earth can a greater variety of animal predators be seen than in Eastern Africa. The region has at least forty-four carnivores that include dogs, mustelids, viverrids, hyaena, and cats. Only the bears are absent.

Conventional theory is that so great an array indicates a rich ecology in which each predator exploits a specific niche. Yet, as knowledge grows, it seems that carnivores are far more ubiquitous than theory allows. While some species do have specific niches, most are extraordinarily widespread and often exploit the same food resources. Many smaller species are as insectivorous as carnivorous, and their diets overlap those of some insectivores.

Africa's animal carnivores are thought to have originated from a common stock, the miacids, which were probably like the present viverrids — genet, civet, and mongooses — in appearance and design. The earliest branch off this ancestral stock gave rise to the mustelids, followed shortly by the dog line, somewhat later by cats and hyaena, each taking an independent track.

Mustelids:

The mustelids — weasels, stoats, polecats, martens, badgers, and otters — did not do well in Africa, possibly through competition from the viverrids. Of those that did carve themselves a place, however, none did so with greater distinction than the honey badger or ratel.

Among Africans the **ratel**, or **honey badger,** is a byword for fearlessness and pound-for-pound strength. One metre (three and one-third feet) long, standing less than twenty centimetres (eight inches) high, prodigiously thick-skinned, squat and broad, enormously well-muscled and heavy-boned, this animal turns aside for no one and readily attacks anything that disturbs it — to the point where it will bite vehicle tyres. It is not nature's most elegant creation — smelling like unwashed armpits.

Slow-moving, the ratel eats a wide range of foods from insects and small fruits, through any small animals — feathered, cold- or warm-blooded — to young antelope if it can take them unawares. It is widely believed that if disturbed by larger animals it will attack the underbelly and, where males are concerned, emasculate them. So impressive is the ratel's implacability that no one acquainted with the species would care to test the myth.

Craving honey, ratels will climb up to beehives and, to get at the combs inside, break them open with their long claws and great strength. Their thick skin protects them from stings, but the ratel also has another defence. It releases a foul-smelling secretion from its anal gland that stupefies the bees — just as apiarists use smoke to drive bees away.

Another mustelid that uses a smell as defence is the **zorilla,** or **African skunk.** Its eye-watering stink lingers and nauseates for days. This small black and white predator lives principally on insects and rodents.

The **striped weasel** is the zorilla's lookalike, and possibly its colouring is defensive mimicry; for any larger predator that has had the misfortune to be sprayed by a zorilla would tend to leave striped weasels well alone, too. Striped weasels are not known in Ethiopia or Somalia, but occur widely elsewhere in Eastern Africa.

The only other mustelids in the region are three otters. One, the **swamp otter,** is a rare western forest form, and may only occur in westernmost Uganda. The **spotted necked otter,** smaller but similar to the well-known European species, is very much a fish eater of the major lakes and rivers. Nearly four times as large as the spotted necked otter is the **clawless otter.** This has a similar distribution to its smaller cousin, but is more an animal of the highland streams, swamps, and backwaters — feeding on crabs, frogs, and molluscs as well as fish.

Viverrids:

This large family of small carnivores is particularly well represented in Africa and tropical Asia. They show many superficial similarities to the mustelids, with whom they appear competitive, being generally long-bodied and short-legged. This may explain why the mustelids are poorly represented in Africa, but more diverse and abundant in the northern temperate zones of both Old and New Worlds where viverrids are few or absent.

The **civet** is Africa's largest viverrid. Weighing up to twenty kilos (forty-four pounds) it occurs throughout Eastern Africa from dense forest to driest savannah. This slow, smelly, nocturnal ground dweller eats fruits, insects, and any small vertebrates it comes across.

For millenniums, civet have provided man with an expensive product. The male's anal glands release a secretion that is used to fix

Above: Large-spotted genet: one of a common look-alike group not often seen. They are strictly nocturnal viverrids — as are the better known mongooses. The cat family may have evolved from a genet-like ancestor.

flower perfumes. The end product, when dabbed on m'lady's wrists and behind her ears, tells little of its origins.

Since Solomon's time Ethiopia has been a major source of civet musk. Although the extraction process is often criticized, the industry is nevertheless big business in Ethiopia — providing valuable foreign exchange, which in turn supports wildlife conservation in the country.

Zanzibar has **Indian civet,** introduced centuries ago for reasons lost with time, living alongside the indigenous African species. In fact, the two are not closely related and belong to different genera, which perhaps explains why they can coexist.

Genet are arboreal viverrids. Their great climbing agility owes much their fully retractable, curved claws. These are so similar to cat claws that it may have been an early genet that gave rise to the cat family.

There are six genet in Eastern Africa, all with pale coats variously spotted with dark brown or black, making it difficult for laymen to identify one from another. They are nocturnal, occur in dry savannahs through to tropical forests, and prey on rodents, birds, insects, and occasionally eat fruit.

The **African palm civet** is like a large, heavily-built genet. Very much an animal of forest and dense woodland, its presence on the Eastern African coast, as is the case with so many forest species, is a reminder that tropical rain forest once spread right across the continent. Though largely arboreal, palm civet are not beyond raiding poultry houses: a trait they share with genet, civet, ratels, and some larger mongooses.

Eleven **mongoose** species occur in Eastern Africa. Two, the **snouted** and **long-nosed,** are forest forms found only in westernmost Uganda and possibly Rwanda. The others range a variety of habitats throughout the region. The largest species, the **white-tailed,** weighing up to five kilos (eleven pounds), is solitary and mainly nocturnal — most commonly seen run over on the roads. The smallest, the **dwarf,** is a highly social, diurnal animal that weighs only 680 grams (just over one pound).

Largely as a result of Kipling's *Rikki Tikki Tavi* the legend has grown that mongooses eat snakes. Since the majority will take anything they can overpower, most species may occasionally kill snakes. None are known, however, to specialize in hunting these reptiles.

Above: Black- or silver-backed jackal.
handsomest of the four African jackal
species.

Right: Golden jackal, found in Asia and
southern Europe as well as Africa, is
perhaps closest of all jackals to the domestic
dog.

Above: Dwarf mongooses are similar to their slightly larger cousins, the banded mongooses, living in small packs dominated by a female. Feeding principally on insects, they also take birds eggs and other small life.

Left: Diurnal and highly visible, the banded mongoose is widely distributed through the more open, wetter savannahs. They are sociable, living in small groups within well-defined territories.

Opposite top: Marsh mongoose: as its name implies, very much an animal of damp habitats. It swims well, and is fond of crabs and fish.

Opposite: The caracal: a bird-hunting cat with prodigous agility once used for hunting in the Middle East. A good cat could knock down several rising pigeons and might be the origin of the term — "cat among the pigeons".

Above: Dwarf mongooses live in close-knit packs under the rule of a dominant female.

Below: African wild dogs hunt in packs. Though not large animals, their group co-operation makes them superbly efficient.

The larger mongooses — the **Egyptian,** **swamp,** and **white-tailed** — kill birds larger than domestic fowl and are unwelcome in the vicinity of poultry runs. On balance, however, their consumption of rodents probably outweighs occasional thefts and their presence benefits man.

Most mongooses are terrestrial and if they climb, it is clumsily. The **slender mongoose** is an exception and this small, long-tailed species that behaves rather like a diurnal genet is an inveterate nest raider.

Two species, the medium-sized **banded mongoose** and the small **dwarf mongoose,** are diurnal and extremely sociable. Both make charming pets and readily adapt to a houseful of children, dogs, and cats. Their groups are strongly territorial and, in the dwarf mongoose, ruled by a dominant female. Moreover, she is the only one who breeds successfully; litters produced by subordinate females are seemingly killed by her. Despite this drastic social control, her young are very much the group's offspring, with all members looking after them.

Both species frequently fall victim to birds of prey, and any moving shadow from overhead is enough to send a pack fleeing pell-mell for cover.

Canines:

The dogs of Eastern Africa are four species of jackal, the four-toed wild dog, the tiny bat-eared fox, Ruppell's fox, and pale sandfox. The jackals — black-backed, side-striped, golden, and Simien — are so close to domestic dogs behaviourally (indeed the ancestor of man's best friend may have been a jackal species) that anyone who has had a pet dog can 'read' them.

Essentially, **black-backed jackal** are arid land animals with two main distribution centres: the Horn of Africa and the Kalahari. However, they are also spread about Eastern Africa in the contiguous better-watered savannahs and woodlands.

Side-striped jackals are savannah and woodland predators, absent from the Horn of Africa and the Kalahari, but sometimes found in semi-arid lands. **Golden jackals** are a Eurasian and North African species found in Ethiopia, Somalia, Kenya, and northernmost Tanzania.

In many places it is not uncommon to find two jackal species in the same general area, and in the northern half of Eastern Africa all three occur side by side — as in the Serengeti National Park. Their diet is wide-ranging and dog-like: some vegetables, insects, frogs, snakes, birds, rodents, and other mammals up to the size of a Thomson's gazelle. They come readily to carrion, wait on larger predators for leftovers, and scavenge about human homesteads.

In their associations with other large hunters one can see how the domestic dog came to be. When man was a hunter he, too, will have been attended assiduously. When a hunting party flushed small game that the jackal could catch the point will have been taken.

A fourth species, Ethiopia's **Simien jackal,** often referred to as a Simien fox, is a lightly built, leggy, red animal of the high grasslands. Not well known scientifically, it is a specialized rodent eater, but may occasionally take carrion. Although there is no evidence, they are also accused of taking lambs, and the hearsay is sufficient to have turned herdsmen's hands against it. The species has been much reduced this century.

For years the **African wild dog** was abused and shot whenever seen — even in many national parks. Indeed, through official edict, it was exterminated in Uganda's national parks. This drastic human reaction stemmed from their efficiency. The species has a high ratio of kills to hunts started, the key to which seems to be a unique degree of co-operation.

Wild dog are harriers that run their victims down. One or two pack members stay close on a victim's heels and the rest fan out behind. As the pacers tire they fall back, to be replaced by another pair. If the victim jinks or changes course, dogs from the rear cut out and head it back. Eventually they close in and tear apart the quarry.

Once weaned, wild dog pups are looked after by all pack members, male and female. Adults gorge themselves and regurgitate part of the meal back at their den to begging pups. They will even feed an adult — if it begs appropriately — and can keep an injured pack member alive until fit again.

Though wild dog are now protected, they have not responded, however, and numbers remain low. They may be unusually prone to diseases such as canine distemper, and this keeps them down. Whether or not this speculation is right, the survival of the wild dog in Eastern Africa is clearly in the balance.

Above: Bat-eared fox, which feed largely on insects, locate prey by using their large ears to detect sound.

Below: Like the dwarf mongooses to which they are distantly related, spotted hyaena society is also dominated by females.

Smallest and most inoffensive of all the region's dogs is the tiny **bat-eared fox.** An animal of the drier grasslands and bushlands, it is another of those animals found in the Horn of Africa and the Kalahari — but not the Sahara or sub-Sahara — suggesting they were linked by an arid land bridge in the past. These small canines are mainly insectivorous, prey being located by sound more than any other sense — hence their huge ears.

Two other dogs occur in the north of Eastern Africa. The first is **Ruppell's fox:** a small, large-eared fox, similar in shape to the European species, but with grey flanks and a pale reddish-brown back. Primarily an Arabian and Middle East animal, it occurs in Africa in northernmost Somalia and in the desert fringes of the Sudan.

The second is the **pale sandfox,** which has been recorded in Ethiopia and Somalia.

Hyaena:

Three hyaena occur in Eastern Africa: the spotted, the striped, and the aardwolf. The first is best known and is found in almost all habitats. The **striped hyaena** is a North African, Middle East, and Indian animal, whose range includes Ethiopia and the Horn, extending southward into northern Tanzania. It is more a dry country species, though it occurs sparingly in some of the moister savannahs of central Uganda.

The **aardwolf,** a highly specialized insect-eating hyaenid, is yet another of those mammals that, like bat-eared fox, black-backed jackal, spring hare, and oryx, are found in the Horn of Africa and in the Kalahari, suggesting again that an arid axis once connected the two regions down the length of Africa.

Physiologically, the hyaenids appear more dog- than cat-like. Yet, as indicated earlier, they are thought to have evolved from viverrids and may be closer to the genet and mongooses than either dogs or cats. With long legs and rather rigid bodies they are better suited to coursing, rather than stalking, and are dog-like in hunting behaviour.

In turn this implies that once they competed with the dog family. Fossil records indicate that there was once a greater variety of hyaena. As the three surviving hyaena are highly specialized, the inference is that the hyaena generally were not successful and may have been displaced by dogs.

Both **spotted** and **striped** hyaenas have massive bone-crushing teeth, an adaptation which suits them to the role of ecological undertakers. This is aided by an extraordinarily efficient digestion which enables them to extract nutrients from waste that regularly includes other predators' dung, old dry bones, and bits of leather.

While the two hyaena became specialized scavengers, the aardwolf freed itself from competition with other large carnivores by becoming an insect eater. Concentrating on termites in particular, it has no use for strong teeth. So where the hyaena have massive molars, the aardwolf has only vestigial pegs.

Because they scavenge, humans widely associate hyaena with death — an association heightened by the spotted hyaena's eerie calls and maniacal laughter; sounds readily associated with the supernatural. Research since the 1960s has dispelled some of this mystical aura and distaste. The spotted species is now well known. Not only is it a scavenger *par excellence,* but a consummate hunter, able to kill animals considerably larger than itself. And in its social organization are traces of its viverrid origins. Like the communal mongooses, spotted hyaena have territories occupied by clans in which hierarchies are dominated by females.

Felines:

Cats are so outwardly alike that, regardless of size, anyone can recognize them, even if unable to name the species. They hunt by stealthy stalk or lie in wait until a victim is within range of a pounce or short, fast rush. It is then seized by the hooked forepaw talons and held, while the jaws find a death grip on some vital point: severing spinal column, major blood vessels, or closing a windpipe. Their deliberate and accurate bite displays an altogether greater professionalism than other carnivores that slash, rip, and maim their quarry. These basic cat techniques are familiar to anybody with a household tabby.

Eastern Africa has seven cat species: wild, serval, golden, caracal, lion, leopard, and cheetah. All but the golden, which is a western forest animal, occur widely and in every one of the region's countries. Similarly, all but the golden are found in a broad range of habitats.

The **African wild cat** was tamed by the ancient Egyptians and is the ancestor of all modern domestic forms. Unlike the direct antecedents of other domesticants — such as

Above: Key to leopard success is a wide and varied diet. Known to have killed full-grown eland ten times a leopard's weight, they also live off rats and carrion.

Opposite: Solitary, silent, nocturnal, and secretive, leopard survive in settled areas long after most other wildlife has vanished.

the dog, horse, and cow, whose ancestors became extinct — the wild cat is still common. So much so that throughout Africa and Eurasia there is widespread interbreeding between domestic and wild cats.

The **serval** is a long-legged grassland species. It has particularly large ears, essential for catching rodents, in which the species seems to specialize. Rats and mice scurrying about in long grass are more readily located by sound than sight. The hunting serval will jump into a grass patch and then stand motionless, listening. When a rat is heard, it pounces accurately at the source of sound, even if this entails pinning it down under the grass.

In keeping with the general carnivore rule of opportunism, however, serval not only eat rodents, but anything from grasshoppers and small birds to hare and the smaller antelope. Though usually a leopardine yellow with black or brown spotting, black servals are common on the high wet moorlands of Kenya's Aberdare Mountains, where they may even outnumber normally-coloured individuals.

The **caracal,** or **African lynx,** is similar in size to the serval and, like it, rather long-legged. In colour, however, it may be any shade from russet-red to pale grey, and has black, long-tufted ears. Primarily a cat of the dry lands, it is also found in small numbers in some wetter savannahs. Its distribution is pan-African, through Arabia and the Middle East, and across Iran and Afghanistan into western India.

Whereas the serval is a rodent specialist, the caracal hunts birds. It will also take any small animal, including the smaller antelope. It is primarily nocturnal and many birds are taken at night as they roost. In daylight, the caracal is adept at catching ground-feeding species: guinea fowl, francolins, bustards, pigeons, and sand grouse.

At one time in India and Persia, caracals were caught, tamed, and used to catch game birds. In a single leap at a rising flock, a good cat could knock down several pigeons. From this, the term 'cat among the pigeons' may have derived.

Above: Lion, the only social species of cat, live in prides of related females. Litters of up to six cubs are common and several lioness often give birth within a few weeks of one another. They readily suckle one another's cubs, enabling young to survive when lactation fails or death occurs.

Opposite: Though only two-thirds the male's weight, lioness make most kills.

Overleaf Left: Young males leave the pride to become wanderers until fully mature, when they take over a pride by deposing the ruler in a savage battle for power — until, in turn, they too are deposed. Weighing over 250 kilos and able to eat up to seventy kilos of meat at a sitting, adult lion are second only to tiger in cat hierarchy.

Overleaf Right: When it comes to eating the rule is biggest and strongest first. In times of little small cubs past weaning may starve.

In Eastern Africa **golden cats** are found only in the forests of Uganda and western Kenya (although, as with so many western forest species of similar distribution, there is the tantalizing prospect that they may also occur in the imperfectly-known western Ethiopian forests). Similar in size to caracal and serval, they are stockier and shorter-legged,

varying in colour from a deep, golden-red to grey with dark brown to black spotting, which also ranges from heavy and general to indistinct. As is so often the case with forest animals, golden cats are not easily observed and little is known about their hunting and behaviour.

Leopard, the most widely distributed of

Above: Lioness tend to stay with their maternal pride, forming collections of mothers, daughters, grandaughters, sisters, and cousins.

Opposite: Odd cats out, cheetah have sacrificed strength for lightness in the interest of speed.

African and Eurasian carnivores, occur in as broad a range of habitats as man. They are at home in forest, woodland, savannah, semi-desert, uplands, and lowlands. But where lion are abundant, they avoid open grassland.

All the larger carnivora, excepting extreme specialists like aardwolfs, are opportunists. They not only kill the same prey, but also hunt one another. There is a strong competitive hostility between them: a leopard's appearance will stir lion into action when an antelope might arouse little interest.

In open places like the Serengeti Plains, where there are no trees to climb for refuge, leopard are few because of their vulnerability to the far larger lion.

Not long ago it was widely believed that leopard were declining through overhunting. Their handsome, spotted coats are prized trophies. But recent research has shown that the species is still abundant and widespread. The impression that they were endangered arose partly from their nocturnal way of life. In many places, even though present, they are

seldom seen.

Perhaps the most striking example of this occurred in the Kenya capital, Nairobi, in the 1960s. A leopard escaped from a trapper's compound within the city limits. Traps were immediately set to catch the runaway but it was never seen again. To the community's amazement, however, two unknown wild leopard were caught.

An equally impressive illustration of leopardine ability to survive is their presence on Zanzibar. A small, densely populated island is the last place that one would expect one of the Great Cats to hold out. Leopard survive in densely settled areas because of both their secretiveness and very general diet. Inveterate scavengers, they come readily to carrion and waste, but will also live off very small animals — rats and their like — as well as larger species, including man. Though leopard do not turn to man-eating often, when they do their hunting skill makes them very dangerous indeed. In recent years, in western Kenya, there have been several instances of

Above: Female cheetah are solitary except when mating or raising dependent cubs. Males often live in pairs or trios.
Opposite: Drinking regularly when water is available, cheetah can go long periods without water — surviving on the body fluids of prey.

such man-eating.

Like serval, black leopard occur and are relatively common both in India and in the Ethiopian highlands.

In many cultures **lion** epitomize ferocity, strength, courage, dignity, and majesty. Second only to the tiger in size and weighing up to 238 kilograms (523 pounds), they are emblems of the power men crave. You have only to see a lion in its tawny prime, with flowing patriarchal mane and implacable golden stare, to appreciate why the species is so prominent in human mythology. Small wonder, then, that of all the wildlife the visitor to Eastern Africa wishes to see, lion tops the list.

Lion are unusual in that they are the only social cats. Like leopard, they, too, are opportunists who readily scavenge carrion and rob other predators of their kills. Part of their opportunism leads to man-eating and stock-killing, still common in many parts of Eastern Africa. Though reinforcing our instinctive awe, it's also a portent of their future. Although lion still occur widely, they are gone from all the highly settled, cultivated regions, and many

developed ranches. In the long run their survival in the wild depends on the continuity of Africa's national parks.

Beautiful and inoffensive, spurning carrion, never known to have killed a human, altogether lacking the feline aura of ferocity inherent in lion and leopard, **cheetah** are the odd cats out. Hunters of the open, they secure prey through a high-speed sprint of up to 600 metres (780 yards) which, initially, appears a very uncat-like method of hunting. But closer examination indicates that the technique is not quite so aberrant as it might seem.

The basic cat approach is a slow, stealthy crawl to within a few paces of the victim, taking advantage of every bit of cover and, when close enough, pouncing or closing through a short, fast sprint. These basic elements are all in the cheetah technique. The major difference is that the sprint is much longer.

Presumably the system evolved in open country where lack of cover made close stalking difficult and the cat had to develop some other way of getting up to its victim. The

Above: Mother and three near-adult offspring on an impala kill. Cheetah also catch rats and, occasionally, animals as large as hartebeest.

conventional short sprint had to be maintained for a greater distance. This led to several modifications in basic cat physiology. The legs lengthened and the back became elongated to give a greater stride. Weight was shed, but at the expense of muscle mass and a corresponding loss of strength.

It meant that the cheetah was unable to wrestle victims to the ground or bring large animals physically to a standstill before killing. The drawn out sprint, however, accommodated the loss of brawling power. A chase at top speed — the cheetah is the world's fastest land animal and may touch 110 kilometres (seventy miles) per hour — over several hundred metres leaves the victim so breathless that it has little strength left to fight when seized.

And a runner without the strength to seize and hold quarry has no need for the retractile 'butchers' hooks' that form the foreclaws of all other cats. The cheetah's claws are blunt and only semi-retractile: all but one, that is — for the cheetah dew- or wristclaw is as sharp and hooked as any cat's.

When a cheetah closes with a victim and swipes it across hind legs or rump, this sharp, curved dewclaw hooks it off balance. Unstable at speed, the quarry tumbles. Before it can regain its feet, the cheetah seizes its throat and closes the windpipe. Desperate already for oxygen, the prey has no reserves left to struggle and loses consciousness very rapidly. The system is neat — almost surgical — and effective. So important is the need to leave the victim breathless that the hunt is often abandoned if it doesn't make a break when the cheetah emerges from cover.

The cost of surrendering strength for speed has put cheetah at a disadvantage to other predators. They cannot risk physical confrontation. In places like Serengeti National Park, where other hunters are relatively abundant, cheetah are robbed of kills and many of their cubs are eaten. Even a scruffy jackal can drive a cheetah off a kill. Consequently, some of the richest national parks may not be ideal for cheetah.

Today the species is still widespread with strongholds in the Horn of Africa and around the Kalahari. It is in these semi-desert environments, where competition is low, that it appears to have the best chance of long-term survival.

Chapter 8 Grazers and Browsers

All ungulates, or hoofed animals, are predominantly, if not entirely, vegetarian. Eastern Africa has a greater variety of them than anywhere else in the world. The vast numbers of grazers in the Serengeti-Mara ecosystem of Tanzania and Kenya evoke visions of an Africa untouched by man. The spectacle of more than a million wildebeest mingling with hundreds of thousands of zebra, gazelle, and other antelope is magnificent. Yet the idea that this is how it was long ago may only be an illusion. Indeed, for numbers and variety the migration may be greater now than it has ever been.

But since nostalgia for a greater wildlife history is so strong, the evolutionary record is worth considering briefly. The African elephant, for instance, creates an impression of timelessness; a feeling that it must have been on earth for millions of years. This is not so. Though descended from a large and ancient

family, it may well be younger than a million years — younger, even, than man.

The horse family, to which the zebra belong, goes back more than fifty million years and has produced many forms. But equine species have declined in number during the last five million years. Similarly, starting some thirty-eight million years ago, the rhino did well initially, but the number of species has been diminishing for the past twenty-five million years.

Against this, the bovids, which include buffaloes, cattle, sheep, goats, and all the antelope, are recent newcomers. Beginning some twenty million years ago, they have produced a wide array of forms — particularly in Africa — nearly as big today as at any time. Indeed, it is thought that this great increase in bovid species caused declines in other herbivores — the once successful horses being a case in point. Their reduction was most pronounced

Above: Elephant young play like children. When fully grown at around six tonnes, bulls may fight in earnest. Gestation takes twenty-two months and from around fourteen to sixteen years old a female may produce a calf once every four years until in her fifties. Occasionally twins are born.

Above: Elephant have to eat between four and six per cent of their body weight daily — 300 kilos for a big male.
Opposite: Elephant as far apart as five kilometres communicate with a variety of vocal calls too low for the human ear to detect and also by body postures and gestures such as shaking or flapping their ears.

when the bovids underwent their greatest expansion.

If an observer were caught in a time warp that could transport him back more than twenty million years, he might see many animals. But they would not include today's antelope. Instead, the plains would be covered by a variety of horses, and possibly some of the last big hyraxes.

The fact is that evolution is a relentless process of change in which species compete with other species, and eventually displace them. In reality, there never has been a balance of nature. Consequently, the present-day diversity of Eastern Africa's herbivores in all their magnificence is unique, and as modern as mankind.

Elephant:
Foremost among the herbivores is the **African elephant.** Although some fossils date back 700,000 years, it does not appear to have 'taken off' and become dominant in Africa's ecosystems until as little as 45,000 years ago — long after mankind attained its modern, sapient form. Yet, despite this late start, the elephant's influence is second only to man's.

For centuries knowledge of elephant was governed by myth rather than fact. Only after the Second World War did it acquire a firm scientific base, when a Dr Perry was commissioned by the Uganda Government to investigate elephant reproduction.

Intense conflict between farmers and elephant had raged throughout the century. But despite shooting thousands, the problem in the 1940s was as acute as it had been in 1910, and officials wanted a scientific explanation for the seemingly endless supply of elephant.

In hindsight, it is obvious that all through this period expanding humanity had steadily eaten into elephant ranges and the conflict arose, not from any exceptional capacity to replace lost members, but constant human encroachment of their habitats. Throughout the 1950s, 1960s, 1970s, and up to the present,

103

Perry's findings were followed by a succession of studies into other aspects of elephant biology and behaviour. Today the species ranks among the best known of all wild animals.

No aspect of this creature fails to impress. It is intelligent with a social organization like our own. It lives nearly as long as man and enjoys a long childhood. Although it has been long known that elephant have an exceptional sense of smell, nothing explained the ability of both herds and individuals several kilometres apart to act in unison. Scientists dismissed the idea that they could communicate. Recently, however, Dr Kathy Pane discovered that elephant 'talk' to one another with sounds at frequencies too low for the human ear. Such low frequencies carry a long way.

The African elephant uses as wide a range of habitats as man. Like us, it can change woodlands into grasslands, find water for other species by digging in a manner that they can't, and radically modify environments. It can subsist on a vast range of vegetation, including every food crop man grows — except narcotics, tea, coffee, and tobacco — and every plant that domestic livestock eats as well.

Biologically, elephant compete with mankind completely: the expansion of one can only come about at the expense of the other. From this and past centuries, there are well-documented instances of human communities forced to migrate because elephant damage to their farms was so severe. Now, in the face of unparalleled human increase, the elephant is giving way virtually everywhere in Africa. The pressure has been aggravated substantially by demand for ivory.

But there is hope. Elephant biology is understood. Scientists know what is happening to them and why. Their survival lies within the national parks where elephant and human interests can be kept separate. Although their numbers outside the parks must inevitably decline, elephant have good prospects for survival in most Eastern African countries, except Burundi and Somalia where there are no effective parks.

Rhinoceros:

Two rhinoceros species are found in Africa:
the **white,** or **grass,** rhino and the **black,** or **browse,** rhino. In Eastern Africa, white rhino only occurred in a limited area of northern Uganda, west of the Albert Nile. Outside the protection of any national park, in the mid-1960s a number were caught and transported east of the Nile into Murchison Falls National Park, where they prospered.

But during Idi Amin's dictatorship, all white rhino were exterminated — both west of the Nile and in Murchison Falls National Park — giving the species the dubious distinction of being one of three thought to have become extinct in Eastern Africa this century. The other two are the giant or Lord Derby's eland, which had a similar range to the northern white rhino in north-western Uganda, and the okapi, from the Bwamba forest in Uganda.

The future of the black rhino is also critical. This century its range has steadily decreased everywhere in Eastern Africa — a process that began at least as early as 1920. The main reason has been competition with man for living space. The starkest illustration of this was the slaughter of more than one thousand black rhino in little over a year in Kenya's Makueni sub-district in the late 1940s to make way for settlement.

More recently this decline has been dominated by hunting for rhino horn, a commodity so highly priced that it offers quick wealth to poor peasants. Though it is unlikely that the species will become extinct, it has been reduced to small populations in a few tiny sanctuaries.

Horses:

Two zebra occur in Eastern Africa: the **common,** or **Burchell's,** and **Grevy's.** Grazers, they are found mainly in grasslands. The common zebra, the more widespread, occurs within reach of water in every Eastern African country. But it avoids wetter areas where grasses are uniformly higher than one metre (three and one-third feet) and too tough and rank, and, inexplicably, the Ethiopian highlands — although it does occur in very large numbers in the country's Nechisar National Park.

Grevy's zebra, a larger, more densely striped animal, is a Somalian species, unique to the

Opposite: Black rhino have been severely reduced by poaching for their horn, which was worth $1,000 a kilo in 1988.

Top: White rhino, an exotic species from South Africa, were introduced to Kenya's Meru National Park.

Above: Knocked out by a drugged dart, game rangers capture a black rhino for translocation to a protected area.

Above: Widespread in eastern and southern Africa, the common or Burchell's zebra is always within daily reach of water. Mature stallions gather small harems of mares and, even when they congregate in their thousands, it is not difficult to pick out these basic social units.

Horn of Africa's arid climates, that extends into Ethiopia's Ogaden and southern lowlands as well as northern Kenya. A small number, released in Kenya's Tsavo Park, have become too scattered to do well.

A third horse, the **wild ass,** also occurs in the driest areas of northern Ethiopia and Somalia. Likely ancestor of the domestic donkey, it closely resembles the grey Maasai form, although it is somewhat larger and has striped 'stockings'.

There are two races, similar in appearance. The **Nubian wild ass** is present in small numbers in north-westernmost Ethiopia against the Sudan border. The **Somali wild ass** is present in the Danakil and Ogaden parts of Ethiopia and neighbouring areas of northern Somalia. Both live in virtual desert and are seldom seen by visitors to Eastern Africa.

As with the common but little seen leopard, this led to the false belief that wild ass were rare. But, given their severe habitat, they are not particularly scarce. In the Danakil, for example, believing that the progeny will be larger and stronger, local tribesmen try to mate their domestic mares with wild stallions.

Pigs:

Eastern Africa has three pigs: wart hog, giant forest hog, and bushpig. The first two live overwhelmingly off grass. The third is omnivorous, consuming both plant and animal matter. Like its domestic counterpart, it unearths subterranean tubers with a plough-like snout.

Turning up wherever grasses grow in highlands and lowlands, **wart hog** are ubiquitous. Their underground dens are invariably abandoned aardvark burrows which they always enter backwards so that any animal following them underground faces their 'sharp ends'.

Giant forest hog are yet another West African forest fringe species that adapted to highland forests in Kenya during a wetter era. When the western forests retreated, they stayed in the mountains and in the gallery forests on the lower slopes. They are also present in some lowland Uganda forests, and are much more common in Ethiopia than previously thought — found on both sides of the Rift as far as Jibbat, north of Addis Ababa.

The largest African pig, weighing up to 275

107

Above: Grevy's zebra, larger than Burchell's, are confined to the arid Horn of Africa and found in Somalia, northern Kenya, and Ethiopia's southern and eastern lowlands.

Above: Grazing pigs, wart hog are found throughout Africa's grasslands.

Right: Unusual among pigs, wart hog live in underground dens — often an abandoned aardvark burrow. The young are born below ground. Whenever a wart hog is chased, it will make for the nearest burrow, entering tail first so that its 'sharp end' faces any aggressor.

Overleaf: Related to pigs, hippo spend the day in or near water, but graze away from it at night. They lead a curious 'Jekyll and Hyde' social life — highly gregarious in water, they are solitary on land.

kilos (605 pounds), giant forest hog need a year-round supply of green fodder and are typically animals of forest glades.

Bushpig like dense cover and are thus animals of thicket, forest, and relatively wet areas. Inveterate and competent crop raiders, they are greatly disliked by farmers.

Branching out as a distinctive form just over ten million years ago, the **hippopotamus** derives from the pig lineage. It evolved into several forms. One, similar to today's common hippo, had eyes on stalks, like periscopes,

allowing it to spy out the land while submerged.

The **common hippo** is one of the largest land animals, a big male weighing up to 3,200 kilos (7,000 pounds). A grazer, it mows grass — not with its teeth, but with its sharp-edged horny lips. Though it sometimes walks a long way from water — usually in cool, wet weather — it normally spends its non-grazing hours partially submerged.

Because water is a separate habitat from mankind's and hippo graze at night, the two

often live close together. Long after other wildlife move away, hippo persist in the midst of human settlement. As a result, the two meet fairly frequently. Since hippo are short-tempered and armed with huge, cutting canine teeth, the outcome is that they probably cause more human death than any other herbivore in Africa. In some places, their toll exceeds that of the great cats and crocodile combined.

An unusual herbivore, the **water chevrotain** is denizen of the wetter West African and Zaire basin forests and Uganda's Bwamba forest. Superficially like a small, stocky antelope, standing thirty-six centimetres (fourteen inches) at the shoulder and weighing up to fifteen kilos (thirty-three pounds), it is a primitive relic from an era before deer or antelope existed.

Branching off the parental stock some fifty million years ago, at about the time that the pigs established their identities from the same roots, they show some similarities. Instead of horns, they have tusk-like canine teeth, as do the pigs — using them effectively in combat and defence. Unusual among mammals, males are smaller than females. Found in the densest forest, the species swims readily and hides in water when chased.

Giraffe:

Two members of the giraffe family occur in Eastern Africa: the **common giraffe** — its name deriving from the Arabic *zarafa* — and the **okapi**. Giraffe are found in all Eastern African countries except Rwanda, Burundi, and Malawi. Animals of open woodland and of *Acacia* savannah, particularly; nonetheless there are some curious gaps in their distributions.

In Tanzania, for example, they do not occur south of the Rufiji River. In Zambia they only occur west of the Zambezi River, along that country's western border, and as an isolated population in the Luangwa Valley. And, despite suitable habitats, there are none between the Victoria Nile and the Kagera River in Uganda. Seemingly, such large rivers are difficult to cross.

There are several races of the common giraffe. The most distinctive and handsome is the **reticulated giraffe** of northern Kenya, southern Ethiopia, and Somalia. In this subspecies the characteristic blotches are so large that the animal appears a rich, liver-coloured brown, covered with an irregular network of white tracery. Contrastingly, the **Maasai gi-**

raffe have irregular blotches on a yellowish background. **Rothschild's giraffe** of Uganda and north-western Kenya is an intermediate between the Maasai and the reticulated form. Within any group, there are many local variations in colour and patterning. In all, particularly the males, colour tends to darken with age.

Predominantly leaf eaters, a long, prehensile tongue enables giraffe to strip foliage from twigs with extreme delicacy. In some areas, among them Nairobi National Park, they

Overleaf: Giraffe — bulls reach up to five and a half metres tall — feed off leaves out of reach to all other large mammals except elephant.

Opposite: New-born Rothschild giraffe is welcomed by its mother.

Below: Despite their great height, giraffe give birth standing up; the calves routinely surviving their abrupt arrival.

Above: African buffalo are found widely throughout Eastern Africa — virtually everywhere there is grass and access to daily water.

Opposite: Male reticulated giraffe — the race found in northern Kenya — in ritual combat. Taking turns, they slog one another with their stubby-horned heads until one has had enough and gives up.

browse trees so heavily they control their shapes, rather in the manner of topiarian gardeners in Europe's parks. A striking feature of the young is the speed at which they are weaned. They eat leaves at two weeks and within a month can go without milk.

The okapi is a member of the giraffe family, exclusively confined to Zaire's dense eastern Ituri Forest. Standing 1.6 metres (5.2 feet) at the shoulder, weighing around 220 kilograms (500 pounds), this leggy, forest leaf-eater has a shorter neck than its plains relatives. Its background colour is deep reddish-black — almost purple. This striking colour is accompanied by brilliant white leg-spots and some almost zebra-like striping on the hindquarters and upper forelegs and pale-coloured sides to the head.

Zaire's okapi in the Ituri Forest on Uganda's western border once occurred in the contiguous Bwamba Forest. Strays may still enter the area. But this interesting forest giraffid may soon share the white rhino's and giant eland's status of being declared extinct in Uganda and Eastern Africa.

The Bovids:

The *Bovidae* family differs anatomically from the deer, *Cervidae,* in several features. Most obvious are the permanent bovid horns, keratinous sheaths growing about bony cores. The cervids shed and regrow their horns annually. Probably because of intense competition from bovids, deer never established themselves in sub-Saharan Africa and none exist there today.

African bovids fall into three divisions. The first contains a single species: the **African buffalo,** related to both the Asiatic buffaloes and domestic cattle, is similar in many ways to both. Buffalo are gregarious, sometimes living in herds of more than 2,000. Recently they have been successfully domesticated in Zimbabwe.

Bold and big, hunters rank them among the most dangerous of animals, a belief borne out

117

Above: Two bull eland, the largest of the antelope family.
Opposite: Male bongo; secretive and seldom-seen forest dweller.

by the number of deaths and injuries they inflict each year. Old males are usually the culprits. Leaving the herd once past their prime, they live in small bachelor groups or alone. It is these elderly and not particularly watchful individuals that people tend to stumble on at close quarters. When this happens, the animal feels threatened and attacks.

In herds, buffalo are seldom dangerous. With many eyes on the alert, people rarely run the risk of getting too close before being spotted and the buffalo make off. However, buffalo can mount an effective defence against large carnivores. Should they detect a lion or leopard, or if one of them is caught and bellows, they will attack *en masse*. Many a lion has met its end this way.

Buffalo occur wherever there is grass and access to water, whether in forest glades or dry savannah. There are two forms: the large, black **Cape buffalo** and the much smaller

West African forest race. Bulls in the Cape race weigh up to 850 kilos (1,870 pounds), whereas those of the western type reach little more than 320 kilos (704 pounds). The two meet in western Uganda where herds often display a range of hybrids. Similarly, the buffalo of western Ethiopia appear to be intermediates, hinting of bygone western connections and the possibility that other lowland forest species might occur.

The second bovid group contains the wild sheep and goats. Two subspecies of the heavily-horned **palearctic ibex,** found only in northern Ethiopia, represent this group in Eastern Africa; reminders of that not-so-distant time when Arabia was part of Africa. The **Nubian ibex** lives in the arid Red Sea hills of Eritrea, while the **Abyssinian,** or **Walia ibex** is found in the steep gorges and precipices that rift and ring the Simien Mountains at altitudes between 2,200 metres (7,500 feet)

and 4,000 metres (13,500 feet) above sea level. Both races have been hunted to the brink of extinction.

The third division of African *Bovidae*, the antelope, are a spectacular evolutionary success. Radiating into many species which took advantage of all available ecological niches, this group seems to have displaced the other vegetarians — particularly the horses.

There are fifty-four antelope species in Eastern Africa. All are generally handsome, but one group stands out: the tragelaphines, or spiral-horned antelope. It contains the **giant,** or **Lord Derby's, eland.** A large male will stand 176 centimetres (five and three-quarter feet) at the shoulder and weigh up to 907 kilos (1,995 pounds), bigger than a full-grown male Cape buffalo.

This rare species had a similar range to the northern white rhino and was found in northern Uganda west of the Albert Nile. It is not known if any are left in this area. In all likelihood it has joined the white rhino as an animal that once occurred in Eastern Africa. The giant eland gets its name not from its overall size, but from the length of its horns, which may be up to 123 centimetres (four feet) long.

In body size the **common eland** weighs less than the giant eland up to (700 kilos — 1,540 pounds) but is a touch taller (178 centimetres).

Top: In Eastern Africa, though it occurs in patches throughout the region, the stately greater kudu is most readily seen in Zambia, Malawi, and southern Tanzania.

Above: A harsh bark or the flash of white tail are often all that is seen or heard of the male lesser kudu, shy denizen of the dry Horn of Africa.

120

Above: Young male and female mountain nyala. Sound conservation measures have made this once seldom-seen animal easy to approach and watch.

Wide-ranging, it is found all over Eastern Africa except Burundi and Somalia. This open woodland and savannah species is surprisingly selective in what it eats, perhaps the most nomadic and mobile of all the antelope — other than the true desert forms. Once there were great hopes that eland might be domesticated as substitutes for cattle in much of Africa, but these were dashed by their need for mobility and very large ranges.

Yet another relic of the days when forests stretched across Africa between the Atlantic and Indian Oceans is the **bongo.** This large, striped, chestnut forest dweller — males weigh up to 405 kilos (891 pounds) — occurs in the western forests, but has a series of isolated populations in Kenya's highlands on the Aberdare and Mau Ranges, Mount Kenya, and the Cheranganis (there may be none now left in the latter). Paradoxically secretive, it is not timid. Surprised at close quarters, it has

been known to charge with buffalo-like determination and, brought to bay, is a fearsome adversary. For unknown reasons, Kenya's bongo populations fluctuate between abundance and rarity.

Most stately of the big tragelaphines is the **greater kudu.** Its great, corkscrew horns measure up to 180 centimetres (five and three-quarter feet) long. The species is ubiquitous in the woodlands of southern Africa and the 'miombo' belts of Zambia, Malawi, and southern Tanzania. In northern Tanzania, Kenya, north-eastern Uganda, Ethiopia, and Somalia, it is more an animal of árid hills and scarps.

The **lesser kudu,** half the size of the greater kudu, has an altogether smaller range, found only in arid Somalia, Ethiopia's Ogaden, northern and eastern Kenya, and the most arid parts of northern Tanzania north of the Central Railway Line. The species is also found in the Yemen on the other side of the Red Sea: yet

121

Above: Endemic to the Bale Mountains of Ethiopia, mountain nyala — like a stocky, shaggy version of the greater kudu — only became known to western science in 1910.

Above: The little red steinbok of open woodland and lightly grassed areas is perhaps the only antelope which will go down an aardvark burrow if pursued.

another reminder that Arabia and Africa were once linked.

Perhaps the most unusual tragelaphine is the swamp-dwelling **sitatunga,** which weighs up to 125 kilos (275 pounds). Confined to wetlands where there are tall reeds and papyrus — Uganda's numerous papyrus swamps, the Malagarasi and Moyowosi swamps of Tanzania, and Lake Bangweulu in Zambia — it is common enough and likely to stay so, as the terrain makes hunting difficult. A peculiar feature is the animal's greatly elongated hooves that enable it to walk on floating vegetation. When chased it dives under water and hides with only its nose showing.

Two species of **nyala** occur in Eastern Africa. Both look like kudus, though, like the bushbuck, males tend to be dark, while females are more red. The smaller, more numerous nyala of southern Africa became so abundant in Malawi's Lengwe National Park that numbers had to be reduced. Handsome as this sitatunga-sized animal is, it is only half the size of the **mountain nyala** of Ethiopia's Bale and Arussi Mountains. This shaggy-coated, high altitude, heathland animal has a very restricted range. Within this it is well conserved and abundant.

The smallest tragelaphine, the **bushbuck,** is also the most widespread. In white spots and stripes against backgrounds that vary regionally from russet-red to dark brown and black, the species turns up wherever there is thicket or forest.

Bate's pigmy antelope, weighing three kilos (six and two-third pounds) is the smallest ungulate in Eastern African and occurs in western Uganda's forests. Somewhat larger, but still tiny — up to nine kilos (twenty pounds) — is the dull brown **suni** of Kenya's and Tanzania's central and coastal forests. Even where numerous, neither of these little forest dwellers is commonly seen, due to the thick cover they use.

Similar in size to the suni are two more open-country antelope, **Sharpe's** and the **common steinbok.** Small, upright-horned, and russet-coloured, Sharpe's occurs in pairs through the open woodlands of Zambia, Malawi, and southern Tanzania, while the common steinbok is found in yet more open country in both southern Kenya and the northern half of Tanzania.

Similar to the steinbok, but twice their size, straw-coloured **oribi** are readily identified by

Above: A pair of dik-dik — small grey antelope of the dry lands.

a large black mark, a gland, below each ear. Very much a grassland animal, it lives in small herds, whereas steinbok are solitary or go in pairs.

The **klipspringer** is Africa's answer to the chamois. This eighteen-kilo (forty-pound), straight-horned antelope is found only on cliffs, rocky hillsides, and mountain screes — some separated from one another by tens, if not hundreds, of kilometres, of unsuitable klipspringer terrain. Although some of these isolated locations are so small they can hold only tiny populations that, in theory, should fail through inbreeding, there is no evidence of this. It suggests that some klipspringers must occasionally move across country entirely unsuited to them — an event that is seldom, if ever, witnessed.

Dik-dik are small, grey, suni-sized antelope of the arid zones. There are four species, all similar in habits. One, the **beira,** is found only in coastal Somalia. The other three are **Salt's** of Somalia and arid Ethiopia, **Guenther's** of north-eastern Uganda, Kenya, and

northern Tanzania, and **Kirk's** of central and southern Tanzania. Interestingly, Kirk's also occurs in Namibia: yet another clue to that arid link that must have once prevailed right across the continent from East Africa to the Kalahari.

Dik-dik live in pairs and mark their territories with little piles of dung, wherein hangs an African fable. Long ago a tired dik-dik was returning home after a hard day. Not looking where he was going, he stumbled into a mountainous elephant turd that lay in the path. Outraged by the elephant's arrogant disregard for others' sensibilities, the dik-dik determined to have its revenge. But clearly a dik-dik dropping on its own is of no consequence to an elephant. If, however, it always used the same site and heaped them together, one day it might accumulate a pile large enough to trap an elephant and get its own back. That is why, to this day, says the tale, dik-dik pile their droppings in one place: so that in due course they will avenge their ancestor.

Duikers are antelope of the forests. Of thir-

123

teen species in Eastern Africa only one — the **grey duiker** — lives outside them. Small- to medium-sized, hunch-backed, and mostly solitary, they prefer the gloom to sunlight. Browsing on the forest floors, almost all eat fruit as well as herbage. The best chance of seeing them is to sit quietly near a fig tree in fruit. Duiker take advantage of the fruit knocked down by birds and monkeys as well as those that fall naturally. Indeed, at least two species — **Aders** and **Harvey's** — and probably several others routinely follow troops of monkeys to benefit from anything edible they may drop or knock down.

Eight of the forest duikers, *Cephalophus* — **Harvey's, Natal, Ader's, black-fronted, Peter's, Ruwenzori, red-flanked** and **white-bellied** — are basically chestnut-red animals with black and/or white somewhere on their coats; for example, black 'stockings' or white belly. The largest, the **yellow-backed duiker,** is mahogany-brown with a bright yellow patch on the rump. Endemic to Tanzania's mountains, **Abbott's duiker** is the next largest, also dark brown, but without the yellow rump patch. The smallest is **Ader's duiker** which occurs only on Zanzibar and in Kenya's Arabuko-Sokoki coastal forest.

Above: The klipspringer, as agile as a chamois, is found only on rocky outcrops, cliffs, and steep screes.

The **grey duiker** of Africa's savannahs is ubiquitous. More than any other antelope it adapts to farmland. It still occurs, hiding out in patches of secondary thicket and weed beds in places where there are more than 500 people to the square kilometre (1,280 to the square mile). In both Uganda and Zimbabwe, Government efforts to eradicate tsetse flies involved the wholesale slaughter of wildlife in certain areas. Some species were exterminated or greatly reduced, but grey duiker actually increased. The group's name derives from the Afrikaans for 'diver' — because of its habit of diving into cover when disturbed.

The kob or 'reduncine' antelope — reedbuck, waterbuck, kob, and lechwe — are a group of medium- to large-size grazers that associate, for the most part, with wetlands or relatively moist grasslands. Only the males have horns. Largest of them (300 kilos — 660 pounds) is the **waterbuck.** Stately, grey, shaggy, and strong-smelling, waterbuck tend to occur, as the name implies, in wet areas and close to rivers and lakes.

The **kob,** a stocky, russet antelope, half the waterbuck's size, occurs through the moister savannahs that stretch from Senegal to Ethiopia and south into Uganda and western Kenya (they may be extinct in Kenya). Two races occur in Eastern Africa. **Thomas's,** or the **Uganda** kob is the subspecies which occupies most of Uganda. The **white-eared** kob occurs in westernmost Ethiopia, south of the Baro River, and may extend occasionally into northernmost Uganda.

Where habitats are suitable and stable — as in Uganda's Semliki Flats — kob live in dense sedentary populations running to tens of thousands. Where food supplies are seasonal, they often move between ranges. The white-eared kob exemplifies such a migratory life style. Its main population perhaps numbers more than a million animals that migrate seasonally on and off flood plains in rhythm with the rise and fall of the Nile, resulting in a spectacle that echoes the better-known Serengeti migration of wildebeest.

Kob also illustrate a third life style. Across vast stretches of their range, they live in small groups, without the huge communal display 'arenas' that are such a feature of their big populations. It illustrates the point that social behaviour varies to ensure survival in a wide range of circumstances.

The **puku,** or **Vardon's kob,** occupies similar latitudes south of the Equator as the previous species north of it. They are found along the margins of lakes, swamps, rivers, and on flood plains in Zambia, Malawi, and southern

Above: Northern, or Bohor, reedbuck, most commonly found singly or in pairs in the medium height grasses that grow on open, seasonally swampy ground.

Tanzania. It, too, is a stocky, red, medium-sized antelope. The males horns are lyrate, but rather heavy and short.

More aquatic by far is the elegant **lechwe** of Zambia's wetlands. In dimensions and red colouring still obviously a kob, though somewhat less stocky, lechwe occupy the flooded grasslands that occur in the upper Zambezi basin and, particularly, on the Kafue flats. In herds of thousands, there they spend much, if not most, of their time in water up to two feet deep. They are found in similar numbers in Lake Bangweulu, where the old males assume a handsome black coat — qualifying this population as a subspecies. Local lion have adapted their hunting techniques to stalk lechwe through water — only their heads showing above the surface.

Just as the puku replaces the kob in southern latitudes, so, too, is there a lechwe north of the Equator. Occupying the same ecological niche as the red lechwe in Zambia, the dark brown **Nile lechwe** lives in the flooded 'toich' grasslands to the south of the sudd and also occurs in westernmost Ethiopia, along the Bara and Gilo rivers in the Gambella area.

Three very similar-looking **reedbuck** complete the reduncine group. Two of these medium-sized, yellowish antelope, the **Bohor** and the **southern reedbuck,** are animals of rank, medium-height grasslands.

The Bohor is found in Ethiopia, Uganda, Rwanda, and Kenya; the southern in Zambia, Malawi, and Tanzania.

The third, the **mountain reedbuck,** is an animal of grassy hillsides more than 1,500 metres (5,000 feet) above sea level. Somewhat greyer and a little smaller than the other two species, the mountain form has a curious African distribution, for it occurs in three widely separated clumps: southern Ethiopia, Kenya, and northern Tanzania; South Africa; and Mount Cameroon in West Africa. Separated by thousands of kilometres, these three outposts again make the point that at one time a common environment linked them and demonstrate how Africa's climates must have changed.

Gazelle specialize in arid lands, so it's no surprise that the Horn of Africa has more species than any other part of Eastern Africa. Most are sandy to russet coloured above with white underparts and stockings. Of the true gazelle, **Pelzeln's** and **Speke's** are found only in northern Somalia and along Ethiopia's Red Sea coast: the driest part of the whole region. **Soemmering's gazelle** has the same heartland, but is also found in central Ethiopia and possibly northern Kenya, again confined to the harshest environments.

Grant's gazelle, of which there are several races and which some authorities feel may be a subspecies of Soemmering's, extends this range throughout northern Kenya, into northeastern Uganda, and down through the arid central core of Tanzania.

Combine the Soemmering's and Grant's gazelle distributions and you have most of the **gerenuk's** range. This gazelle shares the group's ability to survive without free water, but has also evolved a long neck to exploit the *Acacia* shrubs and trees that typify semi-desert lands. Standing on its hind legs, the long neck gives it a reach of nearly two metres (seven feet).

Another gazelle that has evolved a similar long neck and general gerenuk configuration is the **dibatag,** occurring in northern Somalia and south-east Ethiopia.

Odd man out among the gazelle is the small **Thomson's gazelle** or 'tommy' of the open Maasai plains in Kenya and northern Tanzania. It is an exception in that it cannot go for extended periods without water. One-third the size of the similar looking Grant's gazelle, both species have a black flank flash separating the dun-coloured back from the white belly — although not all Grants have this marking.

Cheetah prey extensively on gazelle. Given gazelle fleetness and that they are animals of dry open lands, it is reasonable to suggest that the cheetah developed its characteristic hunting technique specifically to exploit gazelle.

With their liquid, lustrous eyes and general grace, gazelle and antelope have long been used as analogies for feminine beauty. Yet no swain would win favour claiming his beloved looked like a **hartebeest,** even though, when a Somali tells his true love that she looks like a camel it indicates the utmost endearment.

Long-faced, mournful, with large foreparts and small hindquarters and an odd, bounding

gallop, the hartebeests, or alcelaphines, are the ugly sisters of the antelope family. Thought to derive from the gazelle lineage, retaining the latter's ability to run, they have increased their body size, become grazers, and remained animals of open places.

The reddish, medium-sized **hirola,** or **Hunter's hartebeest** is perhaps a relic species that developed early in the divergence from gazelle. Fossils of similar forms are widely found, but today the hirola occupies a small range astride the Kenya-Somalia border and numbers perhaps no more than 40,000. Superficially at least, there appears to be nothing special about this range, so it is puzzling that

Below: The slender gerenuk gazelle has evolved long legs and an even longer neck to feed on Acacia leaves two metres above the ground. Its greatest reach is achieved by standing on its hind legs.

they do not occur more widely. Perhaps, as an 'old' species, it is just 'tired' and unable to compete with more modern forms.

Nearly three times as heavy as this ancient founding form are **red** or **reddish harte-beests,** which occur in the savannahs and woodlands from Senegal to the Cape in several forms. Seeing the **Senegalese** form next to the **Cape** variety, it is easy to accept that they are different species. The differences between neighbouring subspecies, however, are far less apparent and it is clear that the races represent a continuous but gradual variation in form across Africa, questioning the yardsticks which define a species.

Close cousin to the red hartebeests is the **topi** — also called **tiang** or **tsessebe,** according to regional preference. These are slightly more graceful members of the family, with handsome coats of black and gunmetal patches against dark brown backclothes and fawn 'stockings'. Found in all Eastern African countries except Burundi and Malawi, they are confined to short grasslands in well-watered areas or, in drier climates, in sumps and flood plains. Their distribution is sporadic, but where they do occur, it is usually in dense populations.

For sheer density, however, the current star is the **wildebeest.** By virtue of a single population in the Serengeti-Mara region of Tanzania and Kenya, they have established modern concepts of both Pleistocene abundance and mass migration. More than one and a half million wildebeest move seasonally between the dry short-grass Serengeti Plains and the wetter Mara pastures. Similar mass movements have been reported from Botswana.

Yet the idea that wildebeest are 'mega-herd' animals *per se* would be wrong. Wildebeest occur in small herds in scattered pockets between southern Kenya and Botswana. Like the kob, they show that small static herds may suit one set of circumstances, while massed groups may suit another. It illustrates an adaptability that may well have played an important role in establishing antelope dominance in African ecosystems.

Below: Soemmering's gazelle, relatively common in the lowland areas east and south of the Ethiopian highlands and in Somalia.

127

Top: Male Grant's gazelle, of the type that occurs in Kenya's Mara and Tanzania's Serengeti regions.

Above: Male Thomson's gazelle disputing a territorial boundary.

Top: The impala, perhaps Africa's most graceful antelope, is often classified as a member of the ugly-looking hartebeest family.

Above: In contrast to the jet black adult sable, female and young are reddish in colour.

Overleaf: Wildebeest hordes arrive at the Mara River on their annual migration from the Serengeti before surging across in their thousands when hundreds drown. So great are their numbers this loss makes little impression.

Top: Ugly sisters of the antelope family — a Coke's hartebeest with its new-born calf.

Above: Oryx drink when water is available, but have to go without free water for long periods.

Top: Sentinels of the plains, topi often rest on anthills or slightly raised ground, good vantage points for spotting approaching predators.

Above: Rapier-horned and dangerous if cornered, the fringe-eared oryx has been domesticated successfully in Kenya.

Top: Imperious black male sable, Angola's national animal.

If hartebeest are awkward and the wildebeest is a clown cobbled together from other animal parts, then the Cinderella among these ugly sisters is the **impala.** Perhaps the most beautiful of all antelope — the nearest African likeness to Disney's 'Bambi' — impala occur widely in Eastern Africa but not in Ethiopia and Somalia. Those in the northern half of this range are at least a third again as large as those in Zambia and further south. They occupy the fringes between woodland and grassland.

The last group, the hippotragine, or horse-like, antelope are represented by three species — the **oryx,** the **roan,** and the **sable.** The oryx occurs in three forms: the **beisa** of Somalia, Ethiopia, eastern Uganda, and northern Kenya, the **fringe-eared** of eastern and southern Kenya and northern Tanzania, and the **gemsbok** of the Kalahari and its surrounds. Rapier-horned, gregarious, and weighing over 200 kilos (440 pounds), the oryx is a truly desert-adapted species that has been experimentally domesticated in Kenya as possible substitute for cattle in very dry areas.

The **roan** antelope — or, to translate its scientific name, the 'horse-like horned horse' — is the largest hippotragine, reaching 300 kilos (660 pounds). Widely distributed through the deciduous woodlands north and south of the Equator, it is nowhere abundant. As a rather coarse grazer, its numbers may be determined by the relative sparseness of grasses in woodland, combined with a pronounced sense of territory that restricts the size of herds.

Slightly smaller, the black-garbed and scimitar-horned bull **sable** is the most austerely beautiful of all antelope. Females are russet-coloured and shorter-horned. Like roan, sable are an open woodland species nowhere abundant.

In modern times the sable has been confined to south-eastern Africa: Tanzania, Zambia, Malawi, Zimbabwe, Mozambique, and the northern tip of South Africa. Small, fringe populations occur in Angola, northern Botswana, and coastal Kenya. For hunter or photographer, an adult male sable is the ultimate antelope trophy.

134

Chapter 9 Birds

Eastern Africa is rightly famous for its bird life. There may be other similar-sized regions of the world with as many species — the Amazon watershed, for example — but a large proportion live in tall rain forest canopy. As such, they are inaccessible, if not invisible, to most people, while Eastern African birds are incomparable for their visibility. Because of the many open habitats, they are seen relatively easily.

The diversity of bird life comes about because of the variety of habitats: from desert to wet forests, from sea level to snow-capped mountains. Where steep, forested mountains and hills plunge down to savannahs and deserts, radically different species are brought close together.

This diversity is also enhanced by the phenomenon of migration. Through flight, birds follow environments of their choice to a degree unknown to other vertebrates except bats. Thus species which specialize in the burst of insect life that characterizes the onset of the rains may follow the Intertropical Convergence Zone backwards and forwards in its annual north-south movement. By so doing, they live in perpetual 'spring'. Others may move into normally dry, inhospitable areas when it rains to take advantage of brief green seasons, leaving again as they dry out.

As so many of these inter-African migrations take place across vast tracts in which nobody records them, they are poorly understood. Far more is known about the annual inter-continental bird migrations from the Palaearctic region — temperate and arctic Eurasia. Every year many species which spend the northern summer above the 45° latitude move south to the African tropics to avoid inhospitable northern winters. Whether they are African birds which breed in Eurasia, or Eurasian birds that winter in Africa, is debatable. But as many migrant species belong to families that have far more members resident year-round in the tropics, the former is more likely.

The classic migrant is the **Arctic tern,** which annually travels between the Arctic and Antarctic over the Atlantic Ocean. There are some, however, which undertake traverses just as long, between Siberia and the Cape of Good Hope, passing through Eastern Africa en route.

Eastern races of the **curlew** breed in the tundra of easterly Siberia and winter on South Africa's shores, a trip as long as the Arctic tern's. And some specimens of the **lesser cuckoo,** *Cuculus poliocephalus,* may move equally far between Japan and southern Africa.

Distance is not the only striking feature of these migrations. Many small passerine warblers fly, not along welcoming corridors such as the Nile Valley, but across the inhospitable Sahara itself.

With their present dispositions the origins of these migrations are difficult to comprehend. But seen in the light of a past in which Africa and Eurasia lay closer together they become more understandable. Then the Sahara was a series of dry cells in a savannah matrix; Lake Chad was as big as the Caspian Sea; and many now distant habitats were far more extensive.

In this context it is easier to envisage inter-tropical seasonal movements gradually developing into inter-continental travels. The ancestors of the birds that now cross the Sahara once skirted the dry cells. As these slowly expanded, corners had to be cut and by gradual evolution this corner-cutting developed into trans-desert migration.

As geological and climatic forces produce change, they will continue to modify bird migration. If the Sahara expands — either naturally or through human intervention — many small migrants may well be unable to cross it. And as Africa continues to drift away from Eurasia, this may stop soaring birds crossing the intervening sea, since the thermals on which they depend do not rise off water. Already most soaring birds migrate across the Straits of Gibraltar or the Isthmus of Suez.

Migration is but one intriguing aspect of bird mobility. Another is their ability to locate habitats. Semi-deserts are as far removed from water bird requirements as it is possible to conceive. Yet if a freak storm produces temporary pools, or a dam is built, within weeks, sometimes days, water birds are using it.

How did they find it? Perhaps they have constant scouts flying to and fro over all habitats in the hope of occasionally coming across something new and suitable. Such scouts,

however, are seldom seen and the idea presumes that many probably die by going too far into unsuitable habitats. Random scouting does not seem a tenable idea, so the question remains.

Birds are perhaps the best-known zoological class — open to investigation and observation by any interested person. Ornithology has been so well served by amateurs that it has long been at the forefront of progress in biological science. Nowhere is this more apparent than in Eastern Africa.

Until the last decade of the last century the region received scant attention from western science. Yet by 1914, more than ninety per cent of the region's birds had been described. By 1930 this had risen to perhaps ninety-eight per cent. Descriptions of their structures and origins were accompanied by details of their biology, distribution, diet, breeding, nesting, and eggs.

There can be few parallels in the annals of natural science where information was collected so comprehensively as during the 1890-1930 era in Eastern Africa. Many early explorers and administrators were keen naturalists — Sir Frederick Jackson in particular — but they were aided to an unequalled degree by people in many walks of life.

Yet, despite the competence of these early ornithologists, occasional discoveries are still made. In May 1984, for example, a new species of cliff-swallow was found at a lighthouse off Port Sudan in the Red Sea. Appropriately named *Hirundo perdita,* literally the **'lost' swallow,** this is still the only known specimen.

The bird was dead, but whence had it come? Where is the species' normal habitat? There are several types of cliff-swallows, all South or West African, but none occur in Eastern Africa. Perhaps it came from the crags and cliffs of northern Ethiopia, or from the rugged Yemen across the Red Sea. Some lucky amateur may yet solve this enigma.

An idea of Eastern Africa's range of bird families and number of species is given in Tables 1 and 2. These are incomplete: indeed, other than fleetingly, no list will ever be complete. With environmental change so prominent in African ecology, new surprises will always turn up, and occasional deletions take place.

Passerine (literally sparrow-like, but denoting birds with normal 'perching' feet) species greatly outnumber non-passerines. The

Opposite: Black-and-white plumage of the fish eagle serves as a distinctive territorial marker, particularly when seen, as by other fish eagles, from above.

Below: Steppe eagle with engorged crop — as with many predators, when a kill is made they consume large meals to counterbalance sporadic hunting success.

Top: Ruby eyes, ginger tonsures, and cobalt-blue waistcoats are distinct trademarks of vulturine guinea fowl of arid Somalia, eastern Ethiopia, and northern and eastern Kenya.

Above: Yellow-necked spurfowl — Africa's answer to European partridges.

Above: Noisy residents on all fresh-water lakes, dams, and larger rivers, Egyptian geese are found the length and breadth of Africa.

largest family is *Passeridae,* containing 163 **sparrows, weavers, waxbills,** and associated species.

Actual populations of some — **quelea,** for example — may run to hundreds of millions. The family's diversity and abundance is not surprising, however. Predominantly grass-seed eaters, their evolution reflects the great savannah continent of Africa where grasses are the most abundant vegetation. In economic terms this seed eating makes the family important, for, together with the smaller **finch** family, some of its members eat such vast quantities of grain that they are major pests.

The worst of them are quelea. These neat, small, dun-coloured seed eaters form such large flocks that from a distance they look like large, dense clouds of smoke. They follow the rain zone as it moves north and south over the savannah grasslands in their millions. When they land in grain fields, they ruin crops and farms in days, even hours, like locusts. Consuming grain by the tonne, every man's hand is against them.

Governments employ special teams to destroy quelea. One technique used to be placing dynamite amid drums of diesel fuel under the trees, or in the reed beds where they roosted, then blowing them up and burning them at night. Now their roosts are sprayed from the air with an extremely toxic chemical. In Zimbabwe a plan is afoot to catch them in their millions and market them in southern Europe, where any small bird was once a culinary prize.

The Indian Ocean and Red Sea that bathe the coasts of Eastern Africa are not particularly rich in oceanic bird life, probably because these waters are not very fertile. Nonetheless, in addition to at least twenty-six **gulls** and **terns,** there are at least fourteen species of **petrels** and **shearwaters,** four **gannets** or **boobies,** two **frigate** birds and three **tropic** birds.

An unusual feature of the Red Sea is the high density of **ospreys** about its shores. Though found worldwide, perhaps nowhere is the species more numerous than in this area. In Djibouti harbour it is common to see several at once, sitting on buoys and vantage points like so many gulls. But elsewhere in Africa ospreys are uncommon. Seemingly, competition from the ubiquitous **fish eagles** keeps osprey numbers low. But fish eagles do not

Opposite: Cramped for nest space, three young darters wait for a parent to bring a meal.

Left: An adult darter dries its plumage after a fishing foray. As they swim almost completely submerged, this drying out process is frequent.

occur in the Red Sea.

The **African fish eagle** attracts attention with its wild, yelping call. Associated with all the lakes and rivers, this unusually noisy bird of prey has become the clichéd voice of Africa. By preference a fish eater, it readily kills other water birds and mammals up to the size of a hare. Any flamingo gathering of size is attended by several fish eagles, for ailing individuals are always easy game.

The range of raptors in eastern Africa is particularly impressive. Of the thirteen true **eagles,** the two largest are the **martial** of the open savannahs and the **crowned** of the forests. With a greater wingspan, but somewhat lighter bones, the martial spends hours aloft at heights at the edge of human vision. They hunt either from the air, attacking in a long flat glide, or dropping onto a victim from a dead tree or other elevated vantage point.

Their wide grasp and long toes suggest that martial eagles are principally bird hunters, taking **guinea fowl** and **francolin.** However, their choice of prey is both general and opportunistic, with largest kills around the size of a jackal or Thomson's gazelle. A martial has been known to kill a small lion cub.

Shorter-winged but more sturdily built than the martial, the crowned eagle is the one bird of prey in Africa reputed to have hunted humans. In the 1930s, the game warden of Uganda, Captain Charles Pitman, documented a case on the slopes of Mount Elgon. A crowned eagle swooped down and seized a baby lying at the side of a field its mother was cultivating. But it failed to get a proper grip and, about ten feet off the ground, the child fell out of its loose swaddling, little the worse for wear.

As with martials, crowned eagles are opportunists and kill a wide range of prey. They are adept monkey hunters, taking victims out of tree canopies. But frequently they sit motionless on some bough watching the forest floor, dropping on to any suitable quarry which passes below. The largest victim recorded by that famous eagle-watcher, the late Leslie Brown, who made a particular study of this bird, was a female bushbuck. It was far too large for the bird to lift. They kill with a grasp powerful enough to crush a cat's skull, that drives inch-long talons deep into the victim's vitals.

Many large birds of prey soar: stiff-winged, they use thermals and updrafts in the same way as sailplanes. Height governs the distance they can glide; the higher they are, the more ground they can cover before having to regain height to repeat the process. Soaring birds watch one another continuously for evidence of strong updrafts. If one rises steeply, others immediately glide towards it to share the strong lift.

So ingrained is this economic behaviour that if any see a light aircraft make more than three or four consecutive tight circles, they will endeavour to join it: a habit not without hazard for the pilot and any passenger.

Vultures, all accomplished soarers, spend the warm hours of the day moving from thermal to thermal, usually at heights above 150 metres (500 feet), watching the ground for signs of death. When travelling across coun-

141

142

Above: Strange little stork of Africa's inland waterways, the hammerkop builds a nest so large it can hold a man's weight without collapsing.
Opposite top left: Lilac-breasted rollers. Top right: Blue-eared glossy starling.
Centre left: Male golden weaver bird and nest. Centre right: Little bee eater. Bottom: Grey-headed kingfisher.

try, between feeding grounds and nesting sites, they frequently fly much higher.

A conspicuously big raptor is the black-bodied, white-winged and stub-tailed **bateleur**: nature's original delta-wing. It soars well below 150 metres (500 feet), much lower than most other large soaring birds, in characteristic long, fast traverses. Stiff-winged, it rocks in jerky erratic response to every air current, no matter how slight.

No other land bird shares this ability to glide in straight lines in apparent defiance of gravity. The rigid wings and irregular flight recall a tightrope walker juggling for balance with his pole: hence the name — bateleur — from the French for juggler. This aerial predator has more secondary wing feathers than any other bird, giving it exceptionally low wing-loading; the key to its unique gliding ability.

Bateleurs scavenge, and from their low altitude often see small or hidden corpses that the higher-soaring vultures miss. Consequently they often arrive first at small kills but,

because they are watched by the vultures, they have to feed quickly and leave before the mob arrives. In some places they patrol country roads before the vultures are up, looking for small animals hit by cars the previous night.

Besides scavenging, bateleurs hunt competently, killing a variety of prey up to the size of a hare. But they have a particular preference for snakes. In this they betray their relationship to the **serpent eagles.**

Bare-legged and not true eagles, there are four members of this family in Eastern Africa. Though they specialize in snakes, they also take lizards and small mammals — rodents and dwarf mongooses among them.

Nineteen falcon species, including the **peregrine,** range over Eastern Africa. An aberrant and unusual member of this group is the **cuckoo-falcon,** so called because it looks more like a large cuckoo than a bird of prey. It hunts chameleons, methodically looking over tree and shrub foliage, until it sees through the cryptic camouflages of these reptiles.

143

Opposite: Yellow-billed storks advance with open beaks, gently swinging their heads from side to side. Touching a fish or frog, the bills snap shut, gripping the victim.
Left: Hovering between three and five metres over the water and scanning for fish below, the pied kingfisher is perhaps the most obvious of a big family.

Opposite bottom: Stately saddle-billed storks tend to keep to themselves — usually hunting frogs and fish in marshy areas.
Overleaf: Roseate lesser flamingos massed at the water's edge. Here and there among this beautiful rabble are a few aristocratic greater flamingos — whiter and twice the height.

Yet another specialist is the **bat hawk.** Falcon-like in appearance, with pointed wings and high speed, this raptor is really closer to the kites in kinship. It is found near any big bat colony at dusk, when bats leave their roosts. But watching them catch bats before their 'radars' are properly warmed up as they emerge from a cave or crack is poor sport. Far more exciting is to see the pursuit of a bat that is fully warmed up.

When contact is established, the hawk accelerates after its victim, following every move. Any watcher will be convinced that the bat's sonar equipment provides accurate all-round 'vision'. Each jink, twist, and turn shows that it is clearly aware of the hawk's exact position, moving as if it had good eyesight. But unless it can gain cover, even the fastest bat is usually doomed. Such a chase — with sonar sensing system pitted against visual detection — epitomizes evolution's 'ingenuity'.

The tiny **pigmy falcon** is at the other end of the raptor spectrum. More like a shrike than a falcon, this resident of the drier *Commiphora* and *Acacia* country normally catches insects and small lizards. Occasionally, betraying its true affiliations, it will chase a dove bigger than itself.

Which of the 1,480 and more species is Eastern Africa's most beautiful bird? Though a common question, there is no set answer. Not only do different ornithologists have different choices, but their candidates change over time.

Vivid colours abound. Non-iridescent blues, bright, soft and light, belong to the **kingfishers** and **rollers.** They also appear in the **bee-eaters** and the **cordon bleu seed eaters.** Hard, dark, iridescent blues are **starling** insignias, together with equally hard violets, but both appear more softly among the **sunbirds.**

The male **violet-backed starling** flashes brilliant red through to midnight blue, depending entirely on how the light is refracted from its feathers. Iridescent greens are sunbird colours, but receive their most brilliant expression in the **emerald cuckoo.** And **Narina's trogon,** named after its discoverer's Hottentot sweetheart, has a shining, dark bottle-green, seldom appreciated in the deep forest shades the bird frequents.

Non-shining greens, very much a bee-eater colour, are also prominent in the **green pigeons,** some **parrots,** and the **turacos.** Reds, not greatly in vogue, find rich, gorgeous expression on the **scarlet-chested sunbird's** bib; as startling crimson flashes in **turaco** wings, and as an overcoat for the splendid **carmine bee-eater.** Yellow is overwhelmingly the **weaver's** badge, though **orioles** lay equal claim to it.

So if colour be the criterion of beauty, then the palette is so wide and the combinations so many that they defy a common choice. Indeed, when many little brown birds are examined closely, their exquisite patterns and blendings of browns, greys, and creams put them well forward in the opinion of many.

As for singing, the consensus is that one group excels: the **robin-chat** genus, *Cossypha,* of which there are at least ten species in Eastern Africa. All are birds of thicket or forest that adapt well to suburban gardens. Delicate browns or greys above, often with some red-

dish-brown through to deep orange beneath, several sport a prominent white stripe over the eye.

These glorious songsters are also magnificent mimics and incorporate other bird calls into their singing. Parts of these mimicked repertoires are handed down from generation to generation, for it is common to hear robinchats imitate crowned eagles in parts of Nairobi where these big raptors have been absent for years.

Birds often reveal human habits and none more so than **kites, pied crows, white-necked ravens** and **marabou storks.** Their presence is a measure of municipal hygiene. They are abundant in areas where garbage is plentiful and lies in the open.

Sadly, some of their biggest numbers occur around national park lodges — that indolent mob of marabous about the waterhole does not typify the unspoiled African wilderness, but tells of a septic rubbish dump close by.

A crow poses the biggest threat to many African birds. In the last century, Asian traders brought **Indian house crows** to Zanzibar and Djibouti, where they flourished. Since then, brought from Zanzibar to Mombasa, they have spread up and down the Kenya coast. They only do well where there are many people, but when established they rapidly reduce the numbers of indigenous birds, pillaging their nests.

The abundant colonies of **golden palm weavers'** nests in the coconut fronds that were once a feature of Mombasa are gone, along with many other species. In the next century Indian house crows are expected to spread inland from the coast with dire consequences for many birds that presently are such an attractive feature of Eastern Africa.

Opposite: Ruppell's griffons and white-backed vultures conduct last rites for a young wildebeest.

Opposite bottom: Marabou storks, white-backed vultures, and Ruppell's griffons quarrel over a carcass.

Below: The secretary bird's name stems from the time when secretaries rested their quill pens behind their ears.

Overleaf top: An ostrich with quarter-grown chicks. The raised wings are alarm signals.

Overleaf bottom: Crested crane — Uganda's national emblem.

TABLE 1:

A list of non-passerine bird families and a minimal number of species in them.

Family	No of Species	Family	No of Species
Ostrich	1	Grebe	3
Petrel/Shearwater	14	Tropic Bird	3
Gannet	4	Cormorant	3
Darter	1	Frigate Bird	2
Pelican	2	Heron	20
Hammerkop	1	Shoebill	1
Stork	8	Spoonbill/Ibis	8
Flamingo	2	Duck/Goose	30
Secretary Bird	1	Vulture	8
Falcon	19	Kite	3
Eagle	13	Sparrow Hawk	13
Serpent eagle	7	Buzzard	6
Other Raptors	14	Francolin/Guinea Fowl/Quail	32
Rail/Coot etc	23	Finfoot	1
Crane	5	Bustard	11
Thick-knee	4	Jacana	2
Plover	32	Painted Snipe	1
Wader	25	Courser/Pratincole	11
Phalarope	1	Skua	3
Gull	10	Tern	16
Button Quail	3	Sandgrouse	8
Pigeon/Dove	28	Cuckoo/Coucal	21
Turaco	17	Parrot	15
Roller	6	Kingfisher	16
Bee-eater	16	Hornbill	20
Hoopoe/Scimitar Bill	11	Owl	20
Nightjar	19	Mousebird	4
Trogon	2	Barbet	33
Honey Guide	10	Woodpecker	22
Swift	14	Broadbill	2
Pitta	2		

Total: 54 families with 661 species (all raptors counted as one family, hoopoe and scimitar bill as separate families).

TABLE 2: A list of passerine bird families with a minimal number of species in them.

Family	No of Species	Family	No of Species
Lark	34	Wagtail	32
Babbler	12	Thrush-Babbler	7
Bulbul	37	Flycatcher	58
Thrush/Robin-chats	87	Warbler	132
Swallow	28	Cuckoo-shrike	6
Drongo	3	Helmet-shrike	7
Shrike	53	Hypocolius	1
Tit	13	Oriole	7
Crow/Raven	10	Starling	38
White-eye	8	Sunbird	56
Creeper	1	Sparrow *	163
Finch	21	Bunting	12

Total: 24 families with 826 species.

* The sparrow family, *Passeridae,* includes all the weavers, waxbills, mannikins, bishops, widow birds, and whydahs etc.

Combined passerines and non-passerines have 78 families with at least 1,487 species in them.

Chapter 10 Fish

Fresh Water:

Perhaps more than other animal order, fish are at the mercy of geological forces. When the old, pre-Miocene African land surfaces buckled, cracked, rose, or sank, many river courses and drainage systems changed radically. Headwaters feeding westerly rivers were now connected to those flowing east, mixing different species of fish.

The Kafu River in Uganda illustrates this process. Draining a series of northward-flowing swamps and sumps, it used to flow eastwards into Lake Kioga. But the flat land through which it runs has begun to tilt the other way and now the river also drains west over the Rift Valley escarpment into Lake Mobutu and is at a point more like a canal when water can go either east or west. Eventually, it will drain westwards, but for the moment it cannot make up its mind.

Because of such past geological mixing, Africa's freshwater fish communities contain many common elements. Yet despite this, three major divisions are apparent: the Nile fish, the Congo or Zaire basin fish, and those of southern and eastern Africa.

West African fish are a mixture from the Nile and Zaire systems, because the Niger once flowed northwards and eastwards and had connections to the Nile. Subsequently it was 'captured' by the southerly flowing Benue system that had affinities with the Zaire basin rivers. Similarly there were once connections between the southern Zaire basin systems and Southern Africa, and the two regions have some fish species in common.

Eastern Africa's waters have representatives of all three divisions. In western Ethiopia, Uganda, Rwanda, northern Burundi, north-western Tanzania, and Kenya west of the Rift Valley, they are all Nilotic. So, too, are the fish of Lakes Baringo and Turkana in Kenya and the waters of Ethiopia's southern Rift Valley.

Western Tanzania and northern Zambia are in the Zaire system. The fish of the rest of Zambia, Malawi, southern and eastern Tanzania, Kenya, and Ethiopia east of the Rift and Somalia, are in the southern and eastern grouping.

When the Rift Valley formed it captured rivers, cutting them off from past connections. They headed toward the valley's deeper spots to form saline sump lakes that have no outflows. In isolation, and as they became progressively more mineralized, they produced new environments to which their fish had to adapt.

As fish are ancient, most families were well established when Africa was still low-lying and uniformly hot. The relatively recent uplifting of the last two million years produced some cold waters, to which the fish were ill-adapted.

The glacial torrents from the Ruwenzoris, Mount Kenya, and Kilimanjaro, and the cold streams flowing off all the other highland massifs, were alien environments. And with no large bodies of water — either in river or lake form — in any of the highlands, there was no evolutionary 'factory' to turn out fish adapted to the cold. As a result the number of species in Eastern Africa declines rapidly with rising altitude and there are few in the highland rivers.

Generally, Eastern Africa's freshwater fish are not so well known as its birds or mammals. Yet, within the region, there are at least twenty families, containing more than fifty-two genera which, in turn, have at least 220 species. And this minimal list does not include the vast species, 'swarms' of haplochromid fish, that are particular features of Lakes Tanganyika, Malawi, and Victoria. If these were included the total would exceed a thousand species.

Research has concentrated on commercial potential, directed at the large, warm, lowland waters where most species occur. Thus the fish of Uganda and Malawi, both countries dominated by big lakes, are well known. In Kenya and Ethiopia, however, where many miles of highland streams held little commercial promise, research into their fish fauna has, at best, been light.

Visitors are often confused by local fish names: an example is '**barbel**'. Technically, a barbel is a fleshy filament or 'whisker' hanging from or about a fish's lips or mouth — found on many species world-wide. The term derives from the Latin barba for beard. And because a silvery, carp-like European fish has such whiskers from its lips, it is actually called a *Barbus* scientifically or barbel colloquially. Since there are few bewhiskered fish in Europe, this is appropriate.

But Africa has many such fish—none more so than the catfish family. Indeed, they are called catfish because, cat-like, they have such prominent whiskers. In South Africa, someone understandably called the catfish barbels. So the misnomer caught on, despite the fact that Africa is also well endowed with many species of *Barbus* that, by European precedent, are equally entitled to be called barbels. Yet, while confusion may reign over what fish a barbel may be, it gives an added dimension to fishermen's legendary exaggerations of those which got away.

The two largest fish families in Eastern Africa's fresh waters are Cyprinidae—a family also well represented in Eurasia and of which the common carp is a member — and the Cichlidae. The two most prominent cyprinid genera, *Barbus* and *Labeo*, occur widely throughout the region. The **barbus** family has many small, minnow-like species seldom longer than twelve centimetres (five inches) and these, perhaps more than any other group, have adapted to the cold highland streams.

The larger barbus and **labeos** may run to over thirty kilos (seventy pounds) in weight — for example, the Tana River barbus — though most species do not exceed ten kilos. Several larger forms of both genera make pronounced seasonal spawning runs, moving out of lakes into inflowing rivers when in spate. Though they are not regarded as great sporting fish in Eastern Africa, the reverse is true in Southern Africa.

Commercially, the region's most important fish family is the cichlids (*Cichlidae*) which include the best-eating of all African fish — the 'tilapias'. The word tilapia was derived from the Setswana word 'thlape'. By the time the fish came to be named formally, the outlandish pronunciation of thlape had become tilape, which was rendered in Latin as *tilapia*.

The tilapias occur in both lakes and rivers and are also cultivated widely in fish ponds. Primarily plankton eaters, some species also eat aquatic vegetation. As a rule they do best in waters with temperatures between 28° and 32° C. In temperatures well below 20°C they grow very slowly. Tilapias also tend to tolerate salty water. Indeed, some tilapias have been grown successfully in the sea.

The most striking example of their toler-ance of extreme temperature and salinity is found in Lake Magadi and Lake Natron in the Kenya-Tanzania section of the Rift Valley. Both are at low altitudes in a volcanic area where soils are highly sodic. Daily temperatures are frequently above 40° C. As neither lake has any outlet, all water loss is through evaporation. Charged by hot, mineral-laden springs that bubble up about their peripheries, both lake beds form huge deposits of dirty white trona which, at Magadi, is exploited commercially for potash, salt, and so forth.

Yet in these incredibly hostile environments a species of tilapia thrives: the **white-lipped** or **alkaline tilapia** — *Oreochromis alcalica*. The Magadi subspecies, *Oreochromis alcalica grahami*, is also known locally as **Graham's tilapia.**

It lives in the small hot springs that feed both lakes where the water temperatures are 41°— too hot to immerse your hand in, except briefly. The 'water', in fact, is a nearly saturated solution of various salts with a pH of between 9 and 10, thus the fish is well-named. Shoals live around the edge of each spring in water that has cooled slightly to between 36° and 4O°C. Yet if threatened, they will dash briefly into the lethally hotter water at the very lip of the springs.

Not only do they live in a hotter, more saline environment than any other vertebrate, they also tolerate abrupt changes that few fish could endure. The Magadi and Natron springs are so small that a heavy tropical downpour can temporarily swamp them with water little above freezing. And, as rain is slightly acid, their environment may temporarily, but dramatically, change from highly alkaline to neutral or even acid.

But the little fish — seldom longer than ten centimetres or four inches — survive these severe changes and are well adapted to live at the fringes of life's limits.

A number of cichlids, including the tilapia genus *Oreochromis*, are known as **'mouth brooders'**. The males make 'nests' — shallow depressions — and through colourful displays entice ripe females to lay their eggs in them. As the female does so, the male sprays milt, fertilizing the eggs. The ritual completed, the female gathers them in her mouth and for the next few days goes into seclusion, brooding the eggs.

They hatch into larval fish that gradually emerge into the world outside their mother's mouth. At the slightest sign of danger, however, the female makes a ritual movement and the whole shoal of tiny fry rush back into her mouth for safety. Until able to fend for themselves, it remains the centre of their world.

Some of these mouth brooders are found in three of Africa's Great Lakes — Tanganyika, Malawi, and Victoria. These were lakes that were formed either in circumstances that prevented their colonization by many African fish families, or experienced catastrophes that eliminated whole families from their waters. But all three acquired or retained some member or members of the cichlid genus *Haplochromis* which, like some tilapias, are mouth brooders.

In an impressive demonstration of adaptive radiation the haplochromid ancestors of Malawi and Tanganyika found many unoccupied ecological niches. Since nature abhors an ecological vacuum, just as it does the physical, these founding species set about filling the gaps.

In time they produced predators which ate other fish, egg snatchers that stole other species' eggs, snail eaters, weed eaters, plankton sievers, bottom dwellers, mid-water dwellers, and pelagic surface swimmers for the deep, open waters.

The result is an abundance of closely-related fish that live in different ways and, despite their genetic affiliations, often look different. Larger than normal, big-mouthed and sharp-toothed, the predators are fast-swimming with streamlined torpedo-like bodies. The snail eaters developed shell-crushing teeth.

The egg snatcher is particularly interesting. Skulking about the breeding grounds, it nips in and steals eggs as they lie briefly in the bottom of the male 'nest' hollow, before the laying female can gather them in her mouth.

Each of the three lakes now has a 'swarm' of closely related *Haplochromis* species descended from common ancestors, but no two swarms are the same.

As cases of adaptive radiation they are exceptional. By comparison, Darwin's finches in the Galapagos Islands, which are normally cited to illustrate the phenomenon, are crude. In Lake Malawi, for example, there are over 400 species found only in its waters. Speciation has been so vigorous that the lake contains thirty per cent of the world's known cichlid species.

There would be little point for fish that dwell in turbid waters, where they cannot be seen, to evolve bright colours; which may explain, generally, the dull colours of fish in many African rivers and lakes.

Lake Malawi and Lake Tanganyika are so clear, however, that no such barrier exists. Many of their haplochromid species are as vividly and variously coloured as the fish of the tropical seas. Divers familiar with coral reefs who visit either of the lakes find the underwater scenery and fish just as impressive.

But though a wide range of haplochromids has evolved in Lake Victoria, its waters are not as clear; therefore they are not so colourful.

Lake Tanganyika's most sought-after fish are **'dagaa'**, *Stolothrissa tangayikae*. These small sardine-like fish are pelagic and live in vast numbers in the lake's open waters. On moonless nights fleets of fishing boats leave the harbours on the shores of Burundi, Tanzania, Zambia, and Zaire to drift over the fishing grounds with a bright light hanging from the bows. Drawn to the lights, the dagaa are scooped out by the tonne with dip-nets. From a distance the hundreds of bobbing lights appear as small towns out on the waters.

That part of the catch that cannot be sold fresh is laid out on the fine, white beaches and dried, to be marketed later throughout the region. Dagaa, introduced into Lake Kariba on the Zambezi, are the basis of an equally impressive industry there, though referred to by another local name — 'kapenta'.

The open-water pelagic habitat occupied by dagaa in Lake Tanganyika is taken up by an altogether unrelated species on Lake Victoria, a small cyprinid, *Engraulicypris argenteus*, which has adopted this sardine niche to exploit the Lake's plankton. Locally these are known as **'omena'** (Luo) or **'mukene'** (Luganda). They too, are attracted to bright lights and dipped out of the water.

Obviously, drought, and waters that dry up periodically, have been part of the African scene for a long time. Two fish families have evolved strategies to cater for this. The **lungfish**, between 150 million and 300 million years old, are thought by some to be the link between aquatic and terrestrial vertebrates. With swim bladders that act as primitive lungs in addition to their gills, they can breathe air as well as draw oxygen from water.

As waters dry up, the adult lungfish burrows into the muddy pool bottom and makes

Above: Turkana youngster at Ferguson's Gulf, Lake Turkana, with giant Nile perch.

Above: Staples of Africa's inland fisheries. From top — tilapia, Nile perch and black bass.

a cocoon of slime, keeping a channel to the surface open so that when all the water is gone it will still have a supply of air. Encased in slime in the cracked and drying mud, the fish becomes dormant — aestivates — until the rains once again fall and it can emerge to live a normal life.

Five lungfish occur in Eastern Africa. One genus — *Polypterus* — has two species, both covered with thick, bony, rhombic scales and a line of up to eleven finlets along their backs. Seldom longer than forty centimetres (sixteen inches), both occur in the Nile drainage system up to Murchison Falls, but not above, and in the Omo River and Lake Turkana.

The other three — *Protopterus aethiopicus*, *Protopterus amphibius*, and *Protopterus annectens* — are long and rather eel-like in general appearance. The first, common in many Uganda lakes including Victoria, occurs throughout the Nile system and is by far the largest, attaining a length of two metres (six and two-thirds feet) and weights of more than forty-five kilos (100 pounds).

The second, *amphibius*, is somewhat smaller, seldom exceeds ninety centimetres (three feet) or ten kilos (twenty-two pounds), and occurs east of the Rift Valley as far south as central Tanzania. The third, *annectens* — a name meaning connecting, deriving from the belief that the fish represented the fossil missing link between fish and land animals — is a southern

form from Zambia and Malawi similar in size to *amphibius*.

Protopterine lungfish do not have individual teeth but upper and lower tooth plates that come together like sheers. They bite readily — a large fish could easily sever a human finger.

The other arid zone adaptation concerns a group known to aquarium enthusiasts as **'killifish'**, *Nothobranchius*. These tiny fish are seldom longer than five centimetres (two inches). Their tactic is to produce eggs that can survive dessication in the brick-hard mud that forms at the bottom of seasonal pools. As soon as rain falls and pools fill, the eggs hatch. Growing fast, the young mature within weeks. Then, as the pool begins to dry up, they court and breed. Eggs fall to the pond bottom and will not hatch until they have been through the dry, dessicating phase. Adults, like insects, seldom survive more than a single wet season.

The **catfish**, or **silurids**, are also well-represented in Eastern Africa. Without scales, flat-headed, small-eyed with wide mouths surrounded by long barbels, they are unattractive. When alive, some are also dangerous to pick up: the leading edge of their pectoral fins and, in some, the dorsal fins as well, contain a large, needle-tipped spine whose rear edge is at least roughly serrated and, in some, heavily barbed.

When the fish is in trouble, these spines can be locked erect. If the fish thrashes about, they

156

are easily driven into an assailant's flesh. The barbs, coated with a mucus that is a powerful irritant, ensure that withdrawal is extremely painful.

Even more shocking, quite literally, is the **electric catfish**. Light brown, blotched with darker brown, it reaches a metre (three and one-third feet) in length, though it is uncommon over half this length and is readily identifiable as it has no dorsal fin. It produces a powerful electric current which, while obviously applied in defence, may also be used to stun prey. The shock is powerful and might be lethal to any unwary angler with a heart condition.

Most catfish weigh under a kilo. The largest, however — the **vundu**, *Heterobranchus longifilis*, found in the rivers of Zambia, Malawi, and southern Tanzania — exceeds forty-five kilos (100 pounds). It is one of the clarias family; a group that can breathe air having a 'branchial organ' — a form of lung — in addition to gills. Though they cannot aestivate like the lungfish, they can live in liquid mud and water devoid of oxygen, and survive situations which kill fish that only have gills.

The most ubiquitous of the **clarias** — *Clarias gariepinus* — is found the length and breadth of the region in rivers, lakes, and pools less than 1,500 metres (5,000 feet) above sea level, that do not dry up completely or which are occasionally connected by floods with permanent waters. This fish actually moves across land from pool to pool, 'walking' short distances on its pectoral fins. A relative, the walking catfish of Asia, also a *clarias*, which has developed this ability even more, was introduced into Florida, where it has become something of a pest, moving at will from water to water.

Indigenous 'game' fish are the giant **Nile perch** and the **tiger fish**. Nile perch, which belong to the *Centropomidae* family, are unusual in that most members are marine species. As indicated by its name, the species distribution is the Nile drainage and ex-Nile connections such as Lake Turkana and the River Niger in West Africa.

Curiously, though the fossil records indicate that it was in Lake Victoria some millions of years ago, in recent times the species did not occur above Murchison Falls in either Lake Kioga or in Lake Victoria. It was reintroduced to both Lake Kioga (in 1955) and Lake Victoria (in about 1966) where it has done prodigiously well. Indeed, those who made the reintroduction have been much criticized. Within two decades Nile perch have come to dominate Lake Victoria so much that scientists fear for the survival of many haplochromid and other cichlid species. Some Nile perch weigh more than 227 kilos (500 pounds), but the largest caught on rod and line was under 136 kilos (300 pounds).

In their Latin name, *Hydrocyon*, tiger fish are aptly referred to as water dogs. Ferocious predators with mouthfuls of dagger-like, razor-edged teeth, the large southern species, *vittatus*, of the Zambezi basin and Tanzania's Rufiji and Rovuma Rivers, is held by many to be the world's premier freshwater sport fish. Two other species — *forskali* and *lineatus* — just as game, but too small to attract wide interest, occur in the Nile drainage. However, as was the case with Nile perch, they do not occur above Murchison Falls or in Kioga or Victoria.

Rainbow and **brown trout** have been introduced into nine streams in Ethiopia's Bale Mountains, most streams in Kenya above 1,970 metres (6,500 feet) high, and a few in Tanzania and Malawi. Similarly, **large-mouthed black bass** from the USA were brought via South Africa to stock many of Kenya's highland dams and Lake Naivasha.

As in temperate zone waters, a number of fish commute between the open sea and the rivers that empty into the Indian Ocean, four **eel** species among them. In reverse manner to the temperate-zone salmons that are spawned in fresh water, go to sea to grow, and then return to fresh water to breed, the eels spawn in the ocean, enter the rivers to grow, then return to the sea to breed and die.

The most sinister of the sea fish that enter Eastern Africa's rivers is the **Zambezi shark** — *Carcharinus leucas*. Despite its name, this shark is widespread in tropical oceans and is unusual in its occasional habit of going up freshwater rivers. One was caught 1,600 kilometres (1,000 miles) up the Amazon. A dangerous species, it hunts right along the shoreline in knee-deep water, though not where there are fringing coral reefs. Over the past decade many people have been killed by sharks — probably this species — in Mogadishu harbour and elsewhere on the Somalia coast. And, further south, it takes bathers off the beaches at Durban, South Africa.

Salt Water:

The Indian Ocean and Red Sea off the African coast have a typical Indo-Pacific fish fauna. No detailed check-list of all species has yet been published for the region, but the total will probably lie somewhere beyond 1,000 species in at least 120 different genera.

The sea fish are divided into two basic groups: those with a true bony skeleton and those which lack true bone with skeletons of hard cartilage. The latter group includes all the sharks and rays. In Eastern Africa's waters there are more than twenty shark species.

The largest is the **whale shark,** the world's largest fish, which may exceed fifteen metres (forty-nine feet) in length and weigh more than thirty tonnes. These huge animals feed off plankton and very small fish and are harmless to man. They spend hours basking at the surface and allow boats to come alongside them. Gogglers can swim with them and touch them with small risk. However, they are often accompanied by other less amiable shark species with whom liberties should not be taken. The fishermen of Zanzibar have a belief that catching and landing a whale shark will bring calamity to the community. They point out that immediately prior to the bloodshed and revolution that gripped the island in 1964, two whale sharks had been caught in a seine net and hauled onto one of the beaches.

Of the other big sharks found in tropical seas and dangerous to man, the largest occurring off Eastern Africa is the **great white,** which grows to nine metres (thirty feet), but it is uncommon. There are at least two species of **hammerhead** sharks, the largest growing to over eight metres (twenty-six feet), which are relatively common. Nearly as large and just as common is the voracious **tiger shark. Mako sharks,** which grow to four metres (thirteen feet) in length, are occasionally caught — the only shark which qualifies as a 'game' fish.

All these man-eaters are principally fish of the blue waters. They may occasionally be seen along the seaward side of the coral reefs, but are virtually never encountered on their landward side. Consequently there are no known cases of shark attack off the tourist beaches of either Kenya or Tanzania.

Exceptions to the freedom from shark danger are the coast of Somalia, where there are no fringing coral reefs, and Mombasa's deep-water port of Kilindini. Over the years,

there have been a number of fatalities to swimmers, presumably inflicted by oceanic sharks that have followed ships for the garbage and waste they discharge. It is also possible that Zambezi sharks might be a threat in river deltas and estuaries anywhere along the Eastern African coast. But curiously there are so few records of fatalities between Mogadishu and Durban (where sharks are common), local people hardly give them a thought.

In addition to the large sharks, there are a greater number of smaller species that are no threat whatsoever to man.

Also classified as cartilaginous fishes and related to sharks are several **'sandsharks',** bottom dwellers that look like crosses between sharks and rays, and a number of true rays.

The largest of the rays and one of the world's most impressive animals are two species of **manta ray.** More like delta-winged aircraft than fish, a big manta measures over six metres (twenty feet) from wing tip to wing tip. And among the most spectacular of all sights at sea is to watch mantas 'fly'. Despite weighing several tonnes, they build up sufficient speed under water to enable them to leap three or four metres (ten to thirteen feet) clear of the water, to which they return with a thunderclap of a splash.

Of the other rays, all are bottom dwellers which spend a great deal of their time partially buried in sand or mud. At least six are **sting rays.** These have a long, whip-like tail which is a sharp and sometimes serrated spine. This defensive weapon can be jabbed into anything which molests its owner and, as it bears a strong poison, can cause great pain and is sometimes fatal to humans. After catching any of these rays, the first thing local fishermen do is cut off the tail.

One ray which has no sting but is far from defenceless is the **torpedo ray.** Like the electric catfish, it can give a powerful electric shock to any who disturb it.

The bony fish far outnumber the cartilaginous forms. There are so many of them that it is not possible to list or describe all here. However, a general overview might place them in three different groups: the **blue-water** or **pelagic,** offshore, fish which are free swimming and have no particular ties to the ocean floor, the **inshore** fish associated with the shallows and tidal zones within a mile or two of the high tide level, and the **demersal** fish associated with the coral reefs and ocean floor

Above: Lion or scorpion fish should be treated with the utmost caution. Each dorsal and pectoral spine, needle-sharp, is connected to a poison gland. A simple prick from one of the spines injects the virulent venom, inflicting a dangerous and painful wound.

and its various features. There is considerable overlap between all three categories, but from the visitor's point of view, they are easy enough to comprehend.

The first group, the fish of the blue, offshore waters, are likely to be encountered by those who go big game fishing. The most obvious are the several small **bonito** and **frigate mackerel** species that seldom exceed four kilos (nine pounds) in weight — all members of the tunny or tuna family. They feed principally off anchovies (*Engraulidae*) which are found in dense shoals all along the coast. Numerous fish-eating birds, particularly bridled and sooty terns, also live off the anchovies, which are most easily caught when a shoal is driven to the surface by feeding bonito. Thus a mass of plunging terns reveals the bonitos' whereabouts to fishermen, who in turn catch bonito as bait for bigger fish.

Aside from bonito, the most commonly caught game fish off Eastern Africa's shores is the **yellow-finned tunny** or **tuna.** These exceed 100 kilos (220 pounds) when mature, but the majority, taken within twenty kilometres (twelve miles) of the shore, are immature,

weighing far less. The next most frequently caught blue-water fish is the **dorado** or **golden one** (*felusi* in Kiswahili). Many of these open-water fish display a wide range of colours; none more so than dorado. At times blue and silver, at others green and yellow, in death a drab blue/green above and pale yellowish below, it takes its name from the iridescent gold it assumes when under stress. This colour is difficult to describe in terms that do it justice, but it must be one of the most striking exhibited by any living animal.

Third on the list of the game fishermen's catches is the **Indo-Pacific sailfish.** One of the 'bill' fishes whose nose ends as a long, rasp-rough spike, 'sails' are avidly sought and caught. Their name derives from the dorsal fin which, when its owner is excited, can be raised like a huge sail that runs the entire length of the fish and is twice as deep as the fish itself. In life, the sailfish may appear chocolate brown with silver flanks on which there may be several dark, vertical bars. However, seen close to, the sail is interspersed with the deepest royal blue and relieved with a scattering of violet spots which come and go.

The **marlins** are relatively common: **striped, black,** and **blue.** The first is both the smallest and the most commonly seen. Like the sailfish, they have long bills or bowsprits. The purpose of these long 'swords' is not entirely clear. Game fishermen assert that they are used to whack and stun their prey which, for the most part, is other fish. However, the hydrodynamics are akin to waggling a stick on the front of a fast-moving torpedo, which doesn't make good sense and some better explanation is still wanting.

The **broad-billed swordfish** occurs off Eastern Africa, but is not often caught. Seemingly it is far more nocturnal than other bill fish, spending the daylight hours way below the hundred fathom mark beyond the anglers' reach. However, when enthusiasts have set out after dark with broadbills specifically in mind, they have been successful.

Many sharks are caught, including Mako; **wahoo, kingfish** (Spanish mackerel) and **barracuda** are secured in fair numbers. The most commonly practised deep-sea fishing technique is trolling a lure — either a small fish or an imitation fish or squid — behind a boat. However, pundits maintain that the best of all blue-water baits are **flying fish,** of which there are at least six species. These herring-like fish have enlarged pectoral fins that they can

Above: Wizard of camouflage, the delicious crocodile fish blends perfectly with its background, fooling both predators and prey.

Opposite: Three species of rock cod or grouper. Top, *Epinephelus tauvina;* centre, *Cephalopholis miniatus;* and bottom, *Cephalopholis pachycentron.* The largest of this family weighs over 450 kilos and could swallow a man.

160

Above: A shoal of gaterins opens for the diver to pass through.

Opposite top: Blue-spotted box-fish in its predominantly yellow juvenile colouring.

Opposite centre: Surgeon fish, *Acanthurus dussumieri*, so named for the scalpel-sharp blades at the base of its tail which can inflict deep wounds.

Opposite bottom: Reticulated moray eel lurk in crevices and holes during daylight, but swim about as scavengers and predators after dark. Evil-looking and able to inflict a severe bite, unless disturbed they generally leave divers alone.

extend like wings. When chased, they accelerate to over thirty kilometres (twenty miles) an hour, shoot out of the water, extend their 'wings', and glide for several hundred metres to escape their pursuers.

Flying fish are not the only marine animals able to fly. Certain species of small squid also use the same tactic. However, squid use jet propulsion — pumping water at high pressure through a tube — to gain their speed. Instead of the long gliding pectorals of the flying fishes, their wing is the fleshy frill that occurs around the lateral edge of their bodies. The lift this provides is augmented by the aerodynamic lines of the squid body.

The inshore fish — those of the mangrove areas, the tidal mud flats, and estuaries away from the coral reefs and beaches — are the least likely of the region's fish fauna to be noticed as their environments are relatively unattractive. Yet among mangrove roots and along rocky shores there are at least twenty-five species of **mud hoppers** and **rock hoppers.** For the most part these are small, cryptically coloured fish that can stay out of water for protracted periods. They normally draw attention to themselves as they skip away across rocks, roots, and mud when approached by a human.

Periodically huge runs of **sardines** (Kiswahili — *simu*) move along the coastal shallows — the sea seemingly solid with fish. These shoals are attended by numerous predatory fish and birds — as well as fishermen.

One of the most characteristic inshore predators, seen in all the creeks along the coastline, is **garfish.** Long and almost eel-like,

Above: Yellow-spotted angel fish surrounded by cardinal fish courtiers.

these silvery hunters have jaws similar to a gharial crocodile's, full of needle sharp teeth. White-fleshed and good-eating, their bones are bright green.

The estuarine areas and muddy bottoms are where most of the local flat fish — **soles** and **flounders** — which number at least a dozen species, are found. They are also the places in which dangerous stingrays are commonly caught.

Perhaps the most typical of all the coral reef fish are the **parrot fish,** with more than forty species. The largest exceeds 1.5 metres (five feet) in length, but most are far smaller. The majority are brightly coloured, though in pastel shades. Their name derives from their teeth, which are fused into bony plates similar in form to a parrot's beak. As powerful pincers, they break off large lumps of living coral which are then crushed and swallowed. The living organisms digested, the ground coral is then excreted as white debris which, in due course, is washed up on beaches throughout the tropics—thus parrot fish play an important part in creating the blindingly white beaches characteristic of all coral seas.

Equally characteristic of the coral reefs is the family *Pomacentridae*. A large group of more than forty species, they are all small and brightly coloured and include the confident little **damsel fish** which feature so prominently in underwater photographs. Too small to warrant catching, the damsels tend to be left alone by spear fishermen. Not quite so fortunate are the **gaterins.** Gaily coloured, somewhat larger than the damsels and very good eating, they, too, are very confident. Because of this they are among the first reef denizens to be shot out and disappear with the arrival of spear fishermen.

Three large families which associate with coral reefs, but also have some members who live on sandy bottoms or away from coral formations, are the **wrasses** (*Labridae*), the **snappers** (*Lutianidae*) and the **groupers** or **rock cods** (*Serranidae*).

The largest wrasse is the **humphead,** which exceeds two metres (six feet) in length and may weigh over forty-five kilos (100 pounds). However, the majority of the sixty or more species are far smaller and some are tiny. Among them are some of the highly specialized **'cleaner' wrasse.** These small fish run cleaning stations and obtain their food by

Above: Blue-spotted sting ray, one of the species that inflicts painful and dangerous wounds with a poison spine located halfway along its whip-like tail.

grooming other larger reef-dwelling species. When one of these clients feels itchy from sea lice and similar parasites, it goes to its nearest cleaner station. The resident cleaner wrasse go to work, methodically nibbling away all parasites and eating them. The task is done thoroughly: lips, teeth, and the inside of the mouth and gill covers, as well as the scales and fins.

The snappers, of which there are more than twenty-five species, are best known for their excellent eating qualities and are much sought after by fishermen. They are not quite so tied to the coral reefs as the preceding families, but are commonly seen in their vicinities by divers.

The groupers number some forty species, ranging in size from brightly-coloured forms that never grow more than a few centimetres long to the giant *Promicops lanceolatus,* which exceeds 450 kilos (1,000 pounds) in weight. All the groupers are carnivorous, and the largest specimens are big enough — and have sufficiently large mouths — to swallow a man whole. Although there are no known cases — at least in recent times — in which a human has been swallowed by a **giant grouper** (*tewa*

in Kiswahili) local mythology claims that they are to be feared more than sharks. A point on Mtwapa Creek, twenty kilometres (twelve miles) north of Mombasa, is known as Shimo la Tewa — the tewa's hole. It commemorates a legendary tewa which, in bygone times, swallowed people foolhardy enough to swim there.

And there is an apocryphal story about a sceptical scuba diver who, at Watamu — further north along the Kenya coast — went down to see some legendary tewa that lived, he was told, in a vast, coral cavern. He dived and swam along the reef edge. After a minute or two he spied the large cave, very much as it had been described. He swam to it with the intention of going inside to see the great fish. But as he paused at the entrance to fumble for his torch, the cave abruptly closed. It was no less than a tewa's mouth.

Among the most sinister reef dwellers are the small, brightly coloured **scorpion fish.** In body conformation, they look somewhat like a small grouper, but their fin rays are extremely long and the raggedy trailing edges of the membranes give the impression of a fish bedecked with streaming ribbons. Watching

Above: Parrot fish eat live coral and the crunched limestone passes through the fish eventually to form a dazzling white tropical beach.

Preceding pages: Exquisite tableau in gold.

the approaching goggler, they are completely unafraid: hanging in the water, gently moving their bedecked fins, almost inviting him to touch them. The temptation should be resisted, for the fin spines are needle-sharp and connected to virulent venom glands. The very least that anyone pricked by a scorpion fish spine experiences is great pain, and most victims become extremely ill.

Even more dangerous than the scorpion fish are the eight species of **stone fish** which inhabit coral shores. These are all very well camouflaged and lie still, looking — as their name implies — like a piece of weed-covered stone. Often only their eyes reveal their presence. Each of their dorsal spines, thick and sharp, is grooved like a snake's fang and connected to a gland that produces a powerful neurotoxin. When the spines penetrate the sole of a careless reef walker's foot, they discharge the venom. The result is immediate, intense pain, collapse, and, not infrequently, death. And in those cases where the victim recovers, the wound is usually seriously infected.

More sinister looking than either scorpion or stone fish are the **moray eels.** Snake-like and heavy fanged, they watch divers from holes and crannies in rock and reef face. There are at least twenty-four species of moray, and the larger forms, which may exceed two metres (seven feet) in length, are as thick as a man's calf. They can inflict a severe bite, but their appearance belies their nature. Unless provoked, they are not aggressive. They are predators and scavengers: the hyaena and jackal of the coral reefs.

Chapter 11 Snakes

No vertebrates are more difficult to see in anthropomorphic terms than cold-blooded reptiles. And snakes are the least lovable of all. An almost innate revulsion towards them prevails throughout mankind, even among communities that have no first-hand experience of them. Freudian explanations connect the phobia about serpents with sexuality but, more likely, widespread fear derives from their sinister poisons.

As with much of the unknown, knowledge reduces fear. Once the phobia is replaced by understanding, snakes become as fascinating and complex as any other animal group. Relatively, Eastern Africa is as rich in serpents as it is in mammals or birds. Because they are cold-blooded, there are more species in warm areas, and there is a general dearth of snakes in the higher, montane forests, and on the moorlands above the tree line. Within this broad generalization, however, snakes are abundant.

Yet despite their numbers, surprisingly few snakes are seen by lay folk. This is because they are timid, well camouflaged and move away or hide from human activity. Only the experienced collector sees them. No one ever made this point more sharply than the late C. J. P. Ionides, or 'Iodine' as he was affectionately known. As a game warden in southern Tanzania, he became an authority on African snakes, travelling widely to collect them. Many times he arrived in an place hitherto unremarkable for snakes to confound his hosts by finding snakes both in abundance and variety right beneath their noses.

In Eastern Africa there are six snake families — Pythonidae, Boidae, Colubridae, Elapidae, Hydrophiidae, and Viperidae. Between them there are at least 130 species, the majority of which — around seventy-five per cent — are not venomous.

Pythons:
The pythons have but two members: the **common African python,** and the **West African python** — also known as the **royal, ball,** or **pigmy python.** The first is both the largest and most widespread, occurring throughout Africa south of the Sahara below 2,200 metres (7,200 feet) except in semi-arid and arid zones. It is particularly common about water and

swamps, swimming readily. Specimens up to six metres (twenty feet) have been widely recorded. Pythons of between six and nine metres (twenty and thirty feet) have been measured but never verified scientifically. Claims of even longer African pythons have been lodged, but if such sizes do occur, they must be rare indeed.

Common pythons seize prey with their heavily recurved teeth, then coil their bodies round the victim's thorax. Once the quarry is enveloped, the coils are tightened until it suffocates. Big pythons regularly take mammals up to the size of a large dog. Larger prey is taken infrequently, though there are authentic cases in which humans have been caught, constricted, and swallowed.

Pythons lay clutches of between thirty and fifty orange-sized eggs in secluded, sheltered sites. These are actually brooded, the female coiling around them until they hatch.

The **West African python** is a much smaller snake, seldom reaching 1.5 metres (five feet) in length. Beautifully coloured, rich brown and bright yellow, this species has been recorded in western Uganda, but nowhere else in Eastern Africa.

Boas:
Boas, of which the Amazon's mighty anaconda is one, are poorly represented in Eastern Africa. The single species, the **sand boa,** is an arid land snake from the red soils of Somalia, southern Ethiopia, northern and eastern Kenya. Bright orange, banded and blotched with black or very dark brown, this stubby constrictor reaches lengths of only thirty-five centimetres (fourteen inches). It is seldom seen, other than in very wet periods, for it spends most of its time buried in loose earth.

Colubrids:
The colubrid family is by far the largest, containing some seventy per cent or more of the region's snakes. Of thirty-nine Eastern African genera, twenty containing fifty-four species are venomless. Many are small, inconspicuous denizens of leaf litter or spend much of their lives below ground. Some are highly specialized, none more so than the members of the genus *Duberria*, whose diet is mainly

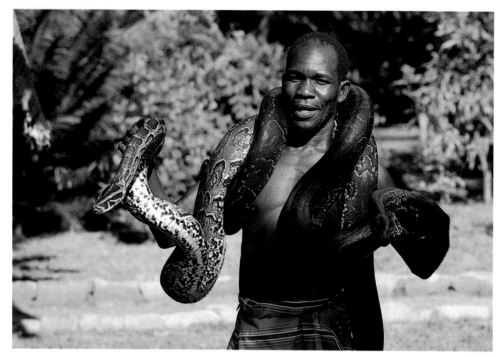

Above: African python. Large specimens exceed six metres in length. There are some rare, but authentic, records of them killing and swallowing humans.

slugs and snails, but which occasionally turn cannibal and eat their own species.

Some species, such as those aptly-named **house snakes** in the genus *Boaedon*, benefit man as the larger forms eat rodents. Indeed, the abundance of rats about houses is why the **brown house snake,** in particular, is so common in and around homes. Lacking poison, they constrict prey as the pythons do.

Among the most unusual of the venomless colubrids are the egg eaters of the genus *Dasypeltis,* which live exclusively off birds' eggs. The egg is swallowed whole — a snake less than one metre (three and a third feet) long can take a hen's egg — and held in the throat. Bony processes protruding downward from the spine into the top of the gullet act as saw teeth and cut the egg in half lengthwise. Having done this, the contents are swallowed while the eggshell is neatly folded, one half inside the other, and regurgitated.

Though harmless, the egg eaters ferociously mimic other dangerous snakes, lashing out at any molesters with fearsome displays. One species, the **common egg eater,** adds to this by rubbing its rough scales together to make a coarse hiss, plausibly imitating the very

170

poisonous, arid land **carpet viper.**

At least nineteen of Eastern Africa's colubrid snakes are 'back-fanged'. They have two elongated teeth far back in the upper jaw. Each has a groove down the length of its rear edge along which poison trickles when the snake bites. Injection is inefficient and the snake usually has to chew on a victim to use its poison effectively. This is good enough to subdue prey that is held in the mouth or thoroughly encoiled, but relatively ineffective in defence.

Most back-fanged snakes cannot open their mouths wide enough to get their poison teeth into so large a victim as a person and, even if they could, it is highly unlikely that they would be given much opportunity to chew. Moreover, the poison of most back-fanged species is not lethal to man. Many might create slight soreness at a bite's site, but little more. Some, among them the **sand snakes** in the genus *Psammophis,* can cause headaches and persistent nausea for several days.

But while most back-fanged colubrids are essentially harmless, four tree-climbing and four ground-dwelling species are dangerous. Four are arboreal and feed at least partially on

Above: Python swallowing a Thomson's gazelle it killed by asphyxiation.

active birds, which may be why they have evolved a fast-acting venom. The first is **Blanding's tree snake,** a black (males) or brown (females) western species that is widespread in the warm forests of Uganda and western Kenya.

Commonly longer than 2.5 metres (over eight feet), it is a big snake. Able to open its jaws almost 180°, its exceptional gape allows it to employ its fangs in a manner unusual for a back-fanged species. Not much is known about its venom, but because it is so big and can employ its fangs against an aggressor, it should be regarded with caution.

The second is the **boomslang** — Afrikaans for **tree snake** — a slender, tree-dwelling, chameleon and bird-eating species widespread throughout Africa. With colour variations ranging from black through dark browns to greys, many shades of green from olive to brilliant apple, and more rarely to a light blue, this snake cannot be readily identified by colour.

Sometimes more than two metres (seven feet) long, the rather large back fangs of the boomslang are relatively far forward and contain a virulent poison, lethal to man. But to get sufficient venom into a person, the snake

would have to chew on its victim.

The third and fourth are **vine snakes,** so named because their slender bodies are camouflaged to look like thin vine stems. Remaining immobile for long periods, they look sufficiently like the surrounding vegetation to fool both predators and prey. These very slender, long-headed snakes seldom exceed 1.25 metres (four feet) in length. They are gentle and retiring. Like the boomslang, they cannot readily inject venom into a human, but should this happen it could kill.

As with the venomless colubrids, many of the back-fanged species are small and specialized. The eight species of one genus, *Aparallactus,* are specialized centipede eaters. The specialization is curious, for centipedes are themselves venomous and armed with formidable 'jaws', which are actually legs modified to bite and inject poison.

The four poisonous, terrestrial colubrids are related to the centipede eaters. All are in the genus *Atractaspis.* All are under a metre (three and a third feet) long, very dark brown or black, glossy and smooth with small scales, with heads never wider than their necks: a shape ideally suited to burrowing for they spend a great deal of time underground.

Above: A water snake, Lake Malawi.

All four feed on rodents, lizards, and other small snakes. They are unusual for colubrids: not only are they venomous, but they have exceptionally well-developed fangs. Indeed, in some individuals these are so big that the tooth actually projects beyond the angle of the jaw. Another peculiarity is that the fangs are too big to bite with conventionally. Instead, each fang can be pulled forward slightly to protrude from between the snake's closed lips on either side of the lower jaw. Yet more unusual, each fang can be deployed independently of the other.

Because of their astonishing fangs these snakes were long considered unusual members of the viper family and are still incorrectly referred to as **'burrowing vipers'**. The ability to use their long poison teeth with closed mouth is an adaptation to life underground. A snake burrowing through loose soil or in the confines of a narrow subterranean tunnel would find it difficult to strike in the conventional open-mouth manner. Coming across a victim in such circumstances, a burrowing viper does not open its mouth. Instead, it forces its head between prey and the confining earth, then reverses. As the head is pulled

backwards, one of the projecting, rearward-pointing fangs catches the victim like a hook and venom is injected.

Burrowing vipers have caught many an aspiring herpetologist by surprise. Picking up one of these harmless-looking snakes conventionally, with a tight grip on the neck, the collector has been surprised by a slight downward or sideways bend of the snake's head and a needle-like fang piercing forefinger or thumb. The virulent venom is capable of killing a child.

The three remaining families — the elapines, hydrophids, and viperines — are all venomous. All are front-fanged: they have poison fangs protruding beyond their other teeth at the front of the upper jaws. With the elapids and hydrophids these fangs are rigid and short enough for the mouth to close without inconvenience. Unlike the back-fanged colubrines, these have a canal through the centre down which poison pours when they bite. In effect, they serve as short, rather inefficient, hypodermic needles. Where people are concerned, they do not penetrate deeply and thick clothing reduces their effectiveness considerably.

Above: Beautiful but deadly green mambas.

Such inefficiency is not the case with viperines. Their fangs form much longer hypodermics. So much so that, for the snake's mouth to close, they have to fold back against the palate. Thus they are movable, swinging forward when the mouth opens for a bite, and folding back out of the way when it closes. Vipers can inflict deep injections through most conventional clothing.

Man has good reason to fear all of these snakes — elapine, hydrophid, and viperine — for many a death has proved that the inefficiencies in elapine and hydrophid fangs are only relative.

Elapids — Cobras, Mambas, and Garter Snakes:

In Eastern Africa there are only five elapid genera containing fourteen species. Many are large and most are active, lively snakes including both **cobras** and the dreaded **African mambas.**

Four true cobras are found in Eastern Africa, all extremely venomous and potentially lethal to humans, though not all bites are fatal. Cobras like to chew on a victim and, where people are concerned, are not usually given the opportunity. Often they fail to inject sufficient poison to kill, and in other cases medical treatment saves a victim.

The **Egyptian cobra,** as its name implies, is distributed from Egypt in the north to Natal in the south, and from Cape Verde in the west to Cape Gardafui in the east. It is a savannah and arid land species, rather heavily built, that may reach 2.5 metres (8.25 feet) in length. Commonly various shades of brown or grey, some specimens in eastern Kenya have salmon-pink washes on the throat or undersides. By cobra standards the species is docile. But when disturbed it rears up, displaying a wide, conventional cobra hood to great effect. Like most African cobras, the Egyptian prefers to feed on other reptiles and amphibians — including all other venomous snakes.

The largest and heaviest of this family in Eastern Africa is the **forest,** or **black-and-white-lipped cobra,** which is frequently longer than 2.5 metres (over eight feet) and may reach more than 3.5 metres (twelve feet). A species of forests and the wetter types of vegetation with a pronounced liking for water, it comes in two colour phases: dark brown in coastal Eastern Africa and shiny black west of the Rift

Valley. In both forms the underside is a rich creamy-white or pale yellow; these colours come up the sides of the face to interlock with the black from above.

The forest cobra swims expertly and readily catches fish under water. It also takes snakes — poisonous and non-poisonous — other reptiles, and amphibians. When the opportunity arises it will also take small mammals and birds (including domestic duck and chicken) eggs.

Until recently the other two cobras, the **spitting cobra** and the **black-collared spitting cobra,** were considered a single species. Both 'spit' — ejecting venom forwards for a distance of up to two metres (nearly seven feet). Their tubular fangs have openings in the front, facing forwards, sheathed in a movable membrane. This holds back the venom in their poison ducts which is put under pressure when the snake responds to a threat.

Facing the aggressor's head, the cobra simultaneously opens its mouth and raises the retaining membrane. Thus released, the venom spurts forward from each fang like a jet from a water pistol. When the droplets enter the attacker's eyes, they cause instant pain, forcing it to retreat. This entirely defensive process is only used when the cobra feels cornered. By biting in the conventional manner, both spitters can also inject poison and do so in defence when 'spitting' fails, or to kill prey.

Though cobra venom generally is neurotoxic, acting on a victim's nervous system, the poison of both spitting cobras is more like that of the vipers. As well as possessing potent neurotoxic elements, it is also vasculotoxic — that is, it destroys tissues as well as blocking the nerves. Both spitting cobras are more excitable than Egyptian or forest cobras.

The spitting cobra grows to just under 2.5 metres (eight feet) long, but is normally somewhat shorter. Colours range from black through various shades of brown to pale brown. It is a widespread savannah species that prefers reptilian food, including all sorts of snakes, fish, small mammals, and eggs, and its diet is rather more general than its relatives.

The black-collared spitting cobra, characteristically a species of the arid Horn of Africa, is found in eastern and southern Ethiopia, Somalia, northern and eastern Kenya, and north-eastern Tanzania.

Two colour phases occur. One in north-western Kenya is pale grey or light brown; the other, which occupies the rest of the species range, is deep brick to bright orange-red. Some are bright burnished copper and very handsome. As their name implies, specimens of both colour phases have a distinct black band around the neck.

This species, the smallest of the true cobras in Eastern Africa, is seldom longer than 1.5 metres (five feet) and eats the same food as its relatives.

Closely allied to the true cobras is the **tree cobra,** *Pseudohaje,* a West African forest species found in the lowland forests of Uganda and Western Kenya. Black, apart from cream-coloured sides of the face and belly, this species reaches 2.75 metres (nine feet) in length, is arboreal, active, and dangerously aggressive. Its venom is every bit as bad as that of the true cobras and probably worse. In keeping with its propensity for climbing trees, its diet consists largely of frogs and toads.

Lake Tanganyika is home to **Storm's water cobra.** Not a true cobra, this handsome snake is light brown, with several dark brown bars across the upper part of the body. Aquatic, it lives almost entirely off fish. Its highly toxic venom quickly paralyses the slippery, quick-moving prey.

Far more feared than the cobras are three species of the agile mambas: the **black,** the **green,** and **Jameson's.** Their fangs are located far forward under the nose and their venom is probably the most virulent of all African snake nerve poisons. People have died within fifteen minutes of being bitten — though it would normally take longer. This combination of virulent poison and agility makes them extremely dangerous, and they are the source of many terrifying stories. Yet, they are not nearly as bad as their reputation, for all three prefer to move away from people.

Black mambas are never black. Colours range from pale grey-brown, through olive browns, to dark gunmetal. The underparts are invariably paler, and the inside of the mouth of this species — for those who care to get that close — is dark grey to black, a sure identification. The maximum size is just over four metres (fourteen feet) long, making it the second-longest poisonous snake in the world after Asia's king cobra. Such size, however, is rare. A big specimen would measure 3.5 metres (twelve feet) long.

Although very much at home in trees, the black mamba is the most terrestrial of the three

Above: Striped sand snakes, fast moving sun-lovers, are mildly venomous to humans but never bite unless actually seized.

Eastern African species and, as the savannah member of the group, often seen on the ground. Individuals appear to have home ranges and some accounts suggest that, at times, it resents intrusion or disturbance and will attack the unwary trespasser.

By reputation it is the most dangerous of the mambas — large specimens are relatively bold and confident. The black mamba's diet is unselective, but it prefers warm-blooded animals: rats, squirrels, bats, and birds.

The green mamba ranges from coastal Kenya, through eastern Tanzania, southwards through Malawi into Natal. Arboreal, a snake of the evergreen coastal forests and thickets, its bright green colouring is good camouflage. More slender than the black mamba and not as big — 2.5 metres (eight feet) long would be a large specimen — it is also not so bold. Its food is similar, mainly warm-blooded animals such as rats and squirrels, but perhaps more birds.

Jameson's mamba, also bright green and of similar proportions and habits, is readily distinguished by the last third of its length being black. It is a West African snake whose range extends into Uganda and western Kenya, and is also likely to occur in the lower parts of Rwanda and Burundi, where suitable vegetation exists.

At least four **garter snakes** round up the elapid snake family in Eastern Africa. All are small black serpents seldom longer than sixty centimetres (two feet). Usually they have distinct white, orange, or red rings or garters down the length of the body. They are snakes of leaf litter and loose earth, into which they burrow for cover. All four species are lizard and frog eaters. Their bite is poisonous enough to make a person ill, but unlikely to be lethal.

Hydrophid or Sea Snakes:

There is only one hydrophid in Eastern Africa: the **yellow-bellied sea snake** found throughout the tropical Indo-Pacific region. It is a truly pelagic animal of the open ocean that only comes ashore, or into shallow coastal waters, by misfortune. By nature inoffensive, they nonetheless have a lethal venom. Any snake in the sea, on the beach, or coral reef should thus be regarded with the utmost respect. Fortunately they are uncommon along the Indian Ocean coast and are only likely to be seen on the shores of northern Somalia and the entrance to the Red Sea.

175

Above: Sluggish and extremely poisonous — the dreaded puff-adder.

Vipers:

The viper family has at least seventeen species in Eastern Africa. A family characteristic is a head that is pronouncedly wider than the neck, though it doesn't hold true for all species. The genus *Vipera* has one member which is highly unusual — **Hind's viper** of the cold, high moorlands on Mount Kenya and the Aberdare range in central Kenya. No other snake in Eastern Africa is known to have adapted itself to so cold a habitat.

It looks like the common viper of Europe and grows to thirty-five centimetres (fourteen inches) long. Mildly venomous, it lives off the high-altitude skinks and lizards that share the same habitat. Hind's viper avoids extreme cold by burrowing deep into the centre of the large grass tussocks characteristic of the moorlands.

Four **night adders** occur in Eastern Africa. Two of them, the **rhombic** and **green,** occur widely in savannahs and woodlands throughout the entire region up to 1,800 metres (6,000 feet) above sea level. Both are nocturnal toad eaters.

As the name suggests, the rhombic is light brown with dark rhombic markings along the entire length of the back. The green is bright green with dark rhombic markings. Neither grows longer than sixty centimetres (two feet) and neither has the pronouncedly wide viperine head.

A third, slightly smaller, brown and blotched species, the **snouted night adder,** occurs in the coastal regions of Kenya, Tanzania, and farther south. The scale at the snout tip is upturned, but this feature is unlikely to be seen except on a specimen in the hand.

A fourth western forest species of the same size as the rhombic — the **olive-green night adder** — is found in the forests of Uganda and western Kenya. It is distinct from the other three in that its head, in true viper fashion, is obviously wider than the neck. It is a dull olive-green overall with indistinct darker 'V'-shaped markings.

All four night adders are terrestrial and at least moderately poisonous. Their venom would make people feel sore and ill, but is unlikely to kill them.

The only arboreal vipers in Eastern Africa are of the genus *Atheris* — the so-called **'bush vipers'.** All are slender, rough-scaled and, relative to their bodies, have broad heads. Four are of varying shades of green with darker zigzags or other markings and one, the **Mount Kenya bush viper,** is brown with a yellow zigzag pattern above and a bright yellow belly. None grow longer than sixty centimetres (two feet), and seem to prefer rodents to any other prey. Like the night adders, their venom is moderately toxic.

The **carpet** or **saw-scaled viper** is a dull grey-brown snake with a pale, almost white, diamond patterning down its back. Growing as long as ninety centimetres (three feet) but usually half this length, it is a resident of dry, arid Somalia, eastern and southern Ethiopia, north-eastern Uganda, and northern Kenya. It is abundant in some parts — in a relatively small area of northern Kenya in 1965, herpetologists Alec Duff-Mackay and Jonathan Leakey collected 6,933 live carpet vipers in four months.

They are probably responsible for more serious cases of human snake bite — and possibly deaths — each year than any other species in Africa. Though not the most virulent, their venom is extremely toxic, and they strike after considerably less provocation than most other snakes. Cryptic in colour and given to lying under bits of dead wood, the unwary collecting fuel are likely to both surprise the snake and have a hand close to it when this happens. The viper strikes defensively, and another case of snake bite occurs.

Carpet vipers aware of approaching danger hiss loudly, not by exhaling breath, but by rubbing rough scales against one another in a continuous coiling motion of the body. If the warning is ignored they strike vigorously. General in diet, they eat insects, spiders, centipedes, scorpions, lizards, skinks, geckos, frogs, and small rodents.

Quite the most frightening snakes are the vipers in the genus *Bitis*. There are only four in Eastern Africa: the **puff-adder,** the **gaboon viper,** the **rhinoceros-horned viper** and the **Kenya** or **Worthington's horned viper.** The last named is something of an afterthought as it is small — thirty-five centimetres (fourteen inches) long — innocuous-looking, and only moderately poisonous. The other three are gross: their broad, flattened, and angular heads are much wider than the neck and their bodies are extremely heavy and broad — almost bloated.

All three have huge, curved fangs: on large puff-adders and gaboon vipers, these may be four centimetres (1.5 inches) long — enabling them to inject venom deep into prey or enemy. Indeed, they can be driven so deep that, in recoiling, a strong victim may rip out or break the fangs. Provision has been made for this, however. Behind each fang lies a replacement set of decreasing size. When a fang is lost or broken, the next in line is brought into immediate use and rapidly grows to full size.

The volume of venom all three can inject is substantial. The gaboon viper holds the world record for all snakes — around six millilitres in one bite.

Bitis venom produces tremendous tissue damage. Small prey animals — usually warm-blooded mammals — die quickly, but animals the size of a human may suffer for several days before succumbing. Massive swelling about the bite, weeping blood and lymph fluids, and intense pain are early symptoms. Blood vessels break down and so much blood can be lost through internal haemorrhaging that substantial transfusion may be the only way to prevent death. Later, there is massive loss of tissue. Even with medical help, a bite may result in a wasted or amputated limb.

The **gaboon viper** adds more horror to this hideous picture by also combining a substantial neurotoxic component with the vasculotoxic element of its venom.

The **puff-adder** is the most widely distributed of the three, occurring throughout the savannahs and woodlands below 2,400 metres (8,000 feet), except montane or lowland wet forests. The largest specimens are always female and may reach just under two metres (6.25 feet) long with girths of as much as thirty-two centimetres (more than twelve inches). Big specimens such as these can ingest a full-grown hare or dik-dik.

The gaboon viper is a species which occurs in the warm forests of lowland Uganda, western Kenya, and — in a relict population left over from the era when western forests stretched across the continent — in both eastern and southern Tanzania. It is bigger and fatter, with a proportionately broader, flatter head than the puff-adder, growing more than two metres (6.5 feet) long, with a girth of up to forty-eight centimetres (18.5 inches) and weighing up to twelve kilos (twenty-six pounds). Colouring includes a white or cream top to the head, and a patchwork body pattern of sharp-edged black, yellow, mauve, and brown blotches, making it one of the most beautifully coloured of all snakes.

The **rhinoceros-horned viper,** a smaller version of the gaboon viper, is distinguished by two long horns above each nostril and an even more bizarre body pattern. The colours tend to be brighter than in the gaboon viper and include yellows, reds, blues, and greens. In length it reaches 1.5 metres (five feet), but is usually somewhat smaller. Its distribution is again similar to the gaboon viper, being primarily a wet forest species with some relict populations in Tanzania.

Despite their grossly-proportioned bodies, all three of the big *Bitis* vipers climb and swim well. Often sluggish, they hunt by lying motionless on, or beside, a trail. When a victim is within striking distance, the snake lashes out, mouth so far agape that upper and lower jaws are in the same plane, great fangs forward. As they pierce the victim there is a convulsive bite, the huge injection is made, and they recoil.

They sometimes hold on to small victims. Larger animals dash off to drop dead a little distance away. Slowly the viper moves after it, flicking tongue unerringly following the scent trail left by the doomed victim. Reaching the corpse, the leisurely process of engulfment commences.

Lying beside or on a path is what makes these big vipers so dangerous. Usually they warn approaching large animals of their presence by exhaling powerfully: the resultant deep hiss giving rise to the name puff-adder. But they do not move away and are trodden on with dire consequences.

Blind-Snakes, Worm-Snakes, and Worm-Lizards:

Between the true snakes and the lizards lie three groups: the **blind-snakes,** *Typhlops,* with at least eighteen species, the **worm-snakes,** *Leptotyphlops,* with at least six species, and the **worm-lizards,** *Amphisbaenidae,* with at least ten species. As their English names imply, most authorities class blind-snakes and worm-snakes with the true snakes and the worm-lizards with the lizards.

All are largely animals of the underground. They tend to be glossy, black or brown, and sometimes marked with subdued colours and patterns. Most are very small and few ever exceed thirty centimetres (twelve inches) in length. Non-poisonous and living off insects, they are harmless to man. They are, however, superficially similar to small burrowing vipers.

Chapter 12   Lizards, Turtles, and Frogs

Lizards:

At least 165 lizard species occur in Eastern Africa, ranging in size from seven-centimetre (three-inch) long geckos to two-metre (six-and-two-thirds feet) long monitor lizards. The largest family, Geckonidae, has at least forty species, some of which are nocturnal.

The most familiar is the almost translucent **house gecko,** *Hemidactylus mabouia,* ever present in houses on land up to 1,500 metres (5,000 feet) above sea level. Hiding behind pictures and furniture in daytime, it emerges at night to catch the insects attracted to lights. Tourists to Eastern Africa will usually make its acquaintance early on in their visits — often with unwarranted trepidation, for geckos are harmless.

Less readily seen, but abundant and widespread, are the chameleons, of which there are at least thirty-nine different forms. One of these, the giant **Malagasy chameleon,** was introduced into the Ngong forest near Nairobi, but it is uncertain whether it still survives there. Up to fifty centimetres (twenty inches) long, by virtue of size it inflicts a painful bite if handled carelessly. All other chameleons are harmless and best known for their ability to match their colouring to their surroundings. The local myth that if placed on bright red they explode is, however, untrue.

Slow of movement, local legend has it that this is a penalty imposed by the Creator. At the dawn of time the chameleon was sent on an errand, but dawdled. As punishment, all chameleons were condemned thenceforth to a senile, doddering, hesitant crawl.

Skinks, with thirty-eight species, are almost as numerous as the geckos and chameleons. Among the best known of these diurnal, fast-moving lizards is the common **two-striped skink.** Dark brown with two creamy or whitish lines down its sides, it can be seen on almost all stone walls.

Among the most striking reptiles are the diurnal **agamas** or **rainbow lizards** of which there are fifteen species in Eastern Africa. All behave alike. They live in small colonies, each dominated by a large male, up to thirty-five centimetres (fourteen inches) long. In most species these dominant males are brightly coloured, usually the head contrasting strongly with the body. The actual colours vary with species, but are principally oranges, yellows, blues and greens.

A widely distributed species, the **red-headed agama** (*Agama agama*) has a bright orange-red head and deep blue body. These rather garish male colours are used ritually to advertise territory to rivals and consorts. Taking station on a prominent rock or tree trunk, males do series of jerky press-ups, bobbing their bright orange heads in semaphored challenges. Other males take note and steer clear or respond appropriately. Such performances are seen at many tourist lodges in the game parks, where agamas have become so tame that they maintain territories among veranda chairs, tables, and visitors' legs.

Female agamas are smaller, with drab olive or brownish uniforms with occasional brighter spots. Like chameleons, agamas change colour in seconds. If chased, or even if vanquished by a rival, an aggressive male in full colouring turns drab olive. And at night, when sleeping, there is no trace of the gaudy raiment worn in sunlight.

The insect-eating agamas are particularly partial to ants, but also take such unusual foods as scraps of cheese. They eat flowers as well — particularly portulaccas — an unusual item in any lizard menu.

The largest lizards are two species of **varanus** or **monitor.** The **Nile monitor,** slenderly built, up to two metres (seven feet) long, smart olive-green flecked with yellow, lives by the water side. Climbing and swimming proficiently, it preys on fish, any small- to medium-sized birds, mammals, lizards, amphibians, or snakes it can catch, and eats carrion. Many were caught on baited hooks for their skins, which produced fashionable 'lizard-skin' leather.

Nile monitors are great egg eaters, with a particular taste for crocodile eggs. Waiting until brooding female crocodiles move off their nests, they dig up and eat as many eggs as possible before the guardian returns. This must significantly influence crocodile mortality.

The **savannah monitor,** heavier and thicker-set than the Nile monitor, has a similar but more drab colouring. It is found in semi-desert

Above: Savannah monitor lizard.

Opposite top: Chameleon from Malawi; one of thirty-nine different species found in Eastern Africa.

Opposite bottom: Almost every stone house in the region has its resident two-striped skinks.

environments miles from water. In eastern and northern Kenya and in Somalia, it becomes dormant during long dry spells. Climbing high into a shady tree, it goes into a coma-like sleep, hardly moving through the dry months.

Like the Nile monitor, the savannah species is a generalized predator, taking what comes on offer — including large venomous snakes, to whose poison it seems immune. If molested, both monitors can inflict a painful bite and both use their tails as powerful whips. One lash from a big specimen will make a dog howl.

Crocodiles:

There are three crocodile species in Eastern Africa. Two are West African, relatively small and only just enter the region's western fringe. The **long-nosed crocodile,** *Crocdylus cataphractus,* is a secretive species known from western Uganda and also near Ujiji in Tanzania. Of conventional crocodile appearance, it is readily distinguished from other African species by its long, slender snout. Not much is known about its general biology, though like the Indian gharial which it resembles, it is probably a specialized fish eater and not dangerous to large mammals. The species is seldom longer than two metres (seven feet).

The second crocodilian with only a marginal hold in Eastern Africa is the **broadnosed crocodile,** *Osteolaemus tetraspis.* Similar in length to the long-nosed crocodile, this rather dark-coloured species has also been found in westernmost Uganda. At a glance, the layman could well mistake it for the Nile crocodile. Its stubby, broad snout and a somewhat upturned nose, together with the different arrangement of scales and scutes at the back of the head, do not stand out in the field and it could be more widely distributed than

181

Above: Water-loving Nile monitor lizard.

the records indicate.

In at least some parts of its range it spends daylight not in water, but down deep burrows some way back from the water's edge. Eating small animals, particularly frogs and toads, it is not dangerous to humans.

The **Nile crocodile** is the most widely distributed of the three Eastern African species. Growing nearly five metres (sixteen feet) long and weighing as much as three full-grown tigers, the Nile crocodile is Africa's most awesome predator. Where man is concerned, it accounts for more deaths annually than any other vertebrate.

In a form that was well established and functional during the age of the dinosaurs, crocodiles epitomize emotionless, cold-blooded efficiency. The Nile crocodile has excellent vision, acute hearing, and a well developed sense of smell. Primarily a fish eater, it will take any animal that it can over-power. One famous early Kenya photograph shows a full-grown black rhinoceros being dragged to its death by drowning. Only sharks

seem to instil the same cold dread this species inspires.

For a long time, in keeping with general attitudes towards crocodiles, they were considered cannibals: so merciless a creature had to be. Research over the past two decades has shown that this was wrong. Crocodiles are careful parents. The female lays a clutch of eggs in the ground and then guards the site for three months until the young are ready to hatch. They announce their readiness by emitting a short, nasal bleat.

At first one or two call sporadically. Within days all hatchlings are bleating in chorus. Any movement on the ground above them prompts a burst of calling. This stimulates the female to dig them up. With the sand removed, the young break out of their eggshells and clamber out of the nest chamber. With great care, the female picks up several at a time between her fearsome jaws and carries them to the nearby water. She does this, trip after trip, until none remain at the nest. For the next six weeks or so, the young 'crocklings' stay close

Above: The Nile crocodile is perhaps responsible for more human deaths each year than any other vertebrate in Africa.

to their mother, clustering around her head. Only when thoroughly accustomed to the outside world do they gradually disperse and become independent.

Even large males respond to the hatching calls and, given the chance, will also carry the young to water. One large territorial male at a crocodile research station was not so adept as the female in collecting or holding the youngsters and she clearly considered his endeavours unnecessary. But while she took one load to the water, the male took advantage of her absence to collect and transport a small quota himself. Nothing less cannibalistic is imaginable.

However, crocodiles do kill one another in territorial dispute. Large males may destroy smaller males which intrude into their domain and these subsequently may be eaten — by them or other crocodiles.

Turtles:

Four turtles occur off the Eastern African coast: **green, hawksbill, leatherback,** and **loggerhead.** Of these the **green** is by far the most commonly seen and anyone fishing within two miles or so of the shore can expect to see several a day. **Hawksbill turtles** are also common, but probably seen at a ratio of one to every twenty green turtles sighted. Both species nest over the entire length of coastline. The other two species are uncommon.

On inland waters two soft-shelled turtles occur. As implied by its name, the **Nile softshelled turtle** occurs in the Nile drainage, downstream of the Murchison Falls and the Semliki River and in Lake Turkana. The **Zambezi soft-shelled turtle** is found in southern Tanzania, Zambia, and Malawi. They are animals of big waters — major rivers and lakes — and both are large, growing to over thirty kilos

183

Above: Hunter becomes hunted: African python and Nile crocodile locked in mortal combat.

Opposite top: Leopard tortoise.

Opposite bottom: Green turtle returns to the Indian Ocean after laying her eggs in the sand above the high water mark.

(sixty-six pounds) in weight.

Four somewhat similar small water-tortoises occur in small streams, seasonal ponds, and puddles less than 1,800 metres (6,000 feet) above sea level. Their ranges overlap considerably and identification is a job for the expert. All are carnivorous — eating fish, tadpoles, and aquatic insects. In the drier areas these water-tortoises — which are similar in appearance to North American terrapins — bury themselves in drying mud and stay dormant until their ponds and water-holes fill up once again.

One species, the **black water tortoise,** *Pelusios subniger,* has an unusual distribution. Not only does it occur throughout Africa, but also on the oceanic islands off Cape Verde in the Atlantic, and Pemba, Zanzibar, Madagascar, Mauritius, and the Seychelles in the In-

dian Ocean. That it occurs so widely as a single species suggests that it may be swept out to sea in floods and survive long periods adrift until washed up on an island. This must happen frequently enough to keep the various populations genetically similar.

Several land tortoises are present in the region, the most common being the handsome **leopard tortoise,** so named for its mottled black and yellow carapace.

Amphibians:

There are over twenty-nine toad species in Eastern Africa and more than 125 species of frogs. Visitors will probably hear far more of both groups than they see. Both toads and frogs are extremely vocal, and the chorus of croaks, pips, trills, and bleats from ponds and swamps as the rains break can be quite liter-

Above: Highland species of toad from Ethiopia and Kenya — *Bufo kerinyagae* — shows the general toad characteristic of good camouflage.

Above: Handsome green toad — *Leptopelis gramineus* — from Dinsho in Ethiopia.

ally deafening. The largest family within the amphibians are tree frogs, with over sixty-nine species.

The biggest frog or toad in the region is the widely-distributed **eastern burrowing bullfrog.** A savannah species, it is active and abroad only during wet seasons. During dry months it buries itself in the ground and aestivates. Growing to twenty-five centimetres (ten inches) long from nose to tail, this giant of the frog world is a voracious predator. Other frogs, small- to medium-sized snakes, small rodents and birds, scorpions, centipedes, virtually anything that moves and can be fitted into this bullfrog's cavernous mouth, are eaten. In keeping with its size, the species has a powerful bite.

With the amphibians as a whole, identification is an expert's field, distributions are often restricted and, as yet, there are no good, readily-available guides to the frogs of Eastern Africa.

Eastern Africa also has at least nine **caecilians,** or limbless, cylindrical amphibians. The group is little studied and eight of the nine species are extremely local in their distributions. The one widespread form is the **mud-dwelling caecilian** that occurs from coastal Kenya to the Rufiji River in southernmost Tanzania.

Chapter 13   Insects

Insects comprise some seventy per cent of all animal life. More than a million species have been described by science, and these form only a small proportion of what is thought to exist. In 1928 Folson Cording observed that some insects are smaller than the largest protozoa (microscopic, single-celled animals), others larger than some of the smallest vertebrates, such as Africa's pygmy mouse.

Relative to the rest of the world, Eastern Africa is rich in insect life, but one could only make an educated guess at the total number of species: it must run at least to tens of thousands. And in no field does the saying 'Out of Africa something new' have such meaning as in the case of Eastern Africa's insects.

The most detailed study of insects has generally taken place in areas where they effect the health of man and beast or influence crop production. Early explorers recorded their afflictions from mosquitoes, tsetse flies, common flies, body lice, the 'jigger' and other fleas — and they reported locusts and caterpillars devastating crops in a manner unknown in the temperate zones.

As with the other arms of natural history, early amateurs collecting insects out of curiosity laid the ground for what we now know. Intrigued by brilliant colours, bizarre patterns, sizes, and shapes, these avid and descriptive collectors were worthy forerunners to the modern professional entomologists who concentrate their attention on the insects of economic importance to man.

Within the limits of this book any review of Eastern Africa's insects must be very abbreviated. Thus to cover the wide spectrum, reference is only made to the more conspicuous, colourful, grotesque, or weird species and those that have some bearing on man's affairs.

Metamorphosis:

The most striking feature of insect biology is the process of metamorphosis, the four stages of an insect's life that are totally different from the developmental stages of vertebrates.

Life starts as an egg, which may be laid singly, in clusters, or even in a sort of purse — the vetheca — depending on the type and species of insect.

An insect egg then hatches into a larva, which is commonly called a maggot, nymph, or caterpillar depending on the family. This feeds on a vast range of both animal and vegetable materials, which differ according to species, and grows prodigiously. Having attained its appointed size, the larva turns into a pupa: it becomes dormant and changes shape — usually into a legless casing that often looks more like a seed than a living animal. In butterflies and moths, the pupa is known as a chrysalis.

After a period which may be as short as several days or as long as several months or even several years, the pupa bursts open to release the adult insect, or imago. This usually looks so different from the larval stage that unless one has actually followed the process, it is difficult to comprehend that larva and imago are one and the same animal. Even today many balk at the idea that repulsive caterpillars are but a juvenile stage in the life of a gorgeous butterfly.

In their adult stage insects mate, lay eggs, and die, and the process repeats itself.

As is so often the case in nature, there are exceptions. The tsetse fly (Glossina), for example, outwardly reproduces rather more like a vertebrate. After mating the female retains her fertilized egg within her body. There it hatches and the larva grows inside her rather like the foetus in a mammal. Only when it is full grown and ready to become a pupa does the female tsetse 'give birth'. The larva is dropped onto the ground (usually close by the base of a tree or bush), wriggles itself convulsively into the soil and pupates almost immediately. During pupation the perfect adult insect develops, the pupa hatches, and the imago flies free.

Butterflies and Moths:

Since both of these groups are classified as Lepidoptera, it is convenient to couple them for discussion. Some 2,500 species of butterflies (Rhopalocera) are known from Africa south of the Sahara. Because they are diurnal and many are conspicuous and brightly coloured, this group is relatively well known. Moths (Heterocera) are predominantly nocturnal, many are dull in colour and are consequently not nearly so well known. Nevertheless there

Left: Eastern Africa's rich mosaic of butterfly life — a selection of common forest and savannah butterflies.

Above: Congo long-tailed blue butterfly, jewel of the rain forests and woodlands of western Uganda.

Above: These moths display 'aposomatic' or warning colours. When birds swallow them they are sick and henceforth avoid these and similar colour schemes.

may be five times as many moths as there are butterflies (12,500 species) — and many more still await discovery and scientific description.

Butterflies range in size from some in the genus *Papilio* — the **swallowtails** — that have wingspans of up to twenty centimetres (eight inches) to tiny specimens in the genus *Lycaenidae* — the 'blues' — which span less than one centimetre (less than half an inch). The swallowtails are usually brilliantly coloured; blacks with vivid blues, greens, yellows, and stripes, or heavily spotted and patterned. Their flight tends to be rather 'sloppy' and most are resident in forests.

Other brilliant species belong to the *Nymphalidae,* which are often large, have stout, heavy, bullet-shaped bodies and fly fast and direct. They, too, are mainly forest species,

though there are some which occur right through the savannahs and into semi-desert. One spectacular member of the family is a glistening mother-of-pearl; others display crimsons, greens, and yellows.

Intermediate in size are the *Pieridae* or **'whites'.** As implied in their group name, they are mostly white or yellow. Many are open country insects and from time to time some species undergo mass migrations. Millions may move on a broad front — often nearly two kilometres (over a mile) wide — away from their natal area. Sometimes these migrations last many days and cover distances of hundreds of kilometres. Seemingly they move to new areas where their food plants may be more abundant. In addition to the whites, many other species also migrate *en masse* and sometimes several species travel together.

Above: Two fast-flying, nectar-drinking hawk moths (top) and female (bottom left) and male (bottom right) lappet moths of the genus *Gonometa*, that has potential as a silk producer.

191

Above: 'Moon' moth of the saturnid family — found in western Uganda.

The **blues,** so called because many members of the genus have a brilliant, shimmering, iridescent turquoise as their predominant colour. Others display purples and powder blues, a few substitute scarlet or green for the blue, but all are small and perhaps the most exquisite of all butterflies.

Many blues are only known from one or two specimens in museum or private collections. Those living in the rain forest canopies are the least known and are almost impossible to capture. However, when a steel tower was erected in such forest at Zika, in Uganda, in order to investigate the incidence of certain disease-carrying mosquitoes at different levels in the forest, some rare blues were collected.

Other blues are confined to boulder-strewn rocky hilltops with little vegetation. The caterpillars of one species live with the ants inside the galls of the whistling thorn — *Acacia drepanolobium* — pirating food the ants produce for their young.

Giants among the moths are the **'moon moths'** in the genus *Saturnidae*: huge bat-like creatures of wonderful soft colours and patterns. Many species have huge 'eye spots' on both fore and hind wings. These look like pupils and when a moth suddenly opens its wings, a predator that may have disturbed it is confronted by two sets of staring eyes. The largest of the saturnids have wingspans exceeding twenty-one centimetres (8.5 inches). The most lovely is the moon moth, which is a delicate, pale green with long 'swallow tails' off the hind wings. It has a smaller cousin that comes in shades of browns and pinks instead of green and it, too, has long tails.

Very different from the saturnids are the **hawk moths** (*Sphingidae*). With streamlined, torpedo-shaped bodies, and thin wings that beat so fast they literally hum, they are among the fastest of the moths. The largest have wingspans of around fourteen centimetres (5.5 inches), but they range down to minute species which fly by day and mimic bees.

A feature of the hawk moths is an extremely long tongue that, when not in use, is held coiled under the head. It enables the moths to extract nectar from deep within flowers while hovering in front of them. It gives them such reach that some long, narrow flowers need hawk moths to pollinate them.

The hawk moths' caterpillars are formidable-looking creatures. Some have false eye spots that give the appearance of a lizard's head to intimidate would-be predators.

Another group of large moths is the family Lasiocampidae or **lappet moths.** Many of these — particularly those in the genus *Gonometa* — are curious in that the males look so different from the females that most would take them for totally different species. Neither males nor females take any food at all as an adult; they don't even have working mouth parts. The females are large, heavy-bodied, egg-machines which look like saturnids, and can barely fly. The males are small, slim-winged and speedy, like hawk moths with frilly-edged wings. Their mobility enables them to track down females and mate with them in the mere forty-eight hours of life they are allotted. Interestingly, these *Gonometa* moths show promise as a new source of silk for Africa.

Hundreds of moth species are small, with wingspans of less than five millimetres and some under one millimetre. Most are undescribed and unnamed.

Beetles:

There are probably more beetle (Coleoptera) species in the world than any other group of insects. In 1934, entomologist Dr A. D. Imms noted that there were then at least 250,000 species. No one has ever tried to make a check list of those which occur in Eastern Africa.

Among the most conspicuous of all beetles in the region, which are often seen by visitors to national parks or cattle ranches, are those of the family Scarabaeidae — the **dung beetles.** In the big game areas where there are abundant elephant, rhino, and buffalo, at night these often congregate in their thousands about lights. Commonly large, of grotesque shape, armed with horns and spikes, these beetles appear with the rains searching for herbivore dung. Finding new droppings, they form a ball of dung and laboriously roll it a considerable distance — often tens of metres — to a suitable burial site. The dung ball is then buried deep underground, and an egg laid in it.

When the egg hatches in this natural incubator, the larva lives off the dung. When it has consumed it all, the larva pupates and waits until the next heavy rains. Once the ground is suitably moist, the pupa hatches and the perfect beetle makes its way to the surface to start the cycle over again.

There are other dung beetles — some quite tiny, many coloured brilliant metallic blues and greens.

Among the biggest of all beetles, much sought after by collectors of curious insects, are the **Goliaths** — members of the *Cetoninae*. Huge creatures up to ten centimetres (four inches) long, brightly coloured in whites and blacks, or in some species brilliant blues, greens, oranges, and yellows, they feed on the saps and gums that exude from the bark of trees and shrubs. Some are pollen eaters and, by destroying flowers, are horticultural pests. The largest goliath beetle had an unusual role in the Abaluhya (a tribe in western Kenya) circumcision ritual. Live specimens were collected and suspended from a tree branch on long threads. The captive beetles flew in endless circles at the end of their tethers, the droning sound emitted being considered suitable background 'music' for the ceremony.

Above: Buprestid beetles about life size. Larvae of all three bore into timber and many dead trees reveal their tell-tale oval holes.

Yet another beetle group with some very large members are the **long horns** (Cerambycidae). They are characterized by very long antennae, a seven-centimetre beetle having feelers over ten centimetres long. The long horns lay their eggs in timber — most species selecting dead wood, though some choose living trees. The larvae eat and tunnel through the wood. They play a prominent role in weakening dead and dying trees, reducing the time that such timber remains standing.

The largest beetle family comprises the **weevils** (Curculionidae), of which there are at least 65,000 worldwide. Their larvae specialize in eating hard plant seeds and, as they consume stored grains on a vast scale, many species are a serious pest to man.

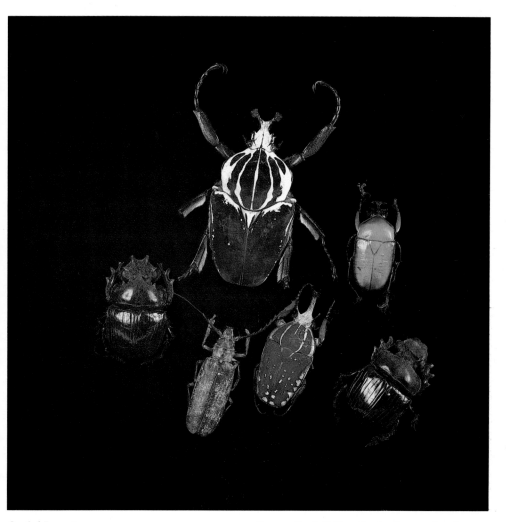

Social Insects:

The order Hymenoptera includes all the ants, wasps, and bees. Although many species are solitary, all three groups are characterized by species that live in matriarchal colonies.

For sheer numbers within a colony, honours must go to the ants and, in particular, to those known as **'safari'**, **'army'**, or **'siafu'** in the genus *Dorylus*. Renowned the length and breadth of Eastern Africa, these vicious, omnivorous insects instil fear and cause discomfort whenever they appear.

A colony of siafu may contain twenty million individuals and weigh twenty kilos (forty-four pounds). As with all colonial Hymenoptera, the colony revolves around a 'queen' — usually a huge, ungainly, fertile female whose role is to turn out an endless stream of eggs and to act as the centre of the community. She

Above: 'Goliath' beetle, twelve centimetres long; two green, cetonid beetles of the chafer family; pinkish 'longhorn' wood boring beetle, flanked by two dung beetles — both larger than match-boxes.

195

Above: Giant grasshopper (top), tree cricket (left), and (right) a terrestrial mole cricket. Members of this large family include the dreaded locusts — scourge of tropical agriculture.

is tended by castes of small 'workers' and both major and minor 'soldiers' equipped with huge biting jaws. All the workers and soldiers are blind, infertile females. From time to time fertile males are produced. These bear little resemblance to the rest of the colony.

They are winged, have eyes and don't look at all like ants to the uninitiated. Periodically (tradition says when the rains are about to break), these males are released from the colony and fly off to find a mate, copulate, and found a new colony. Attracted to lights at night, they are widely known as 'sausage flies' and are harmless nuisances given to crashing into bowls of soup during dinner or into drinks around the camp-fire.

A colony of siafu has a regular territory — several strategically placed underground bases — which are often abandoned termite colonies. Night and day, workers and soldiers stream out in all directions, raiding and foraging. They travel to and from the scenes of action along cleared and well defended trails. At a hunting ground they spill out as a carpet over the ground, swarming up and over trees and bushes. And all creatures caught — other insects, nestling birds, lizards, snakes, chickens, and anything that cannot get away from them — will be torn apart, tiny piece by tiny piece, and carried back to the fortified nest.

After cleaning out the hunting grounds within easy reach of one of their bases, the colony moves into another site in its territory. The huge, ungainly queen is lugged along bodily, surrounded by battalions of soldiers, ready to swarm over anything which moves nearby. In addition, eggs, larvae, and pupae are all picked up and carried to the new site. Once encamped, the relentless raiding commences again and goes on until local resources are depleted and another move becomes necessary.

In the past, the biggest siafu soldiers were used as surgical sutures. The lips of a wound were held together and a large soldier applied so that it bit convulsively across them. Once its jaws were well set its body was twisted off, leaving the clamped jaws holding the wound closed.

Another species of colonial ant in the genus *Messor* lives in grassland and eats grass seeds. One of their colony sites is a conspicuous circular area up to ten metres (thirty-three feet) in diameter in grassland that is completely devoid of vegetation. They collect seeds so assiduously that no grass can regenerate around their colonies and they are much disliked by pastoralists.

The **'cocktail'** ants (*Crematogaster*) often live in a symbiotic relationship with the plants in which they build their colonies. Many of these look like large black lumps and are situated high up in trees. Examined closely, they have the texture of papier mâché.

If their tree is shaken or in any way disturbed, hundreds of these tiny ants rush out of their nests, swarming along the branches in all directions looking for the cause. When agitated they hold their abdomens upright— hence the name cocktail — and when they encounter an aggressor, they not only bite, but sting in the manner of a wasp.

One of the cocktail ants lives in the extraordinary thorn galls on the whistling thorn trees (*Acacia drepanolobium*) characteristic of Eastern Africa's upland, black soil savannahs. Each gall appears as a black bulge up to three centimetres across that develops at a point on a twig where two thorns protrude. Each of these galls is hollow and almost all contain a small colony of 'cocktails'. Presumably there is some connection between the genesis of the gall and the ants.

The ants act as the trees' guardians. Any disturbance and the ants pour out to repel the invaders. Giraffe, for example, like whistling thorn leaves and browse them avidly. However, they only have time to take a few bites before the defending ants are swarming about their muzzles, forcing them to move on to the next bush. Thus one may see giraffe browsing whistling thorns, but it is a case of two or three bites here, move on, two or three bites there and move again. The ants save the trees from being over-used.

Many people mistakenly think of **termites** (Isoptera) or **'white ants',** as they are widely but incorrectly known, as belonging to the same family. In fact, they are not related at all to ants, but to the cockroaches (*Blattidae*). However, as they are colonial, they share some similarities with ants.

Photographers Alan and Joan Root titled their documentary film on termites *Castles of Clay*, and it well describes many forms of termitarium. In a variety of domed and spired shapes, these 'anthills', as they are known, are both prominent and characteristic features of savannah Africa.

Termitaria are rock-hard and laboriously built, grain of sand cemented to grain of sand with a special 'glue' produced by the worker termites. Every grain is brought from below ground, and thus what you see above ground represents the tip of an 'iceberg' of excavation for countless chambers and endless passages down below.

Deep in the subterranean vaults is the queen's chamber, where she lives with her consort. Looking like a large, white, pulsating slug, the female is a great egg producing machine, utterly unable to move. Surrounded by countless workers that clamber about her person polishing, cleaning, and feeding her, she sheds an endless stream of eggs that are rushed off to hatching and nursery chambers where other workers look after them.

And another feature of termitaria are their fungus gardens.

The termites eat fungi. Each species has its own fungus which is cultivated underground in chambers where temperature and humidity are carefully controlled. In turn the fungi are cultivated on a medium derived from cellulose: the basic, indigestible constituent of wood. Above ground termites forage for dead wood — in the form of a piece of paper, dried grass, or tree trunk. They gnaw away and ingest tiny portions. Microscopic protozoa and bacteria in their gut break down the cellulose into components which the workers then transport underground and excrete for the fungi to grow on.

As decomposers, and by opening the soil to allow both aeration and water to percolate, termites play important roles in the basic ecology of many parts of the tropics.

Most termite mounds contain a weird collection of beetles, flies, mites, and other insects known collectively as inquilines or termitophiles. These prey on both termites and one another. Similar creatures living in true ant colonies are known as mymecophiles.

Probably the best known of all social insects worldwide is the **honey bee,** *Apis mellifera.* African honey bees are reputed to be particularly fierce, and probably account for more deaths annually in Eastern Africa than snake bites.

As in Europe and Asia centuries ago, before the cultivation of sugar beet or sugar cane, until very recent times honey was the main sweetener in Africa. Almost all people kept beehives and were adept at extracting honey. Some, such as the Okiek hunter-gatherers of the Mau Range in Kenya, have a culture deeply rooted in beekeeping and honey gathering. So constant and close is their contact with bees that most of the men seem immune to their stings. A honey-based mead, or 'tej', is the potent national drink in Ethiopia, and most households still brew their own.

One of the more unusual relationships between animals and insects is the association between the black-throated honey guide bird, humans, and bees. The honey guide eats honeycomb and its contents, but has no means of breaking into beehives. However, it associates people with this ability and in many parts of Africa leads them to beehives. Honey hunters know this and both bird and people cooperate to locate beehives. Nobody knows how honey guides learn this behaviour. They cannot be taught by their parents because, like the cuckoo, they are parasitic nesters and their young are reared by other birds.

And in areas where sugar is readily available and honey gathering no longer commonly practised, honey guides do not try to lead people to hives, even though both birds and beehives are present. It seems, therefore, that this unusual instinct will fade away and may even become extinct.

In addition to the stinging honey bee, there are a number of stingless bees. None form the large colonies characteristic of the honey bees. Their tiny hives are located in small hollows in rotten wood. The smallest are common in dry country where they come to any source of moisture. Given the chance, they will cluster about human and animal eyes for a drink. Similarly they are attracted to a sweating human — hence their common name **'sweat' bees.** Though never much in quantity, their honey, stored in small, spherical cells, is quite delicious.

There are also many solitary bees and a host of social and solitary **hornets** and **wasps,** most of which share the characteristic of an unpleasant defensive sting. Most prominent are many species of wasps that make mud nests in and about houses. The larvae of many of these mud nest makers are carnivorous. The adult hunts down a caterpillar, stings it — not to kill, but to paralyse — and carries it back to the nest chamber. It then lays an egg on the victim and seals the chamber. The egg hatches, and the larva consumes the caterpillar which, not being dead, has not decomposed. Having eaten, the larva pupates, hatches into an adult wasp, bites its way out of the mud chamber and flies free.

Perhaps the most fearsome of these predatory wasps is a large, steel-blue and orange species that hunts not caterpillars, but spiders — often species larger than itself and just as fearsome. Backwards and forwards, the wasp searches the ground for the holes in which its prey lives. Locating one, it lands and sets about a seemingly impossible task. It has to enter the tunnel, face a predator equipped with large 'fangs' and a poisonous bite, overcome it, and — in the confined space — apply its own paralysing sting. The setting and actors are out of science fiction.

Curiously, the ferocious spiders seldom put up the resistance expected of them. It is as though they are genetically programmed to succumb. Usually, it's only a matter of moments before the wasp emerges with its stupefied victim and, because it is so much larger than itself, starts dragging it back, up hill and down dale, over tussocks and stones, to its own nest site.

An unusual group of wasps, the **'Ichneumons'** and **'Brachonids'**, reproduce by injecting their eggs into other living insects. They are equipped with the necessary surgical equipment: their ovipositors (the tube down which they pass their eggs) are like fine hypodermics. Inserting them gently into the victim's skin, they place one, or several, eggs inside them. When these hatch, the larvae eat their host alive.

One of the most astonishing ichneumonids has an ovipositor some six centimetres (2.5 inches) long. It parasitizes the larvae of beetles and moths that eat wood and live deep inside branches and tree trunks. Walking about on the wood's surface, the ichneumon senses the presence of larva deep beneath — quite how, though, is not known. Having detected a victim, it lowers its hair-thin ovipositor. No mere hypodermic, this is a fine drill as well. Slowly, and with exquisite precision, it drills through the wood and into the larva below. When the victim's skin is punctured, an egg is passed down the drill's core and placed in the victim.

Flies:

Flies, among the best known and least liked of insects, belong to the order Diptera, which comes from the Greek *Di*, meaning 'two', and *pteros*, meaning winged-insects. It is one of the largest insect orders.

The best known of them all is the **common house-fly,** *Musca domestica,* a nuisance and disseminator of disease worldwide. Many flies look sufficiently like the house-fly to be recognized for what they are. Some are large — such as the four-centimetre-long rhinoceros parasite, *Gyrostigma,* a frightening, biting fly that is a glorious blue and orange. Others are tiny, almost microscopic, like the biting **midges** (*Ceratopogonidae*) less than two millimetres long.

Some of these biting flies are the sources of disease; none more so than the **tsetse** flies of Africa. As the vectors of trypanosomes — the thread-like agents of trypanosomiasis, or sleeping sickness, in humans (or nagana in domestic animals) — they have been the source of much misery, directly inflicted by the disease itself.

Indirectly, attempts to eradicate tsetse flies have also caused problems. Immense numbers of wild animals were shot to deprive the tsetse of food — to little avail — and vast areas

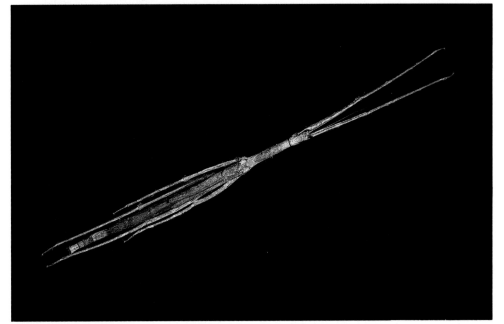

Above: Giant stick insect nearly thirty centimetres long, one of the world's largest insects. Harmless and vegetarian, they are common in Eastern Africa's coastal forests and thickets.

Above: Predatory dragonflies (top and right) and two harmless look-alike 'ant-lions' (left, centre and bottom). Dragonflies are aerial hunters — living off other insects. Ant-lions are the adult stage of the larvae that leave little, conical depressions in all dry dusty soil.

sprayed with noxious chemicals, causing great damage to other life, but still the goal of exterminating tsetse has not been achieved.

And there are flies whose larvae live in animals' stomachs — the so-called **bot flies** — that are either coughed out, or excreted with the faeces when ready to pupate. The elephant, for example, has one such fly, whose eggs are laid at the base of the animal's tusks. Hatching, the maggots creep quickly into the elephant's mouth and are soon swallowed. Down in the the elephant's stomach they feed on what their host ingests, and grow to about five centimetres (two inches) long. Ready to pupate, they wriggle their way back up the

elephant's oesophagus and lodge in its pharynx. Wriggling and tickling, they induce the elephant to cough or snort — and are blown out into the wide, outside world. Landing on the ground they rapidly dig into the earth and change into a pupa. No elephant over the age of weaning is without these bots; seemingly they cause no inconvenience.

There are also flies which live on birds, others on bats, and there is even a tiny one that lives on bees. There are **warble flies,** whose larvae live under the skin of mammals — and a host that live on and in fruit.

Yet of all the fly family, perhaps none cause so much human misery as the **mosquitoes:**

particularly in Africa where they are the vectors of malaria, yellow fever, dengue fever, and spread the filaria which causes the gross swellings of elephantiasis. There are over 450 species of mosquitoes. All their early stages are spent in water: the eggs are laid on water, the larvae live in water, pupation takes place in water — only the adult takes to the air. Many species can make do with the slightest quantity of water — a bottle top is enough. Water trapped in old snail shells, tins, bottles holes in trees, or even a drop of water in a leaf axil, will support one species.

Dragonflies:

Eastern Africa has a rich array of dragonflies, with at least 150 species. These range in size from the large *Anaxtristis,* fourteen centimetres (5.5 inches) long with a wingspan of thirteen centimetres, down to tiny species of only fifteen millimetres in length.

Body colours are often bright: reds, oranges, greens, and blues, though a few are dull and cryptic. The majority have colourless, transparent wings, but some have bright tinges or dark blotches.

All start life under water. While the egg is laid on or at the surface, the completely aquatic larva lives entirely below. The young are ferocious predators, catching and eating anything small enough for them to overpower, including small fish. Some of the smaller species make do with little water — a water-filled hole in a tree branch, for example. The larvae in these cases live off mosquito larvae that breed in the same site, or other small insects.

Once airborne, adult dragonflies continue their predatory lives pursuing and catching small flying insects, and eating them on the wing.

Dragonflies are generally found near water, but some migrate considerable distances from it. Other species are gregarious, flying and resting in companies of tens or even hundreds.

Ticks, Spiders, and Scorpions:

Though not really insects, these arthropods are generally regarded in the same light by lay folk. Ticks and mites (which, as mice are to rats, are really very small ticks) often come to our attention because many are blood feeders. The visitor to Eastern Africa's game parks will note that many of the bigger game animals are parasitized by a variety of ticks. These are usually clustered where the skin is thinnest — on the belly, between the hind legs, under the tail, and about the ears. They also pose difficulties for cattle owners.

Female ticks produce a mass of eggs down among the grass roots. These hatch into a swarm of tiny larval ticks that swarm up the grass stems above them and await a passing animal. Sometimes these masses are so dense they look like grass seeds at the head of a stem. As an animal brushes past, they latch on and set about taking their first meal. As anyone who has had the misfortune to take on a load of these pinhead-sized **'pepper ticks'** knows, it's not long before they make their presence known. Biting down through the skin about the tenderest parts, they cause an excruciating itch.

Having gorged itself, the larval tick that hasn't been scratched or bitten off its host, drops and moults. After moulting, it again climbs up a grass stem and awaits a victim for its next meal. This process may be repeated several times, the tick becoming bigger on each occasion. When the mature, eight-legged adult stage is reached, the tick mates, takes one last engorgement of blood, drops off and, if a female, lays a new mass of eggs.

The foregoing is only a generalized description of tick biology. There are a vast range of ticks and countless variations on this basic theme. Many specialize in certain types of animals and some stick to a single species. There are forms that live off birds, others off mammals, some off reptiles — snakes, lizards, and tortoises — and even some which parasitize insects. Some are long-lived, and many go for years between meals. The characteristic species of African grasslands can even cope with the seasonal grass fires. Sensing the heat of approaching flames, they drop down to the ground and rapidly bury themselves deep enough in the soil to be protected when the fire passes overhead.

Not only are their basic habits unpleasant, but ticks seriously debilitate a host and, more seriously, are the vectors of many unpleasant diseases. In man, they transmit a range of typhus-type fevers.

In addition to the blood-sucking ticks and mites, there are many vegetarian mites that live off plant juices. Most are horticultural pests.

Spiders form a vast group of arthropods. All are eight-legged and wingless. Yet, despite this, they can fly. Many small and immature specimens let out a length of silken thread which, caught by the wind, wafts them through the air. Blown this way, spiders fly between continents. And there is almost no habitat in which they do not occur — from sea level to the highest mountains, from desert to forest, in caves and volcanic tunnels, and in all man's dwellings from grass huts to modern skyscrapers.

Spiders are perhaps best known for their silken webs, used by some species to trap prey, or to line tunnels or hideaways. However, while not all make great use of webs, all are carnivorous, preying for the most part on insects. Some specialize in other animal's food. One group of spiders hunt under water, using their web to make a small air trap, providing a supply of oxygen when they dive. These forms eat small fish, as well as other small, aquatic life.

The largest spider in Eastern Africa is *Megalamorphida cithariscius crawshayi*. The female of this vast, intensely hairy species has a body the size of a small pear and thick legs that span a greater area than an adult hand. On the other hand, the male is a small, insignificant creature. Females are the stuff of nightmares, as ferocious as they look. Residents of the lowland, dry savannahs, they live in subterranean burrows and are seldom seen. Little is known of their biology, but one specimen in a Nairobi laboratory killed and devoured white mice. Sensing movement above ground, it quietly advanced to the entrance of its burrow. When the unsuspecting mouse came close, it shot out, threw itself over the victim and, while holding it in hairy eight-legged embrace, drove two glistening black fangs deep into its body. Injected with venom and digestive juices, all struggles quickly stopped. Human watchers breathed relief that these spiders are no bigger.

Similar to *Megalamorphida* are a group of slightly smaller, but nonetheless impressive, 'baboon' spiders. Common in all lawns, they live in almost vertical tunnels lined with a silken web. Some species make a hinged trap door to close the entrance. They bite freely if disturbed and though not a great deal is known about their venom, it is considered dangerous.

Another large, hairy, and aggressive spider — usually yellowish in colour — that lives on the ground is the 'wolf spider', *Geolycopsa*. It, too, bites readily and is considered highly poisonous — but cases are few and far between and science doesn't know a great deal about their poison.

That most venomous of all spiders, beloved of murder fiction writers, the **black widow spider,** is relatively common in Eastern Africa — as it is widely around the world. Its small size and the minute quantity of venom at its disposal, however, render it a threat only in the realms of fiction.

Some fifty species of **scorpion** occur in Eastern Africa: most in warm, dry areas. They apparently shun forests. Mostly active at night, they are so secretive that one can easily be misled into believing an area devoid of scorpions. But dozens will be revealed in relatively small areas, glowing with a greenish iridescence under ultraviolet light at night.

The largest scorpion in Eastern Africa is the black *Pandinus gregorianus,* which grows up to twenty centimetres (eight inches) long and lives under loose bark on dead trees. Another, *Pandinus cavimanus,* which grows to twelve centimetres (five inches), digs a subterranean burrow that has a typically oval cross-section. Other species live under stones, in nooks and crannies, in leaf litter, and one — *Uroplectes* — is a tree dweller. Scorpion stings are extremely painful but rarely fatal. Smaller species seem to have more potent venom than larger forms, but the worst is probably the medium-sized *Parabatus liosoma*, which is yellowish with a black body patch.

Centipedes and **millipedes** are common, widely distributed, and found in most terrestrial environments. Both have long, segmented bodies supported on many legs. But though their names imply that the former have 100 pairs of legs and the latter 1,000 pairs, this is poetic licence. Centipedes have one pair of legs per body segment — about twenty in all — while millipedes have two pairs per segment; some 100 pairs in all. They can be told apart, not only by the numbers of legs, but because most centipedes are rather flat, while millipedes are round.

Millipedes, feeding mostly on detritus and vegetable matter, are harmless, although some release a noxious secretion when disturbed that can cause blistering on sensitive skin.

Centipedes, on the other hand, are hunters and insect-eaters, capable of inflicting an extremely painful bite. Those who have been bitten by a centipede and stung by a scorpion report that the centipede's bite was the worst.

PART THREE:
SPECIALIST ARTICLES

Above: For most, underwater beauty remains more exotic than anything seen on land, defying description.

Chapter 14 Wildlife Photography

No matter how far modern cameras have evolved, the principles of successful photography remain constant. Certain fundamental techniques must be followed if the final results are to bring you not only happy memories, but pride in sharing them with your friends. Photographing wildlife needs skills, and this chapter — distilled from many years of practice — gives hints and advice to help the novice.

All good photography calls for experience, and those who have graduated over the years from simple non-automatic cameras to today's sophisticated instruments have an advantage over those who are beginning with one of the new 'wonder' cameras.

Modern electronic cameras, with their built-in automation for exposure, flash, film transport, and even focusing, should make photography relatively painless. But, considering the quality and price of the equipment used, results are often disappointing and below expectations. What goes wrong?

It is tempting, when planning a rare overseas vacation, to buy the best camera and lenses you can afford. But disaster lies ahead if you are not careful. Never start a photographic safari with totally new equipment. Theoretically, it may be automatic, but it will be intricate and needs understanding. Familiarity with it is absolutely vital, as photographing animals and birds — which do not pose for you — needs instant reactions. Your mind must be free to concentrate on the subject and not have to contend with whether you have set the correct speed, aperture, and focus.

By all means get new equipment, but buy it in good time so that you can put a number of films through the camera, using your range of lenses. Get to feel totally at home with all of it, for it is too late to learn while on your safari.

With regard to cameras and lenses, my comments refer exclusively to 35mm. equipment, as this size is by far the most commonly used. Most well-known makes have reached a high degree of sophistication. The best is very much a matter of personal preference, and the purchaser should be able to find an outfit that suits his or her pocket-book.

Semi-automatic or automatic cameras with fixed lenses that have focal lengths between 35mm. to 50mm. will produce excellent memory-reviving photos of people and places, and even occasionally of big game such as elephants, giraffes, and zebras. But little creatures will appear disappointingly small in the final results.

To get larger images of them — and of birds in particular — it is necessary to have longer (telephoto) lenses than those normally fitted to the fixed lens cameras. The longer the focal length of the lens, the greater the magnification of the image. This opens up a vast field for the large range of cameras that are designed to take an even bigger range of interchangeable lenses.

What constitutes a satisfactory range of lenses for wildlife photography? There is no easy answer. Some camera *aficionados* collect many lenses, but do not necessarily use all with any regularity. Considered from the most basic needs, the standard 35mm. or 50mm. lens used for landscapes, people, and places should be augmented with at least a 200-250mm. lens, but preferably with two of 135 and 300mm. focal lengths respectively.

The photographer keen on small birds may desire a still longer focal length lens in the 400-600mm. range; but travelling with and using lenses of this size and weight introduces certain complications. You would be well-advised to consider a '2 X' tele-extender which increases lens magnification. These supplementary lenses double the focal length of the lens with which it is used, when introduced between it and the camera body. Thus a 200mm. lens is increased to 400mm. and so on.

However, care must be taken to select a good quality tele-extender, as cheaper models can ruin definition. Besides possible loss of quality, there is another complication. Tele-extenders absorb light, reducing the effective lens apertures by two stops. For example, an aperture of f8 is converted to f4. Consequently exposure times become longer, a major snag in long-lens wildlife photography.

Opposite: Yawning displays are frequently given when hippo are uneasy or slightly disturbed. The slope of the cutting surface on this hippo's lower canines show that it is a female.

Below: Because of their constant movement, small birds call for a tripod and a fast shutter speed. Sometimes snapping one through vegetation — as with this red and yellow barbet — brings pleasing results.

Lenses with variable focal lengths (zoom-lenses) are very popular, and two could cover the entire range of focal lengths required for nature photography, especially if used in combination with a tele-extender. Yet again, it is essential to buy high quality zoom-lenses, as performances vary widely.

One final word of advice on lenses. It is not necessary to buy telephoto lenses with big apertures such as f2 or f2.8. Firstly they are too expensive, and secondly, being bulky and heavy, are difficult to handle. With today's high quality fast films, an aperture of f4 or f5.6 is quite adequate.

Now let us turn to films. They are of two broad categories: negative colour films, from which you get colour prints; and reversal colour films, which produce slides or transparencies. Transparencies can be made from negative film and, vice versa, prints made from reversal film, but the processes are involved, expensive, and quality is reduced. So make sure you select the right type of film for the end result you require.

Colour films are available in a range of speeds from 25 ASA to 1,000 ASA. The higher the ASA number the faster, or more sensitive to light, the film. If you wanted to photograph a black cat in a dark cellar at night, you would use 1,000 ASA film. But in Eastern Africa's normal sunny, outdoor conditions, 100 ASA film is fast enough for most purposes. It is important to bear in mind the general rule that the faster the film, the grainier the texture, with consequent loss in definition. The quality of films has improved so much in recent years, however, that you should not hesitate to use faster film if light conditions warrant it.

Having considered cameras, lenses, and films, it is now appropriate to turn to the technique of wildlife photography, which is essentially a technique of telephoto lens photography. Using a camera with a standard lens for taking shots of African buildings, landscapes, and scenery calls for no difference in technique to that which you would use at home in Europe or America. But when you fit your camera with a telephoto or long focal length lens to photograph wildlife, you may be entering a new field. The rest of this chapter is devoted exclusively to this technique.

The most common error to all novices with a telephoto lens, responsible for more bad photographs than anything else, including inaccurate focusing, is 'camera shake'. Let

Above: Flamingos are among the most rewarding of all photographic subjects — en masse at a distance, or in close-up.

me explain.

Holding a camera with a 50mm. standard lens and an exposure of 1/60th of a second, you photograph your dog. You get what appears to be a sharp picture. Now, from the same position with the dog at the same distance and with the same exposure, you wish to take a close-up of the dog's head, so you fit the camera with a 200mm. lens. This will give you a linear magnification of four, or an area magnification of sixteen. Holding the camera by hand, and with the same exposure as before, you take the picture. But the new photograph lacks crisp outlines.

What happened was that while enlarging the image of the dog's head sixteen times, the telephoto lens also magnified the minute shake of your hand by as much. While this was not obvious on your first photograph with the standard lens, it produced the blurred picture in your second.

Put simply, it's impossible to hand-hold a camera, set at 1/60th of a second with 200mm. (or larger) lens, firmly enough to eliminate the consequences of the minute movements your hands make — hence the expression 'camera shake'.

There are two ways to reduce or eliminate this error. The first is to use as fast an exposure as possible. I have a firm rule never to make an exposure with a hand-held long-focus lens at less than 1/500th of a second. If light conditions make this impossible, I very reluctantly reduce the speed to 1/250th. To comply with the rigid principle, I choose film which is fast enough to allow me to do so. In Eastern Africa's normal sunny conditions, 100 ASA film does the job comfortably.

The second route to eliminating camera shake is to support the camera. While this is best done using proper mounts, tripods, and so on, my rule is that any rest is better than none. Perfection comes with fast film *and* a rock-steady camera.

Much wildlife photography in Eastern Africa is undertaken from vehicles — often safari cars or minibuses modified for the purpose, with comfortable seats for about five passengers besides the driver and a guide. The photographer should have access to a window seat and, at least in Kenya and Tanzania, possibly also the luxury of a roof hatch for both viewing and photography.

Your driver spots an animal and stops in a

Above: Cats spend most daylight sleeping and can be photographically boring.

reasonable position for you to take pictures of it. If the light permits, in accordance with my principle, set the exposure at 1/500th of a second or faster. If possible, also rest the camera against the car window frame or roof hatch. Better still, have some soft shock absorber upon which you can rest the camera. This could be a folded cloth, better a cushion, or, better still, a canvas bag about eight by ten inches (twenty by twenty-five centimetres) in dimension — two-thirds filled with beans or dry sand. When the camera is pressed down on the bag, the contents take the camera's shape and provide a firm support that will let you get away with relatively slow exposures.

A special word of warning when photographing from vehicles. Never let the camera touch or rest on the vehicle if the engine is running, for the vibrations guarantee camera shake. Obviously good pictures call for the engine to be switched off. Similarly, other occupants in the vehicle should be still, for the slightest movement, or shift of weight, will be all too readily recorded by the telephoto lens.

Eastern Africa's wildlife lodges and tented camps provide photographers with many opportunities. Besides supplying food, drink, bed and other comforts, many are situated at sites — rivers, salt licks, and water-holes — that bring animals into close photographic range. These offer excellent prospects, for the camera can be sited at a pre-selected point, on a tripod or some other carefully arranged support, and camera settings can be made without the haste that often accompanies an approach by vehicle.

The hotels and lodges that provide facilities for still-watching wildlife have come a long way since the days of Kenya's original 'Treetops' in the Aberdare National Park salient. The first concept of a small cabin built in a tree over a water-hole has grown into large establishments where artificial moons light up the animals at night so that they are easily visible.

Photographing at night, even with lights which appear very bright, needs exposures of two to three seconds — even on fast films of around 400 ASA. In these circumstances I consider tripods or similar supports a must, though sometimes you get away with it by pressing the camera hard against veranda

Above: From time to time, however, they yawn and expose their fearsome fangs. Watch the animal that has just been roused from sleep.

railings and holding your breath. The results often have a strangely ghost-like appearance and recall the thrills of a night spent in solitude.

Even where the wildlife lodges and hotels do not present big game close up, a number of smaller creatures such as squirrels, wild cats, birds, and lizards become remarkably tame and allow people to approach relatively close. Consequently an early morning or late afternoon walk within the lodge boundaries can be rewarding.

When hand-holding equipment, some photographers use a shoulder-pod (rather like a gunstock) to provide additional support. Others, who have the luggage space and foresight to bring one, use tripods. Even a small one is better than none at all, and it is amazing how useful the lowly monopod (a one-legged support) can be in keeping a camera steady.

Yet, even without these aids, remember that a reasonably fast film of around 400 ASA and shutter speeds of 1/500th to 1/1,000th can give you shake-free exposures, making a walk about the grounds with hand-held camera and telephoto lens well worth your while.

Certainly some of my best pictures have been taken in this manner.

And remember to get up early and make the most of dawn opportunities, when animals and birds which later retreat to the shade are still abroad, and the rising sun's changing light makes for interesting perspectives as it brightens.

Wildlife photography, especially with telephoto lenses, is demanding, but skill is not difficult to acquire. It will provide the most lasting and vivid mementos of Eastern Africa with the unique value of being completely personal; the pictures taken were those viewed through your own eyes. So enjoy your safari and remember — keep your camera steady!

Chapter 15 Underwater Photography

Words can never really describe the beauty that lies beneath our oceans. Most divers give up trying to convince their friends that under-sea life is comparable to the most magnificent flower gardens.

Along the shores of the Red Sea, travellers find only bleak, barren desert, but a few metres away there is a cool, beautiful, underwater coral wonderland. One way to share these joys with your friends is to photograph, film, or record it on video tape.

Photography is difficult enough, but under-water you are faced with more problems: cold, currents, surge, loss of colour, plankton, back-scatter and unexpected movement.

First, you should be a certified diver. It is possible to take shots while snorkeling, but you would have to be extremely good at hold-ing your breath to get good results. Australian film-maker Ron Taylor, noted for his under-water photography, does a fair amount of work with snorkel equipment, but he was once a world-class spearfishing champion.

Once you are a confident diver, your next step is to look at the equipment you need to film the beauty of the underwater world. It's only about twenty-five years since serious underwater photography took off, but all kinds of cameras and underwater housings, from disc devices to the most sophisticated cam-eras, are on the market.

If you want a camera without a housing, the Japanese Nikonos is your answer. Many professionals use this camera, starting at the Calypso and then going through the range of Nikonos 1, 2, 3, and IVa, to the more recent Nikonos V.

All these models have a full range of acces-sories and flashes.

Colour:

One major problem of underwater photogra-phy is loss of colour. The water filters out the light. The first to go, at between four and five metres is red, followed by orange at eight metres, yellow at eleven metres, green at nine-teen metres, blue at twenty-three metres and grey at about thirty-one metres. When you bleed underwater at any depth your blood takes on a greenish hue.

Without a flash, a CC30R filter helps to bring back the reds, but always remember that a flash is an important adjunct of a good underwater photography. When using a fil-ter, make sure that it has drain-holes, for the water to enter and leave the space between the filter and lens, otherwise it may crack. During my travels I have noticed many photogra-phers using a piece of gelatin filter *behind* the lens. I have also seen some photographers covering the flash with a filter.

Strobes:

Nothing is more upsetting than flash prob-lems. It happened to me on the first day of a trip to the Maldives, when I ended up with a flooded strobe and camera.

Today, with the latest technology, flash attachments have become more robust and reliable, and a number of resorts have repair facilities and back-up units available. When buying a strobe you should look for several special features. **Beam angle** is important — it is no use using a 15mm. lens when your flash only covers a 35mm. lens. This can be done, but it enables you to highlight only certain areas of your picture. Wide-angle beam strobes are available, but usually you have to sacrifice at least one f-stop.

Naturally check that you have the correct connector designed specifically for your cam-era. Always take your camera with you to see that the strobe works.

My wife was once sold a strobe in New York that she was assured was the right one, and was told that the reason why it was not working was that the batteries were dead. But when she returned to Africa we found she had been sold an incorrect connection.

Also make sure that whatever model you buy can be recharged on either 220v or 110v. Adaptors are available for changing the volt-age. Beware of plugging your charger into the wrong voltage, as it can cause serious damage.

Another three features worth considering: **Multiple power** — This enables you to vary the power output for varying conditions **Slave** — This leads to some interesting shots, as it enables your strobe to be triggered by another unit; ideal for action shots of another photographer taking pictures.

Automatic Exposure — This feature has now been perfected and, with little effort, perfect exposures can be made almost every time.

Remember that with all these additional features you must ensure that your flash is set for the shot to be taken. It is quite easy to make a mistake, so be warned and make sure your camera is set on correct film speed, aperture, function (i.e. auto or manual), and, of course, distance.

Strobe arms are another important piece of equipment. It is advisable to move your strobe away from your lens to prevent back-scatter when the strobe light bounces off suspended particles in the water.

If it does bounce back, you pick up a 'snow' effect that invariably spoils the shot. The arm enables you to hold the strobe away to the side and above the lens. With a wide-angle lens, a long extension arm held above the top of the lens gives a pleasant effect.

Aiming the strobe is extremely important, as refraction causes the target to appear one-third closer. Compensate for it by aiming beyond the target. Some photographers have a modelling light on top of their flash which helps the arm. Some flashes come with this feature built in, but a Super Q light is a good addition for strobes without it.

Using this feature, the flash can be aimed perfectly. Remember, your equipment is only as good as you maintain it. Keep it clean with the O-rings checked and greased with silicone and you should have few problems. But I have yet to meet the underwater enthusiast who had *no* problems.

If your flash is incompatible when your camera is on automatic, it is essential to have a good quality light meter, such as the Seconic Marine Meter. I have found this device accurate both with cine and still photography.

Photography Techniques:
Taking good underwater pictures comes mainly from experience. If the conditions are such that you cannot get into the water every weekend, either use your pool to experiment or wait until you go on holiday.

Although 'bracketing' is an expensive way of taking pictures, at least you know that one is going to be perfect. It is not possible to get fish to stand still for you, so it is a matter of keeping as still as possible and trying to get them to come up close to you.

Close-up Attachments:
One simple and impressive way of taking underwater pictures is with extension tubes or 'add-on' close-up attachments such as those made in the early days by Green Things. I have one that fits over a standard 35mm. lens, and the results are outstanding.

All come with guide numbers for your strobes, and it is simply a matter of framing your subject and firing away. Significantly, these pictures usually gather awards at any slide presentation.

The more sophisticated cameras can be used for similar pictures.

Above: Like some strange creature from space, a human intrudes into the beautiful realms of the Indian Ocean's coral reefs.

Top: Spiny lobster or crayfish. Above: Spanish dancer. Opposite top: Imperial angel fish. Opposite top right: Clown fish in sea anemone. Opposite centre: Moorish idol. Opposite centre right: Sea cucumber. Opposite: Coachman or pennant coral fish. Opposite right: Sea slug.

213

Above: The delightfully unexpected result of underwater flash — a shoal of tiny, silvery fishes light up like a star-filled sky in an inner universe.

Most amateur photographers make the mistake of swimming over the reef too fast and missing some of the more interesting subjects. With patience, you will be amazed at what you will discover in one small reef area.

Don't forget, when concentrating on your subjects, to have a dive buddy present who might see that big shark coming up behind you. On a number of occasions photographers have not believed other diver's tales of what monsters swam past behind them.

There are two basic methods of taking pictures, both of which work and give pleasing results. The most popular system is to take a meter reading of the subject guide number and hold the flash at a distance to give you the correct exposure.

So if your meter gives you f8, then check the strobe-to-subject distance for f8. This gives a very natural-looking picture.

With a coral and diver subject filled in with strobe and the blue surface in the background with perhaps another diver or boat in natural light, you are set for an interesting shot.

For fish subjects, you can set your aperture smaller than the meter reading and hold your

strobe closer. This will give you a black background with the fish standing out in your picture. Experiment with both these methods. You may find things much easier using an automatic strobe.

Hand-feeding fish, morays, and sharks has added a new, interesting dimension to underwater photography. But don't try it unless you have studied someone else doing it. There are no problems with fish feeding unless a huge cod comes in for his bit — but this does make for some fine action shots.

Feeding moray eels is popular at most dive resorts. These formidable creatures turn out to be docile when treated with respect, but it's dangerous to tease them out of their holes for a better view of their entire body — I have had some nasty moments when the moray makes a grab for the food and attempts to take a piece of finger or hand with it at the same time. Better to begin by letting the food drift towards it, so it can see that your intentions are friendly.

If you're feeling a bit braver, hold the food between your forefinger and middle finger with your hand balled into a fist. In that way your fingers cannot get caught by its teeth. If a moray does grab your finger, *don't* pull it away. Just leave your hand where it is and it will eventually let go.

Shark feeding should be done only after you have studied experienced techniques and listened to a few hairy tales. In the Maldives, the main difficulty is that the moment the boat stops at a shark area, the brutes begin to look for food, which is usually taken down in a bag. Once the sharks have settled down the feeding begins. There is no difficulty by feeding under controlled conditions, but if food is dropped among them, then there is usually a frenzy, that could cause trouble. Nonetheless it certainly makes for excellent underwater photography.

Lenses:

There are many lenses available for the Nikonos range, all of excellent quality.

35mm: This is the standard lens that comes with the camera. It gives excellent results both topside and under water. It has apertures from 3.5 to 22, and it can be focused to one metre. This is a good lens for fish and coral pictures.

28mm: There are two models of this lens made now, one for top shots only, which is splashproof, and the other corrected for underwater work. If it is used on land you have a certain amount of 'barrel' distortion. This lens is excellent for most situations with edge-to-edge sharpness and it can be focused down to just under sixty centimetres.

If I were allowed one lens to take on holiday, I would choose this one. The depth of field is excellent, and the only two criticisms I have is that the figures are rather small and the aperture has no click control. I have used an O-ring slide over the control to increase the drag and so minimize the chance of its being bumped on to another setting.

15mm: This is a marvellous wide-angle, distortion-free lens, and, significantly, the workhorse of a number of professionals.

It has been described by many photographers as the best lens ever made for underwater photography. Word has it that there is a new lens on the market which is compatible with the Nikonos IVa and V on automatic. Both 15mm. models can be used on the full range of Nikonos cameras, although the older model cannot be used on automatic on the IVa and V.

80mm: This lens is not, in my opinion, a good underwater lens. The depth of field is minimal. It is, however, a good lens for top-side shots.

Viewfinders:

Although most cameras have built-in viewfinders, an optical viewfinder makes composition of shots a good deal easier.

The Nikonos optical viewfinder for the 15mm. lens is a must; and for the 28mm. and 35mm. lenses, Nikonos also make a top-quality viewfinder that ensures perfect framing. The only problem I have experienced with this viewfinder is keeping it parallel to the subject.

I have overcome this problem by putting a small dot on the front and rear of the finder in the centre of the glass. Once the two dots are lined up, like a sight, you know you are on target.

Anther problem is that they are parallel — corrected for two metres. As this lens is much used in fish photography, I consider that one metre is better, and I have modified my device to that distance.

Film:

Film — which film, which speed — is a subject that one could write much about, as individual preferences play an important part in the ultimate choice.

Most divers who take up underwater photography are inclined to use the fastest film they can buy. But with experience they find that this is not the best solution. In any event, fast film can detract from quality because it tends to become grainy.

400 ASA film is acceptable, to record a dive but if good quality is required, a slower film should be used — roughly speaking, from 200 ASA down to 64 ASA, or even 50 ASA.

I have always found Fujichrome good, and processing is handled at most resorts. Agfa have good film on the market.

A good pointer is to stick with the film you prefer, as changing brands and speeds can lead to errors.

Open up a new field of beauty for your friends and start taking underwater pictures today. You'll be delighted with the results.
— **B.D.L.S.**

Chapter 16 Heritage of the Indian Ocean

In all its many forms, conchology — the past time (some say art) of collecting seashells — is probably a old as man himself. From the beginning of time the oceans of the world have yielded a vast and varied assortment of seashells ranging in appearance from downright ugly to breathtakingly beautiful, and the rulers of the land have been gathering them as assiduously as the sea has been delivering them.

These days serious shell collecting is largely practised by specialists, scientists, and enthusiastic amateurs, but in the early period it was a labour of necessity and profit. Seashells have played an enormously important role in the economic history of the world.

For centuries the long East African coastline, from the Red Sea southwards, supplied Indian Ocean shells to all of Africa, and many of the cowries used to decorate the shrines and figurines in the ancient Nigerian cities of Benin and Ife originated 5,000 kilometres away on the shores of Sudan and Somalia. They came to West Africa by sea and across the Sahara by camel, becoming a valuable form of currency which found a ready demand in the markets of Kano and Timbuktu as well as the populous tropical coastal centres farther south which we know today as Togo, Takoradi, and Niger Delta.

Early man collected shells for food, adornment, prestige. Certain shells were used in magical ceremonies; others were worn as good luck charms — in particular, cowries were sought after to ensure fertility, as their shape resembled a female reproductive organ. Others were reserved for the use of kings, and even now the golden cowries of Figi and the New Hebrides are worn only by chiefs.

The little yellow money cowrie was once used as currency in many parts of Africa. Threaded on strings, forty at a time, tons of them were transported to West Africa to pay for gold, ivory, palm oil, and slaves. Twenty to fifty thousand would be needed for a slave; sixty to a hundred thousand for a beautiful young wife. One man built a bungalow and paid for it entirely with money cowries — a staggering sixteen million of them.

Shells had other uses, too. The Phoenicians founded a most profitable dyeing industry based on the little murex shell from which they extracted a purple colour as fast as the most sophisticated dyes used in industry today. With the exception of precious stones and rare metals, the most expensive commodity of the ancient world was probably a dye made by the Phoenicians from a fluid secreted within the shells of three marine molluscs — the Banded Dye Murex, the Spiny Dye Murex, and the Rock Shell.

This dye was called 'Tyrian purple'. About AD300, during an inflationary period, a pound of silk dyed in Tyrian purple cost an amount equivalent in purchasing power to about £15,000. Or, to put it another way, a typical silk scarf worn by a woman today would have cost the equivalent of £600.

In the eighth century the British used a shell for dyeing parchment; the little purple or 'dog' periwinkle. The Aztecs, too, used shell for colouring their artefacts. Instead of milking the snails — a custom still practised by the Mixtec Indians of Central America — the Aztecs, like the Phoenicians, either removed the gland or broke open the shell, a wasteful practice that greatly depleted the supply. Fragments from the crushed shells were piled up outside the city in great heaps, and on days when the wind blew onshore the busy streets of Tyre stank abominably.

Shells have provided man with cloth. The pinna shell, a long slim dark bivalve, attaches itself to a solid rock base in muddy sand by a *byssus,* a silky thread that it spins itself. The Romans wove cloth from it, and in the Middle Ages the anchor-cord of the pinna produced the famous Cloth of Gold. Until quite recently, there were still gloves and capes woven from the byssus thread in Sicily, although it was discreetly adulterated with a proportion of one-third silk. The Italians also used tiger cowries to iron their lace and burnish their paper.

Shells have always made excellent utensils and tools from the earliest times. We use them still: some fish dishes are delightfully presented when served in shells, and I use some shells for the arrangement of flowers and others for bird-baths. Before modern society came to

Above: Seashells, like butterflies, flout belief that evolution is all functional efficiency.

rely on plastics, most buttons were made from the shell of the pearly oyster and the *Turbo* and *Trochus* shells. The ubiquitous cowries were used as ballot stones by the Greeks and Romans, and to this day they make ideal counters for games.

Shells are excellent for decoration as well. In the eighteenth century entire rooms were encrusted with shells, and at one stage there was a vogue for grottoes, which were considered incomplete without them. Shells were used on snuff and other boxes, on frames for pictures and mirrors, and as goblets. They were also used as jewellery — and still are — either on their own or as pieces cut from the pearly nacreous inner layers.

Cameos are fashioned from shells, each layer displaying a different hue. The best cameos are made from helmets, *Cassis rufa* and

217

Above: Seashell shapes and forms suggest a burst of creative spontaneity; of glorious escapism — a holiday from common sense.

Cassis cornuta; but in the western hemisphere they use big conch, *Strombis gigas.*

A shell with a very different role is the big triton conch, *Charonia tritonis,* which is sometimes a trumpet. It produces a splendid resonant note and was used by the Polynesians for important ceremonies and on the battlefield. In East Africa triton shells were used in the past to urge ferry hands to greater efforts when cars were pulled across Kilifi Creek north of Mombasa by hauling the ferry along a chain; and when dhows enter Lamu harbour they still announce their arrival with a blast on their shell trumpets, as they have done for centuries. Indians use their sacred chank shell, *Turbinella pyrum,* as a trumpet.

There is a great deal of romance about shells. They speak mutely of the remote regions in which they originated and they charm the soul with their infinite variety. In the past they were an additional source of wonder; great collections were formed by rich and knowledgeable amateurs who sailed remote parts of the seas or had agents buying from those who did.

Nowadays most of the famous collections are in the hands of the great museums, to be enjoyed and studied by all. Yet even the savants are puzzled by some of their rarest specimens; one-of-a-kind enigmas, hailing from heaven-knows-where, unique and irreplaceable.

I once held in my hands a *Cypraea leucodon,* one of only two in the world.

There are other cowries almost as rare: the *Cypraea broderipi* for one, of which only three are known to exist, and the *Cypraea valentia,* of which there are only five. No one knows their origin; they are probably deep-water shells. I have also handled the world-record golden cowrie, *Cypraea aurantium,* and the famous cone shell, *Gloria-maris,* and I have had the fun of confounding the experts — no one was able to identify my unknown *Cymatium;* it was not illustrated in any of their books, so I left it with the specialists for identification.

Exciting as these rare shells are, the greatest thrill for any conchologist is finding his own shells, whether they are rare or not. I can remember how my first white or egg cowrie looked, the primary colour almost hidden in the water by its jet-black mantle and contrasting orange *papillae* (white cowries, *Ovula ovum,* are allied cowries, because they have teeth only on one side).

Within months of my first find I settled down to the serious business of trying to amass the full range of different Indian Ocean cowries that I could find, with every new species an exhilarating discovery. Records show that there are fifty-two different cowrie species in East Africa; I have forty-five, and the last seven are certain to present problems, but I have not given up.

Most beginners are usually first drawn to cowries. The reason could be that these are often the first shells that one finds in the Indian Ocean waters; the tiny *Cyparaea annulus,* or ring cowrie, and the big *Cypraea tigris,* or leopard cowrie. Their shells are radiant and glossy and need little attention once the shellfish has been removed.

But to capture all the fantasy of a fine collection one should see the living cowries in their natural environment; some are more beautiful than the shells they create. *Cypraea nucleus,* the nucleus cowrie, is a small, knobbly, beige shell; the fish inhabiting it has a strawberry-pink mantle with pale-green papillae.

Cowries lay eggs in the form of capsules, little seed-like objects gummed together, usually under rocks. The mother broods over them as a hen does, puffing out her mantle to cover them in the same way that a hen fluffs out her feathers.

The egg capsules vary in colour according to the species, but they also vary within the range of the same species; the reason is obscure, but it might be because of the developing eggs inside. I have seen the leopard cowrie, *Cypraea tigris,* on magenta egg capsules and on greyish-mauve ones. Both the false swallow, *Cypraea kieneri,* and the Chinese cowrie, *Cypraea chinensis,* run the gamut from golden-brown to pink egg capsules.

The lynx varies from cream to lavender; so does the star cowrie, *Cypraea helvola.*

It is important to put rocks and weeds back after looking for shells so as not to disturb any eggs or other marine life that may be adhering to them or sheltering beneath them.

Beneath the sea you soon discover that there are many other interesting shells waiting to be uncovered.

As your cowrie score mounts and the remaining species become more and more difficult to find, most conchologists enlarge their collections to include other shells. The handsome cameo shell, the *Cassis rufa,* with its orange mouth and pink-and-brown flecked back, is one of the first that most are drawn to. Its larger relative, the helmet shell, *Cassis cornuta,* is more difficult to find, as it tends to live in deeper water with a sandy bottom — and both shells tend to bury themselves in the sand — so I kept watch for a helmet.

At last I was rewarded with a beauty. This specimen was resting on the bottom in about six metres of water. Maia Hemphill from Shimoni, Kenya, a well-known authority on Indian Ocean shells, was lucky enough to find one sitting on a sandbank; it was encrusted with weeds, so at first she thought it was a rock itself. Not till she turned it over did she discover its true identity.

After cowries I think the favourite shells are cones. They are interesting and varied; their colours never seem to fade as some of the

Above: Starfish are seemingly designed and coloured on some nursery floor.

cowries' colours do. But they need more work, having to be cleaned outside as well as inside.

While cowries are peaceful browsers, grazing on sponges and coral animals, cones are more active killers, stalking their prey, which include other shells, worms, and fish. Furnished with a poison gland, their barbed tongues can penetrate the human skin easily, and five cone genera are known to cause bad stings. These are the *aulicus, textile, marmoreus, tulipa* and *geographus.*

The last of these is a killer; it should be handled with respect and care, being held from the back and top of the shell, away from its rear aperture.

The spiky murex shells have a great appeal, as have the lesser frilled ones. This species usually lives in rather calm sheltered waters with a muddy bottom, where they prey upon bivalves and other shells. The big triangular *Mures ramosus* with its red aperture and spiky exterior is a handsome variety. I have often found it with a bivalve shell clasped under its aperture, intent on opening the valves to reach the flesh inside.

Harp shells are other handsome carnivores. Their huge pink-and-white flecked feet are very obvious crawling about sand and weed.

Several times I have picked one up to admire its beauty, ribbed with pink, brown, and white and an intricate inlay of the same colours between the ribs, only to be struck by the excessive sliminess of the foot.

On closer examination, I have found crabs in the centre, in the process of being digested.

I have seen the big trumpet shell, *Charonia tritonis,* devouring a starfish, *Culcita schmideliana,* also known as the pincushion of the sea. By the time I arrived a third of the starfish was gone; the part next to the shell was white and rough looking. The role of this shell in preying on the Crown-of-thorns starfish, *Acanthaster plance,* a serious menace in any coral area, is well known. You will find both on live coral in fairly shallow water.

The lamp shell, *Bursa rufa,* also eats starfish. It is often found devouring the common red-and-grey starfish, *Protoreaster lincki.*

A large, beautiful, and common family of shells is the *Strombidae,* which include the finger or scorpion conch shells. They are mainly herbivores and prefer areas near sand and weed. This species often carry cloaks of weed on their backs, which makes a good disguise.

Strombidae are very active; if you hold one in your hand, it constantly reaches out with its

Above: Starfish are sometimes victims of trumpet and lamp shells.

horny operculum in an attempt to turn over and escape. Their shape is most attractive.

Many collectors prefer to collect a sequence of these shells, ranging from juveniles to the most mature, showing how their 'fingers' are produced from the first simple whorl through the scale to maturity and, finally, how the 'fingers' are worn down to stubs by movement.

Sand-shelling can be most interesting, following humps and bumps and tracks in the sand, preferably at night when it is cool, or when the tide is retreating, or just returning. It is at this time that most shells are active.

It is possible to find bivalves, and the long pointed augers, the *terebra* shells that prey on them; also the olives, rather like long, slim cowries with a toothless aperture. In addition there are *mitres*, another handsome family of large and small carnivores, often ribbed.

Indian Ocean shells are found just about everywhere in the ocean, from the most exposed rock faces to the slimiest mud beneath mangroves. Some of the rarest varieties are found in the most unexpected places. By day, most try to escape the sun by hiding in nooks and crevices, in and under rocks, so you have to turn rocks over to reach them.

By night they wander in the open. It is a sight to see a mature cowrie with its glistening mantle spread out like a veil of sheen and colour.

The best hunting ground in East Africa is in the inter-tidal strip. Most specialists prefer to collect shells in forty-five to sixty centimetres of water, chiefly because the rocks that have to be moved weigh less in water. Also, when hunting in a silty area one tends to kick up less mud by flipping about than by treading on the bottom.

Another boon to snorkelers is that it is possible to stir up sand and expose shells that are often buried beneath.

Some shells do not belong to the shore at all. They are truly pelagic, coming in from the open sea.

Janthina, the fragile purple snail, found mainly in tropical waters, makes itself a raft of bubbles, trapping air in a slime that it excretes, and floating free in the ocean. After a storm you can often gather a harvest of these shells washed ashore.

The pearly nautilus comes from Malaya and the East Indies, where its octopus-like occupant hunts crabs and lobsters on the ocean floor in deep water. When it dies, its gas-filled

Above: Tangle of lacey corals and their cryptic guardian — a scorpion fish.

shell floats ashore on the ocean currents.

There are many curiosities in the realm of conchology. The tusk shells, or Dentalia, are buried in the mud — like miniature elephant tusks open at both ends, some ridged and others smooth.

There is also the bivalve *Penicillus africanus,* the watering pot; it starts life conventionally like a tiny butterfly shell, then gradually it builds a long calcareous tube with a little frill round one end speckled with holes, like a garden watering can.

The mystery is how it evolves from the 'butterfly' to the 'watering pot' phase, as no one has ever seen the intermediate stages.

I have only mentioned bivalves as a food of other shells; but they are worth collecting, not only as a food, but in their own right as beautiful and decorative objects. This type varies enormously from the delicate rose-tinted Tellins, the sunset shells, to heavy-ribbed *Tridacna* clams.

The giant clam, often two feet across, disappeared long before the age of man. The Jessop family of Shimoni, Kenya, have a number of these fossilized giant clams in their gardens, set in coral.

Dick Jessop found the rarest shells in Kenya, the volute, *lyraformis,* alive on a sandbank. Most other surviving specimens have been washed ashore dead or brought in by a hermit crab. A number of deep-water shells are brought in that way.

Nowadays, it is more difficult to establish a good shell collection, as the reefs have been overshelled and denuded of everything that can be carried away, often quite indiscriminately. Here collectors remonstrate with people for collecting fragile, immature shells that are certain to be broken before they reach home. It is also unnecessary to take old worn shells that are invariably discarded once they reach the smelly stage; these would be good breeding stock if left alone.

L.L.D.

(Editor's note: Lallie Lee Didham's misgivings about over-collecting unfortunately have been borne out. Unless you are a Kenyan national licensed by the government as a collector, dealer, or exporter, it is illegal to collect shells on the Kenya coast.)

Chapter 17 Ethiopia: a Land Apart

Ethiopians are fond of saying that their millenniums of isolation from the rest of the world in their highland fastness, and the fact that they have never been colonized, have given them their greatest advantages over the rest of Africa, and at the same time their greatest disadvantages.

An extensive montane fortress, with a healthy, temperate climate, fertile soils, surrounded by arid seas of semi-desert, enabled them to thrive with little contact with the outside world. Empires waxed and waned within Ethiopia and without, with little effect on one other. A civilization evolved in these mountains that subsisted easily on nature's bounty, and subjugated the fertile highland plateaux over the ages.

There is little agreement amongst botanists as to what the 'natural' vegetation was really like. Remnants are few and far between, and the same is true of the wildlife. However, vestiges remain at the extremes of altitude and climate, and in the small traditional conservation areas around places of worship and resting places for the dead.

Relicts occur in the steepest gorges and cliff faces. The extremes consist of the highest, coldest heights in the Simien and Bale Mountains, and at lower altitudes wherever cultivation was not possible. In recent times, even these natural barriers have been pushed back by the sheer availability of medicine, by new methods of managing the land, by the demand for natural resources — especially fuel wood and charcoal, and by new strains of crops, capable of withstanding either cold or aridity.

We can date the origins of the bulk of Ethiopia as a physical entity quite accurately. Around forty million years ago lava began to leak profusely from the crust of the earth — not as an eruptive volcanic action, but a massive outpouring of lava upon lava for some twenty million years. This seemingly infinite hot spot, or boil, on the face of the earth sent up an extensive blanket of lava some two to four kilometres deep, and 700,000 square kilometres in extent.

Towards the end of this upward and outwards welling, the earth's crust weakened and split — again over several million years — and began to form a new island to rival Madagascar, through the formation of the Great Rift Valley. The massive block of lava was split from north to south, as much of Ethiopia, Kenya, Tanzania, Djibouti, and all of Somalia began their inexorable journey together, east from the main African continent.

This process continues today at a rate of several centimetres a year, and is nowhere more evident than in the Danakil basin — already more than 100 metres below sea level. Here the Rift opens into a wide mouth facing the Red Sea, and you feel it only needs the effort of an earthquake or a madcap engineer to bring the sea rushing in to fill the basin and perhaps complete the process of splitting Africa from top to toe.

The two highland islands so formed rear up some 2,000 metres above the surrounding lowlands in most places, but at their extremes they are over 4,000 metres high. They form extensive plateaux, that, in the more massive western block, have been shaped and worn by countless rivers into castles, pinnacles and peaks, isolated ridges, and far-flung *ambas* — those amazing flat-topped ridges miles from anywhere, both horizontally and vertically, but on which a village will be perched.

You travel for hours over these extensive flat plateaux, secure in the knowledge that the world goes on for ever, and gravity has little effect upon your life, when suddenly you reach the edge of the secure world, and stare two kilometres down to the next. Gelada and hamadryas baboons bark at your silhouette on the edge, children gather from the villages perched along the precipice while, up a crack in the cliff face below, women toil with their clay pots of water.

Within these vertical kilometres, the crops change before your eyes. You see a microcosm of Ethiopia from desert to semi-arid to montane conditions, camels and goats give way to sorghum and maize, teff and wheat, and finally barley; the sun's glare and baking heat

Overleaf: The most rugged country in Africa — where the Ethiopian highlands plunge thousands of feet down to hot lowlands.

Above: Conservation success story — two decades ago the mountain nyala of Ethiopia's Bale Mountains were shy and seldom seen. Today they are both more abundant and easily viewed.

rise up from the canyon's depths, and the mist wraps itself around your feet.

Yet higher, at Ankober, Simien, Bale, and countless other high points — the pimples on these massive highlands — frosts occur most mornings, lashing hailstorms ensure only the fittest survive, and snow lies for several days each year.

This, then, is the backdrop to the natural world in Ethiopia. What you see has survived the upheavals of the earth's crust, millenniums of inclement weather, 8,000 years of glaciation, centuries of man's wresting a living from the soil, and long isolation by the surrounding sea of aridity from any similar forms of life and conditions.

Small wonder then that Ethiopian wildlife is so different, wary, and unknown. They include the blue-winged goose, whose nearest relative is in the Andes; the mountain nyala, the last new large mammal species to be named by science in 1910; the white-winged flufftail, seen only thirty-odd times here, but also known from southern Africa; the chough — crow of the Cornish cliffs, the Alps, Himalayas, and

the high Atlas; and the giant mole rat, only found in the Bale Mountains.

The literal boiling pot that is Ethiopia continues to surprise scientists and visitors alike in the wildlife field, as it does all those who think they know Africa. They arrive suddenly these days, usually at Bole airport in Addis, and wonder at the contrast to the world they left such a scant time ago — especially if that world was Kenya, the neighbouring country just under a two-hour flight away. Ethiopia is a land apart.

Millenniums of isolation of extensive habitats with unusual conditions in the highlands of Ethiopia have led to the evolution and retention of unique species at all levels, but especially smaller species less able to travel, or be carried across inhospitable habitat.

Other species from temperate regions, finding a similar habitat to their usual homelands, established populations here. This is especially the case with the birds. Endemism is rife, particularly amongst both large and small mammals, amphibians, reptiles, fish, and to some extent the birds. Apart from the 'hangers

Above: Leggy red canid of the high Ethiopian moorlands, the Simien jackal — also inappropriately known as the Simien fox or wolf — is a specialized rodent eater.

on' in the main bulk of the highlands at 2,500 metres, there is little wildlife to be seen. These die-hards, as in the rest of Africa, include the olive baboon, vervet monkey, grey duiker and bushbuck, porcupine, and numerous small carnivores. The rest of Ethiopia's wildlife is found either at the extremes of the highlands in the Bale, Simien, Arissi, and Ahmar Mountains, or comprises more common Eastern African wildlife in the arid habitats of the lowlands.

A glance at the map of Ethiopia shows two conservation areas in the highlands — the Simien and Bale Mountain National Parks, and the rest either down the length of the Rift Valley — Yangudi Rassa, Awash, Abijatta-Shalla lakes, Nechisar, Sanctuary; or in the lowlands surrounding the edges of the highlands — Harer and Yavello Sanctuaries, and Gambella National Park. The final park in the north — the Dahlac Marine National Park — is set in an archipelago of real islands in the Red Sea, with all the biological signs of being stepping stones between Africa and Arabia.

Not all of Ethiopia's special wildlife is confined to the extremes of the highlands. The endemic birds, being more mobile, are scattered in several of the conservation areas, including those at intermediate altitudes in the Rift. Bale, however, tops them all with fifteen of the twenty-seven endemic bird species. Swayne's hartebeest — an endemic subspecies that once occurred from Somalia in a broad swathe through the Ethiopian Rift — now lives in a few scattered populations: Awash (where it was reintroduced), Senkelle, Maze, Nechisar, and Yavello.

The wild ass lives in the remote desert confines of the Danakil depression, and is conserved in the Yangudi Rassa National Park. And wildlife from neighbouring Sudan of a very different ilk occurs in the west, in swampy Gambella, including migrating droves of the white-eared kob, herds of the graceful Nile lechwe in inundated areas, and that anachronism of the bird world — the shoebill or whale-headed stork.

Omo and Mago are famed for their unspoilt wilderness filled with the larger wildlife species expected of bush areas of Africa —

227

Above: The giant mole rat of the Bale Mountains is something of a cartoon character — and prime prey for the Simien jackal.

elephant, giraffe, common eland, buffalo, ostrich, greater and lesser kudu, Grevy and Burchell's zebra. Further north, Nechisar combines spectacular scenery surrounding the two lakes — Chamo and Abbaya, with wildlife such as Burchell's zebra, greater kudu, Grant's gazelle, Guenther's dik-dik, and large numbers of kori bustard and the Abyssinian ground hornbill. The lakes harbour amazing numbers of extremely large crocodile as well as hippo, easily seen from safe vantage points along the steep escarpment roads.

Even further north, Senkelle safeguards the best population of Swayne's hartebeest — over 2,000 of them in a small area, with the familiar problems of an endangered species: overabundance in a tiny area of habitat surrounded by farmland. This sanctuary is managed as part of the nearby Abijatta-Shalla Lakes National Park — jewels in the Rift and, with nearby Lake Langano, part of the Rift Valley recreational area.

Both the lakes in the park are sodic, but while shallow Abijatta fluctuates wildly in size, and harbours thousands of water birds

— especially lesser flamingos and great white pelicans, Shalla, set between tall escarpments and studded with islands used by birds for nesting, emits an aura of mystery. Yet it is almost fishless due to its great black depths of over 250 metres. Hot springs and boiling mud spout along its shores, deep lava caves pierce the earth in the south, and here again you feel yourself close to the split that is tearing apart this great continent.

In Awash you approach the more familiar Africa again. The Rift has opened out until you cannot discern the opposing walls in the haze, apart from the Ahmar Mountains to the south. Huge hot springs of crystal-clear waters well up in the north, lava blisters dot the plain, and Mount Fantalle, with its huge crater and fresh black lava flows said to have occurred in the time of local peoples' grandparents, all keep the formation of the Rift in the forefront of your experience.

These plains, however, are inhabited by Beisa oryx in enormous numbers, greater and lesser kudu, ostrich, Defassa waterbuck, and helmeted guinea fowl. Only Soemmering's gazelle and a few Swaynes's hartebeest give the lie to your being in Kenya's Samburu Reserve, or at the edge of Amboseli. Stoic kori bustard march the plains, appearing to keep the rest of the animals in order, and deigning not to notice the brilliant carmine bee-eaters riding their drab backs as a mobile perch from which to hawk for insects. Ostrich and oryx bear their jewelled burdens in better humour.

On up the Rift, now a wide-open desert plain; stony, scrubby with wait-a-bit thorn, camels, goats, and Danakil and Afar tribesmen, to Yangudi Rassa. Famed as home of the wild ass and not far removed from what seem the depths of the earth — Lake Abbe, and neighbouring sulphur fumaroles, salt mines, and beautiful, wild, and barren desolation. Neither sea nor land, but images from Dante's inferno: no water — but salty; land — but no vegetation.

Also found here is a reasonable cross-section of usual and not-so-usual African fauna, including Grevy's zebra, greater and lesser kudu, oryx, lion, leopard, cheetah, Soemmering's gazelle, gerenuk, and hamadryas baboon.

And above it all, far removed and invisible in the bulk of the highlands, lie the mountains: Simien — a sheer rugged mass of pinnacles and abysses likened to an upside-down table with its legs in the air, and Bale — a solid bulk of high-altitude plateau, aloof from its surroundings, studded with tiny jewel-like lakes, and the odd peaks rising from the Sanetti Plateau, likened to a table the right way up. Both areas are mountainous in the extreme, yet in its way each is unique — and remember they are separated by 700 kilometres, six degrees of latitude, and the Great Rift Valley.

Simien is unforgettable for its sheer, vertical appearance. Travelling around its tiny 220 square kilometres, this is brought to your notice at every turn, as you move from one viewpoint to another to catch a glimpse of the agile walia, so incredibly at home on these cliffs. Rivalled only by the resident klipspringer, it was thought the species was on its way out, but it appears to be holding on with the protection given it here.

The Simien jackal (or fox) in these parts has apparently been less able to cope with the insidious invasion of its habitat by man in past decades, and numbers are now low. Gelada abound on the cliff tops, descending every night to secure cracks and ledges in the abyss edges, while the white-collared pigeons and thick-billed ravens use natural air movements against the cliff faces to rise and fall each evening and morning, between feeding grounds at the top and roosts far below at warmer altitudes. Gracefully they wheel and turn, plummet down, and rush up on invisible air currents, making the walia look like a bumbling old man in comparison.

Come to Bale for the seemingly infinite wide-open spaces and that incredible silence found only in vast mountains. Look out from your tent at night and wonder at the multitude of stars in the clear frosty skies, 'hear' the crackle of the silence of the spheres, stare at the piercing blue of the sky at midday, and marvel at the contrasts that life here has to withstand — some 40°C shift in temperature from night to day — minus 15°C to 26°C in the dry season. One of the first visitors this century dubbed it 'The Sahara by day and Siberia by night'. No wonder the plants and animals are so different.

The stately mountain nyala live at relatively low altitudes around 3,000 metres above sea level, but can also be found on the high plateau to the topmost peak at 4,377 metres (14,360 feet) — Tullu Deemtu. Like a shaggy, stocky greater kudu, to which it is probably more closely related than the nyala of southern Africa, these antelope are the hallmarks of the juniper and hagenia woodlands and high grasslands to the north of the mountains. The spiral-horned males tend to move alone or in small groups, as is the custom in this family, but on occasions over ten can be seen together in the presence of females and juveniles.

The hornless females and their young consort in larger groups, sometimes more than a hundred, but more usually a dozen or so together. High in the mountains they are still extremely shy and disappear over the horizon, amongst the tall spires of rock and lobelia plants, but down in the woodlands they will stand and watch, the result of fifteen years of protection and familiarity with vehicles.

Come to Bale, too, to see the Simien jackal. Variously known as the Simien fox, Abyssinian wolf — and more correctly by its Amharic name of *Ky Kebero*, the red jackal — this animal is most closely related to the jackal but is the red colour of a European fox, and has long legs and a lope like a wolf. It is a specialist, evolved to feed off the incredible numbers of rodents found on the high plateau above 3,700

Opposite: As the species nests exclusively on cliffs, Ethiopia offers Ruppell's griffon more breeding habitat than any other country in Africa.

Right: The soft, booming call of the Abyssinian ground hornbill recalls the cadences of a distant lion.

Right: Aerial rubies in the dry, drab lowlands, carmine bee-eaters are common in southern Ethiopia.

Right: Blue-headed coucal, bird of the high montane forest clearings, catching the morning sun.

metres (12,139 feet). Its elongated snout and hooked teeth are interspersed with large gaps for holding wriggling rats.

Constantly loping through the short grass and herbs, totally undermined by its prey, it relies on the surprisingly frequent instances when a rodent doesn't see it coming to snatch a small meal with a quick pounce. Alternatively, it will scrabble at a hole and breathe down it, pounce to the next and repeat the process, and worry the trembling victim in the warren beneath so much that it rushes out of a hole — only to succumb to the rush and pounce of the jackal.

Sixteen species of rodent are recorded in the area, of which eight are endemic, but of greatest interest to the viewer and the red jackal is the giant mole rat, endemic to these mountains. Weighing up to a kilogram, this marmot-like creature lives underground, but gathers its food above a series of holes served by a network of tunnels. Rarely emerging more than half a body length, it nervously gathers cheekfuls of leaves and grass from the scanty vegetation, before ducking below to deposit it.

Returning several times, it may only spend twenty minutes a day at the surface. The rest of the time is spent below, digging tunnels, plugging surface holes, and sorting out the rubbish from the delicacies it has gathered. Its eyes, on the top of its head like a hippo, are functional — unlike its relative, the common mole rat (a pest of African cultivation) — and protected from the rough soil through which it digs by a set of handsome, stiff, black eyelashes.

This beast resembles nothing less than a cartoon character as it bumbles around, bobbing its head in search of jackal or bird of prey that might attempt to take it. The red jackal has been recorded to spend up to forty-five minutes motionless over a giant mole rat hole, awaiting the eventual emergence of this delicacy, and, at a kilo a time, this effort is well worth it when compared to the eighty grams of the other rodents.

In Ethiopia you feel apart from the world, let alone Africa. Walia ibex, Simien jackal, gelada baboon, mountain nyala, blue-winged geese, Rouget's rail, thick-billed raven, spot-breasted plover, snail-eating frog, black-headed forest oriole, giant mole rat, giant *Lobelia rhynchopetalum* — the list goes on and on; all uniquely Ethiopian.

* Ethiopia has a recorded list of 845 bird species, of which twenty-seven are endemic (3.2 per cent); fifteen of these endemics occur in the Bale Mountains; twelve of them occur in Simien.

* Ethiopia has a recorded list of 242 land mammals, of which twenty-two are endemic (9.1 per cent); eleven of these are recorded from Bale, and seven from the Simien Mountains.

* Studies of amphibians show a definite number of fifty-four species recorded, of which seventeen are endemic (31.5 per cent). However, this could be as high as sixty-six species, of which 45.5 per cent could be endemic. Research and discoveries continue.

Groups of the smaller organisms are less well known, but it is certain that as they are studied many more new and endemic species will be discovered and described. A three-week expedition in the Bale Mountains in 1985 revealed four species of frog new to science. Endemic does not mean endangered — just limited to a geographical, and nowadays political area. Ethiopia possesses a large and isolated area of unusual habitat — the highlands — and is therefore endowed with more than its fair share of endemic species.

So don't expect to see the teeming wildlife of the Eastern African plains, nor the glimpses of truly *wild* wildlife, not even bounded by a national park, as seen on cosseted travels between luxury water-holes through Kenya and Tanzania. Instead, you'll travel long hours, walking or riding on rugged mountain ponies and withstanding hours of cold and mist.

It may be more physically exhausting, but your reward will be breathtaking views of unsurpassed landscapes and images of wild and wonderful animals found nowhere else in the world.

Opposite: Found only in the Simien Mountains, the gelada is unusual among baboons for its very restricted range.

Overleaf: The gelada's long-haired cape is necessary protection from cold at the high altitudes at which it lives.

Chapter 18 Traditional uses of wildlife products

Traditionally, Ethiopians have always been very much aware of their environment. Indeed, their manner of describing the country rests squarely on its ecological characteristics. Ethiopia is divided into altitude/temperature zones that determine vegetation, wildlife, living conditions, and the crops that are grown. From sea level, these zones are: *Bereha*, desert under 500 metres, the lower *Kolla*, land between 500 and 1,000 metres, which together with *Bereha* forms fifty per cent of Ethiopia; the upper *Kolla*, which lies between 1,000 and 1,800 metres and is twenty per cent of the country; *Woina Dega*, between 1,800 and 2,500 metres and taking fifteen per cent of the country; *Dega* at 2,500 to 3,500 metres — which makes up ten per cent of the country; *Wirch*, which is anything above 3,500 metres.

At one time wildlife was as widely used for food and basic materials in Ethiopia as anywhere else in the world. Today, however, general subsistence hunting survives only in the low-lying areas around the highland massifs, particularly in the east, south, and west along the Sudan borders. The Nilotic people in the west bordering the Sudan still eat a wide range of wildlife including rodents, crocodiles, and hippos.

In the south, the Borana peoples still use buffalo skin to make leather buckets for lifting water out of deep wells — as they have for centuries. Ledges are cut into the well walls spaced about a man's height apart. In deep wells there may be as many as fifteen ledges between the water and the ground above. When lifting water, a man is stationed on every ledge. Each passes a full buffalo hide bucket to the man above and at the same time takes an empty one on its way back down. The whole exercise, accomplished with extreme grace and rhythm, is accompanied by wonderful chanting. Sadly, the dearth of buffalo in Ethiopia is leading to a search for alternative bucket materials, such as tough industrial machine belting.

The most prominent use of wildlife products until recently was for warriors' regalia. Oromo and Amhara soldiers made capes and cloaks from the flowing coats of Gelada baboons, still used in traditional dancing. Senior warriors had lion skin capes. Shields were made from the tough, thick hide of either buffalo or rhinoceros, and the numbers required by the armed forces in the past may well have contributed to the decline of both species. The traditional use of hippo hide for horse whips still persists.

Perhaps the most widely known wildlife cottage industry in Ethiopia — one that has been going on since the time of Sheba — is producing musk from captive civets. Records from the fifteenth century indicate that musk was exported from the port of Mit'siwa in the north. Currently between 1,800 and 2,000 kilograms of musk a year, worth US$1,000,000, are exported from Ethiopia. In addition, a small amount is used locally in traditional medicines.

Conservation is not a new philosophy in Ethiopia. Indeed the Menagesha Forest was established by King Zera Yakob (1434-1468) from seeds collected in Wef Washa Forest, between Debre Berhan and Debre Sina. These grew into a 7,300-hectare plantation that was protected by Imperial edict from the 1600s onwards. Emperor Menelik II (1888-1912) employed foresters to protect it, and no trees could be cut without his permission. Thus, though Menagesha has shrunk considerably to 2,700 hectares, it is probably Africa's oldest formally-protected nature reserve and must also be one of the oldest in the world.

Ethiopia's two main religions (Islam and Christian Orthodox) have had a major influence on the peoples' attitudes towards wildlife. The eating of game meat has generally been discouraged, and certain animals and birds are forbidden altogether: odd-toed ungulates, primates, carnivores, pigs, and both water birds and birds of prey. The Christians forbid eating meat, eggs, and dairy products on Wednesdays, Fridays, and the fifty-five days of Lent. On such fasting days fish are the only acceptable animal protein.

Sites of worship and burial places are traditional conservation areas in which no trees may be cut or animals killed. Hence, in a land where most other trees have been cut down

Above: Traditional tribal finery — ostrich feathers, hippo teeth, bushbuck skin, wildebeest tail, and cowrie shells

for fuel over millenniums, they are havens, particularly for nesting birds. The monasteries on the island in Lake Tana are good examples.

The connection between religion and wildlife is also reflected in the idea that some species are present through the activities of saints. For example, the local people believe that the Walia ibex was brought to Simien by the legendary Saint Yared. Churches also used to decorate the topmost cross of the building with an ostrich egg on each of the seven points. Nowadays they do so on the highest point only. Beeswax is another wild product associated with Christianity in Ethiopia as it was used to make candles for lighting churches (as well as rural households).

Religion did not stop the use of certain animal products for medicine. Organs and other parts of many nocturnal animals, such as hyaena and mongooses, are still used as amulets to prevent psychological illnesses. Porcupine meat is eaten as cure for cancer, and the smoke from smouldering elephant dung is inhaled as treatment for asthma.

In the days before rubber teats, the tips of both bushbuck and mountain nyala horns — through which a small hole was drilled — were favoured as teats for babies' bottles. And the tradition still persists today, as it is believed that they impart strength to the suckling infant.

Chapter 19   Ethiopia: Hunting and Fishing Facts

In the early days, most tourists coming to Eastern Africa did so to hunt big game. Today, the majority come to watch and photograph wildlife. In Kenya, all but bird shooting is now banned, and a similar situation prevails in Malawi. There is no wildlife left to hunt in Rwanda or Burundi outside the parks. Licensed hunting is still permitted, however, in Ethiopia, Uganda, Tanzania, and Zambia. In this chapter, Sheila and Jesse Hillman and Abdu Mahamued describe conditions and rules concerning sport hunting in Ethiopia.

HUNTING

Hunting, regulated by the Wildlife Conservation Organization, Box 386, Addis Ababa, is still legal in Ethiopia. But the list of species is periodically revised in the interests of conservation. A strict yearly quota for mountain nyala and elephant is maintained. Though hunting is allowed elsewhere, there are eighteen controlled areas for those who wish to hunt on payment of a special fee.

Four types of hunting licence are currently available:

1.   General hunting licence: Enables the hunting of most crop raiding and smaller animals — bushpig, dik-dik, duiker, hare, wart hog, vervet monkey, anubis baboon, and porcupine. The number to be hunted is limited and the licence is valid for four months only.

2.   Supplementary licence: Under this licence some fifty different species of mammals, and ostrich, are included. The most important are Menelik's bushbuck, crocodile, elephant, Grant's gazelle, Soemmering's gazelle, gerenuk, hippopotamus, klipspringer, greater and lesser kudu, leopard, mountain nyala, oribi, Beisa oryx, Bohor and Chandler's reedbuck, Defassa waterbuck, serval cat, caracal, gelada and hamadryas baboons, buffalo, and lion.
Hunting areas: The hunting area for most of

the above mentioned plains game, leopard, and lion is the Awash valley all year round. Hunting for most species also occurs in the Omo valley in south-western Kaffa from July to January.

Hunting for big game, such as buffalo and elephant, occurs in Gambella from December to May. In Mizan Teferi (montane forest areas of Kaffa and Illubabor), elephant and leopard hunting is from November to May.

Arissi, Bale, and parts of the Chercher Mountains is the area for mountain nyala and, Menelik's bushbuck. Hunting is possible all year round, but is not recommended from July to October because of rain and fog.

3.   Game bird licence: Under this licence, Up to ten of any one species or all species combined are allowed in one day: ducks, francolins, geese, quail, partridge, guinea fowl, sandgrouse, pigeons, and doves. The season is from 1 October to 31 March. The licence is valid for two months.

4.   Snipe licence: All snipes, except painted snipe *(Rostratula bengalensis)* can be hunted — up to thirty in one day. The season is from 10 November to 6 August. The licence is valid for three months.

General information on hunting:
a)   Prohibited areas: Hunting is strictly prohibited in national parks, wildlife reserves and sanctuaries. Hunting without a permit in a controlled hunting area is also forbidden.

b)   Prohibited species:

Aardwolf	Rhinoceros
Dibatag	Wild Ass
Giraffe	Patas Monkey
Aardvark	Cheetah
Walia Ibex	Pelzeln's Gazelle
Speke's Gazelle	Tora Hartebeest
African Hunting Dog	Simien Fox
Beira Antelope	Bat-eared Fox
Dugong	Grevy Zebra
Swayne's Hartebeest	

Above: Hunting party sets off in search of trophies.

c) **Prohibited methods of hunting:** Hunters are not permitted to:
* use fire to drive or surround game
* use any artificial lights for hunting, except for specified nocturnal animals
* use dogs to hunt down and chase any game other than game birds
* hunt during the hours of darkness, except for specified nocturnal animals
* shoot from a motor vehicle, motor driven boat, or aircraft
* use hides or blinds
* use a grenade or explosive, poison, or any toxic substance
* use bows, hand held pistols, air guns, air rifles, and air pistols

d) **Registration of trophy and certificate of lawful possession:** After the hunt, the trophy should be registered, and application should be made for a certificate of lawful possession at the Licensing Office.

e) **Export of Trophy:** Trophies are allowed to be exported only through a Customs Port exit. An export permit for trophies may be issued by the Hunting Licence Office upon the production of a certificate of lawful possession and veterinary certificate. Original receipts of all payments made for hunting licences and professional hunters services must be submitted in order to obtain approval for export from the National Bank. Comparable CITES export permits are also issued by the Licence Office to facilitate import to destination.

f)   Self-defence or defence: An animal may be killed in self-defence or defence of another person. When an animal is killed in such a situation by the holder of a game licence for that species, or by the professional hunter assisting him, the animal will be deemed to have been killed on that licence. In other cases the trophy must be collected and handed over to the Hunting Licence Office.

g)   Wounding of game animals: All hunters are legally bound to follow up and kill any animal they have wounded. In the case of dangerous animals, when wounded and lost, a full report must be made to the nearest official of the Wildlife Conservation Organization, District Administrator's office, or police office in charge of the area.

h)   Fees and Conditions:
1. All licence and capitation fees are to be paid in advance and are non-refundable. There is also an extra ivory payment after hunting elephant.

2. All tourist hunters must be accompanied by a licenced professional hunter on all types of hunting licences. All tourist hunters must also be accompanied by a Game Inspector from the Wildlife Conservation Organization. A fee of Birr 10 per day will be charged for this.

3. The minimum number of days required for hunting plains game is ten, and for big game is fifteen. However, for better results, fifteen days are recommended for plains game and twenty-one to thirty for big game.

i)   Facilities and Services: Six fully-licensed professional hunters are currently operating, providing guns and ammunition, transport, hotel accommodation, hunting licence, taxidermy services, and the shipping of trophies. The Taxidermy Producers Co-operative also provides taxidermy services and arranges shipping of trophies.

Sale of Wildlife Products:
Wildlife products such as skins, horns, and ivory are on sale at authorized shops. Visitors are strictly forbidden to buy any wildlife or their products from unauthorized dealers. No wildlife product is permitted to be taken out of the country without a valid export permit from the Wildlife Conservation Organization. Any unauthorized item will be confiscated.

FISHING

Fly fishing for introduced trout of two species (Brown and Rainbow) is available in the Bale Mountains National Park area. Fish were introduced into nine rivers nearly twenty years ago and have thrived in local conditions. Permits are available from the Ministry of Agriculture offices in the area, or from Addis Ababa.

Fishing is fair at all times of year, but is best at the times streams are rising or falling, in the early wet and early dry seasons. These are the periods from March to June and October to December. There is an excellent lodge, recently refurbished, in the heart of the fishing area at Dinsho, the park headquarters. It is possible to fly or drive to nearby Goba, where there is also an excellent hotel, the Goba Ras.

Coarse fishing is available in most of Ethiopia's lakes and larger rivers, except for those in national parks. Arba Minch is the centre of the best-known area — for Lakes Abaya and Chamo. These are renowned for their Nile perch and tiger fish, amongst others. Other areas include Lakes Langano and Koka for tilapia, catfish, and barbus.

Sea fishing has yet to be fully developed, but it is possible to fish off the coast at both Assab and Mit'siwa. By hand-lining, it is possible to catch rock cod, red snapper, blood snapper, spotted grouper, and Sudan grouper, amongst others. 'White' baits, especially pieces of fish, are the best. Trolling is likely to bring in barracuda, little tunny, and several tuna species. Sharks and rays also occur in the area.

Sport fishing permits must be obtained from the Mit'siwa Fisheries Office. Green Island, opposite Mit'siwa, is a sanctuary where no fishing or collecting of corals or shells may be carried out. The same is true of the rest of the Dahlac Marine National Park, including the islands of Dissei, the Assarcas, Shumma, and Ito Umm Narus.

The months of May to October are hot; brief rains occur between December and March. The temperature at sea and on the islands is 5-10°C lower than on the mainland. Fishing is best in the early morning and late afternoon. Local boats can be hired from Mit'siwa, and there are good camping sites on several of the islands, such as Harmil and Dissei. You must take your own supply of fresh water.

It is advisable to bring most of your own fishing equipment, since little is currently available in Ethiopia.

Chapter 20 Medicine on Safari

In the past Africa was often referred to as 'the white man's grave'. The term had particular relevance to West Africa: hot, low-lying, humid, and a haven for mosquitoes and tsetse flies. It was not unwarranted. Strangers from the temperate zones had little resistance to malaria and many other tropical diseases which flourished there — and few effective drugs with which to treat them. The region's reputation lingers on in history books.

Because it is part of the same continent, Eastern Africa has been tarred with the same brush as West Africa. But this is unwarranted. Even before the present century, much of Eastern Africa — in particular the highland areas — were at least as healthy for humans as the temperate zones, if not more so, a fortunate situation now enhanced by the resources of modern medicine. Today's visitors have little reason to fear for their health. Hundreds of thousands visit Eastern Africa each year, enjoy themselves, and go home without encountering any medical problems. Nonetheless, it's common sense to be aware of any possible risks and take whatever steps are needed to avoid them.

One Basic Rule
If you fall ill within two months of returning home from a visit abroad, tell your doctor where you have been. It will help the doctor diagnose the cause of your problem and may save you much discomfort.

Before the Safari
At home, check the dates and validity of the vaccinations which are usually required: yellow fever (valid for ten years) and sometimes cholera (valid for only six months), particularly if you travel between different African countries.

Other useful vaccinations are:
   Typhoid (Tab)
   Anti Tetanus
   Anti Rabies *
   Anti Hepatitis B *
*Also recommended if tough safaris in very remote areas are envisaged.

Personal Clothing
Preferably light and airy cotton, khaki or light colours (avoid dark blue or black in tsetse areas for they attract these biting flies strongly). Include long trousers, long-sleeved shirts, good light ankle-length walking shoes, warm pullover — nights can be rainy and cool — good hat, sunglasses. Do not forget a **Toilet Kit,** and carry a small **Sewing Kit.** It is sensible to take a small **Personal First Aid Kit,** and don't forget, if on regular medical treatment, to *include extra supplies of drugs needed in case of loss.* If using glasses, also carry a spare pair.

ON SAFARI

Health Precautions:

Camp Sites:
Should be shaded, airy, and clean (clear undergrowth). In the evening:
* wear long trousers and long-sleeved shirt
* use insect repellent
* mosquito coils
* sleep under mosquito nets

Food:
Should be protected from flies (use netting or boxes).
* clean hands when preparing and eating food
* wash and peel fruit
* soak green salads, tomatoes, etc. in weak potassium permanganate solution for at least half an hour

Sanitation:
Bury excreta: there must be a good latrine in camp, otherwise use trenching tool.

Water:
Remember in hot places you must drink a lot.
* Water should be filtered — alternatively, use alum crystals to precipitate particles in turbid water. Then:
* Boil for fifteen minutes — if boiling is difficult, water sterilizing tablets can be used (see instructions on box).

PRECAUTIONS WHEN SWIMMING

In the Indian Ocean:

Shark bites are rare and virtually unknown on the Eastern African coast inside the reefs. Watch out for coral poisoning of wounds. Treat at once with antiseptic — Betadine, Mercurochrome.

Very fine particles of coral can cause extremely painful ear infections. To avoid infection, put cotton wool wad in ear and clean and dry ears after swim.

When walking on the reef wear thick-soled tennis shoes to avoid coral cuts and risk of stings from stonefish or sting rays. Watch out for jelly fish, particularly 'Portuguese man-of-war' — a little transparent bubble with a frilly fringe of blue tendrils that floats on the surface: these trail slim, blue ribbons up to a metre (three and a third feet) long that can inflict most unpleasant burns.

Inland Rivers and Lakes:

Before swimming, wading, or washing in lakes, rivers, and ponds, check with local people as to whether crocodiles and/or hippos are present. If there are no people to ask, behave as though both are present but unseen (remember — the crocodile that gets you is the one you didn't see). Also accept that all water less than 1,800 metres (6,000 feet) above sea level is likely to be a source of of bilharzia (Schistosomiasis) [see below].

AILMENTS

Fever:
Treatment:
Rest, plenty to drink, aspirin — watch out for malaria. If persistent or severe see a doctor as soon as possible.

Toothache:
Treatment:
Aspirin. Oil of clove drenched on a wad of cotton wool in the cavity of the tooth will greatly ease the pain.

Foot Blisters:
Treatment:
Disinfectant — do not take off skin. Piercing the skin, run a needle with durable thread (which has been disinfected in Savlon or spirits) through the blister. Cut the threads, leaving half an inch on each side. The water will

drain out (move the threads a bit to and fro). The skin will dry and protect the blister. Walking is not painful anymore.

Jiggers:
On toes, a round, itchy, whitish lump growing from pin-head to large pearl-size with black centre. The jigger is a female burrowing flea with egg sac.
Treatment:
Can usually be deftly extracted by camp or medical staff using well sterilized needle. Disinfect well and put dressing on afterwards. If detected before the egg sac is apparent, put a cotton wool dressing soaked in lamp paraffin on the site overnight. This will kill the jigger, but itching may follow.

Larva Migrans:
Usually caught at the sea side. Appears as a red, itchy sinuous line on foot or leg, sometimes on the back. It is the larva of a tapeworm burrowing through the skin.
Treatment:
Same as for jigger. A pad of cotton wool soaked in paraffin, extending further than the line, and kept in place for at least two hours will deal with the condition, which can be trying.

Sore Eyes:
Conjunctivitis, sometimes with a pussy discharge, is usually due to dust and dirt.
Treatment:
Clean eyes with warm water and apply eye ointment. By day, wear sun-glasses or broad-brimmed hat.

Prickly Heat:
This is a painful, itchy, rash which usually develops about the less well-ventilated parts of the body — in and about armpits, the groin, and the waist where a belt or tight trouser tops hold clothing tightly against the body, preventing air circulation. Unacclimatized people often suffer from it in hot, humid conditions. Caused by excessive sweating, which can block the sweat gland canals, resulting in itchy pimples.
Treatment:
Try and avoid sweating (don't drink hot drinks), wash and dry body, put on dry, loose clothes. Prickly heat powder and calamine lotion are useful as relief.

Sunburn:

Should be avoided at all costs if you wish to have a comfortable safari. Use an effective sun-blocking lotion. During the first few days, short exposure to the sun of usually covered skin areas will help you get a protective tan. Extensive sunburn on white 'sensitive' skin can be very dangerous as well as painful.
Treatment:
Keep in the shade — don't burst blisters. Keep covered.

Heat Cramp:

Usually experienced in the leg, this cramp is common at night if not enough fluid and salt was taken during the day.
Treatment:
Instant remedy is one-half tablespoon of salt (or Marmite). If occurring in the day, accompanied by dizziness and nausea, rest in the shade — drink fruit squash or water with two pinches of salt in the bottle.

Heat Exhaustion:

Can occur in hot humid conditions with poor ventilation, even in the shade, or in a tent. Symptoms: cold sweats, dizziness, weak pulse, patient can become unconscious.
Treatment:
Lie in ventilated shady place. Place cold wet cloth on head — give hot foot bath if possible, and give drink as for heat cramp.

Heat Stroke:

The most dangerous result of excessive exposure to the sun, often with physical work. The first signs are headache, fast pulse, flushed face. Sweating stops and the temperature rises. The patient may lose consciousness. Particularly dangerous in elderly people as their temperature regulation is not as efficient as when young.
Treatment:
The first aim is to lower the body temperature. Lie the patient in the shade in a well ventilated place, head and shoulders propped up. Leave only underclothes on and pour tepid water on body and limbs. Do not pour very cold or icy water as it contracts the skin blood vessels, allowing the inner body temperature to continue to rise. Vigorous fanning helps. If conscious, give water with pinch of salt as above. With heat stroke the body's heat regulating mechanism is temporarily upset and when the temperature starts to fall in response to treat-ment, it may rapidly drop below normal, calling for reverse treatment in which the patient should be covered with a blanket. This may lead to a rapid rise in temperature back above normal and several alternate cooling and warming steps may be necessary before temperature returns to normal. If possible, therefore, the patient's temperature should be constantly monitored by placing a thermometer in the anus.

Dehydration:

This usually accompanies severe sunburn, heat exhaustion, and heat stroke.
Treatment:
Rehydrate with water or fruit juices with added oralite salts according to instructions for the particular brand used. If no sachets of oralites are available, add a half teaspoonful of table salt per litre of drink taken. A useful home-made solution for rehydration is two tablespoons of sugar, one teaspoon of salt, and any flavouring desired, added to one litre of boiled water. Drink as much rehydration liquid as possible, but slowly — in continuous small sips, rather than large gulps.

DISEASES

Water-borne, Excremental Diseases:

Can be prevented by boiling water. Examples of water-borne diseases: bacillary dysentery, typhoid fever, infectious hepatitis, cholera, amoebic dysentery, bilharzia, hookworm.

Bacillary Dysentery:

A disease of dirt and flies.
Symptoms:
Abdominal cramps, diarrhoea, usually with blood, high temperature.
Treatment:
Rehydration as for heat stroke (even if the patient vomits frequently he should keep sipping the rehydration liquid), antibiotics, Immodium, Intetrix.

Amoebic Dysentery:

Caused by contaminated water or by raw vegetables washed in dirty water.
Symptoms:
Fatigue, lack of appetite, stools can be solid but may be greasy, foul-smelling, and sometimes containing a mixture of blood and mucous.

Treatment:
Rehydration, rest, and treatment with metronidazole (flagyl) — adults: two tablets, three times a day, for one week.

Typhoid Fever:
Caused by Salmonella.
Symptoms:
Starts slowly. No appetite, headache, temperature rises steadily, abdominal pain, light diarrhoea or constipation. Patient is prostrated, sometimes delirious.
Treatment:
Plenty to drink, antibiotics (Intetrix). Patient should be hospitalized as soon as possible.

Infectious Hepatitis:
As the incubation period is three weeks, the condition usually appears after the safari. Most common causes — contact with an infected person or swimming in contaminated swimming pools, rivers, or lakes.
Symptoms:
Nausea, vomiting, loss of appetite, fever, later yellow colouring of eyes and skin.
Treatment:
Rest and light food.
Prevention:
Gamaglobulin injections before your African visit may give resistance, though medical opinion is divided on its effectiveness. A simple measure that may help prevent contraction of this disease (which is widespread about the world) is not to immerse the head underwater when swimming in strange places and ensuring water doesn't enter the mouth and nostrils.

Cholera:
Caused by water contaminated with cholera vibrios.
Symptoms:
The onset can be very sudden — vomiting, continuous watery diarrhoea, muscle cramp, sunken eyes, clammy skin, pulse thready or absent.
Treatment:
Evacuation to hospital is an urgent need. Immediate rehydration (see under heat stroke — keep sipping despite vomiting), intravenously if possible and appropriate fluids and equipment are available. The disease, so fatal in the past, responds rapidly to modern antibiotics such as tetracycline in high doses.

Bilharzia (Schistosomiasis):
Caused by a small worm (cercaria) which enters the body through the skin if swimming, wading, or even washing in contaminated waters where the host snail lives.
Symptoms:
One type causes abdominal symptoms, the other disease of the bladder. These symptoms will usually appear after the safari. They should be suspected, diagnosed, and treated as soon as possible.
Treatment:
Oral remedies are now easy and effective.

Hookworm:
The larva of the worm enters the body through the skin of the feet if one walks barefoot in humid areas. The worm, two centimetres (half an inch) long, lives in the duodenum.
Symptoms:
Anaemia and general fatigue.
Treatment:
Doses of Widespectrum anti-helminthic drugs.
Prevention:
Don't walk barefoot.

Insect-borne Diseases:
Can be prevented by using insect repellent and sleeping under a net. Examples of insect-borne diseases: malaria, trypanosomiasis (sleeping sickness), dengue fever, sandfly fever (at the coast), and tick typhus.

Malaria:
Carried by plasmodium transmitted at night by the bite of the anopheline mosquito. It is common in Africa below 1,250 metres (4,000 feet), particularly in the wet season.
Symptoms:
Recurrent fever, alternative shivers and feeling cold followed by intense heat and sweating. There are four types of malaria — the most dangerous, *falciparum*, which can cause cerebral malaria, is the most common in Eastern Africa, hence the importance of prophylaxis.
Treatment:
Chloroquine: Four 250-milligram tablets to start with, followed by two 250-milligram tablets twice a day for three days. If no response do not try other drugs, but get the patient to hospital immediately.
Prevention:
The risk of infection is very small if you avoid the mosquito — i.e. at night, wear long trou-

sers, long sleeves, use insect repellent and mosquito coils, and sleep under a net. It is also essential to take a prophylactic drug, such as Paludrine (proguanil) — two 100-milligram tablets once a day for adults and a proportional dose for children, taken in the evening, starting on departure and carrying on fifteen days after return from safari. However, no drug is foolproof and if any illness occurs after travelling in an endemic area, tell your doctor you have been in a malaria area and ask for a blood slide to be taken to identify, or rule out, malaria before anti-malaria treatment begins. The symptoms are very similar to flu.

Trypanosomiasis (sleeping sickness):
Found mostly in southern East Africa, Sudan, Uganda, Tanzania, Zambia, and Zimbabwe. It is transmitted by the tsetse fly. There are two types of sleeping sickness — gambiense and rhodesiense.
Symptoms:
In gambiense the symptoms are general lassitude and a sense of malaise; onset is gradual. With rhodesiense, which is the most widespread in Eastern Africa, onset is rapid with high fever and muscular pain.
Treatment:
Suramin (Antrypol). Evacuation to hospital for special treatment.
Prevention:
Avoid tsetse bites. Wear light-coloured clothing and avoid black or blue. Use insect repellent. Ask your tour guide/organizers to tell you if you enter any possible sleeping sickness areas, as only a small proportion of the areas that have tsetse flies carry any risk of human sleeping sickness. If, on returning home, you are taken ill and you did go through such an area, tell your doctor so that he is aware of the possibility of sleeping sickness—faint though it will be.

At the Coast
Sandfly Fever :
Caused by the bite of the very small sandfly.
Symptoms:
Fever with aches and pains.
Treatment:
Rest and drink plenty of fluids.
Prevention:
Avoid sandfly beaches, use insect repellents and sleep under very fine-meshed mosquito nets.

Dengue Fever (Break-bone fever):
Caused by bites from infected mosquitoes — *Aedes aegypti* — the species that also causes yellow fever.
Symptoms:
Recurrent rash, very painful joints, headache.
Treatment:
Aspirin, rest. Leaves one weak and depressed.
Prevention:
Use precautions to avoid mosquito bites as under malaria.

Yellow Fever:
Caused by mosquito bites.
Symptoms:
Black vomit. This is a serious disease, not commonly present in Eastern Africa, but possibly in occurring in the Sudan and western Ethiopia.
Prevention:
Vaccination. Note most governments in Eastern Africa insist that all visitors entering their countries from others where yellow fever is endemic carry vaccination certificates and some insist that all visitors have been vaccinated. To avoid delays and unpleasantness all visitors to Eastern Africa should be vaccinated for yellow fever prior to leaving their home countries

Tick Typhus:
Rickettsial infection transmitted by tick bite.
Symptoms:
The bite may be inflamed with a dark centre, a swollen gland nearby, accompanied a week later by a rash, fever, and headache.
Treatment:
Antibiotics.
Prevention:
Long trousers. Watch for ticks when walking in the bush and if bitten, take out tick with lamp paraffin and disinfect the bite.

Malta Fever:
Also known as Brucellosis, is transmitted through drinking unboiled goat or cow's milk.
Symptoms:
A general feeling of malaise accompanied by a fever (sometimes high) that comes and goes with regularity: hence a third name for the disease — undulant fever.
Treatment:
Antibiotics under strict medical supervision — usually in hospital.

Prevention:
Only drink boiled or pasteurized milk. Milk in the major hotels is usually safe, having been heat treated, but be careful with milk in rural areas. African-style tea, however, is usually safe as water, tea, sugar, and milk are thoroughly boiled together.

A.I.D.S. (HIV):
The disease, though present in Eastern and Southern Africa, is no threat if one avoids the primary source of infection: indiscriminate and unprotected sex, used hypodermic needles, and transfusions of infected blood. If injections have to be given, they should be with disposable needles and syringes taken from sealed packages. In this respect, some travellers now carry their own disposable syringes and needles in case the need for an injection might arise, and it is a sensible precaution. Blood transfusions should be from tested donors only. Razors, toothbrushes, should be strictly personal. Shaving, depilation at the barbers and hairdressers should be avoided.

Bites:
Any animal bite is likely to be infective and should be washed immediately with lots of water and soap and disinfected with iodine or other disinfectant. If a wild game bite — lion, hippo, crocodile, etc. — administer antibiotics and anti-tetanus and quickly evacuate to hospital facilities.

Rabies:
Any mammal bite can transmit rabies. If there is the slightest suspicion of rabies seek immediate medical advice and get active immunization with Merieux Human Diploid Vaccine. Follow makers' instructions.

Scorpion Sting:
Scorpions live under tree bark, stones, and sand and can inflict a very painful sting. In a minority of cases the victim may become seriously ill, in addition to the pain and the shock that this brings on.
Prevention:
Avoid sitting down on old tree stumps or on the ground. Look into shoes, beware when taking up ground sheets.
Treatment:
Get the victim to hold a car engine's spark plug lead and at the same time touch the vehicle's chassis. Get helper to turn key in ignition for just a second -- just long enough for the engine to turn over a few times to create a spark and give an electric shock. The pain of the scorpion sting will start to fade after four or five shocks and be gone by ten shocks. If a petrol-engine vehicle is not available, an electric fencer or electric cattle prod will provide an adequate current. Do NOT, under any circumstances, use mains electricity. There is no scientific explanation for the efficacy of this treatment as yet, but it is extremely effective and harmless. If a suitable vehicle, fencer, or cattle prod is not at hand, any normal analgesics will help relieve the pain.

Spider Bites:
These can be very painful and may be dangerous. It is possible that the treatment for scorpion bite might work with them, but not proven. Oral or local analgesics will help alleviate pain.

Bee Stings:
Remove the stinger left in the skin without squeezing the sting, extracting it with a needle or knife blade rubbed sideways. Antihistamine is useful. In cases of multiple stings, treat for shock with black coffee or strong tea. People who know that they are allergic to bee stings should carry an appropriate antidote in their personal effects when visiting Africa.

Snake bites:
Out of 160 snakes in Africa, only about ten are venomous and common. Often they don't inject much venom in the bite; nevertheless snakes inspire a dread that is out of all proportion to the actual threat they pose. As a result, the psychological consequences of snake bites are frequently worse than any venom injected and greatly complicate medical treatment. The first rule for both victim and anyone treating a case of snake bite is do not panic: keep calm. In this respect, some basic facts may help:
* Few people die of snake bites.
* Most of those bitten by the most poisonous species live.
* When snakes bite defensively they often fail to inject a full dose of venom: full doses are associated with feeding, not defence.
* Harmless snakes bite as readily as poisonous species and, as in Eastern Africa they substantially outnumber dangerous species, most cases of snake bite are inflicted by harmless snakes.

* Except in the case of mambas, the effect of snake bites develops relatively slowly and the victim usually has four to five hours in which to get medical help.

The safest course is to get the victim to a doctor as quickly as possible. What follows is written for those rare instances where the victim will be unable to get medical attention within five hours.

The basic rule for any person likely to be in such a situation is to carry a suitable anti-snake venom serum. That recommended for Eastern Africa is the polyvalent Pasteur Ipser Africa serum.

It is important to know that professional medical opinion varies on the procedures for treating snake bite. Intravenous injection of serum unquestionably obtains the best curative effects, but inexperienced people may find the procedure difficult — and, if it's not done properly, it can be dangerous.

The manufacturers of the Pasteur serum, for example, believe that the problems of intravenous injection by amateurs outweigh the advantages of rapid administration. For the inexperienced they recommend the slower subcutaneous and intramuscular routes. But they also recommend that medically-trained personnel should inject serum intravenously. In favour of the latter, those who are going to spend time in the bush beyond the reach of quick, qualified medical attention should take a first aid course to learn how to give an intravenous injection.

With this in mind, the following procedures are recommended in the case of fresh snake bites.

* Reassure and calm the patient. If necessary give a sedative (valium, etc).
* Lie them down and apply a very tight bandage — not a tourniquet — fifteen centimetres (six inches) above the bite and another, if possible, at the root of the bitten limb.
* Study the bite to confirm that fang punctures are present. If a single bite is involved in the case of the more dangerous species, these are likely to be one or two quite distinct punctures. If a single bite produces many little prick marks, it is likely to have been inflicted by one of the non-venomous or mildly venomous species — though this evidence is not infallible.
* Try to identify the snake.
* Note the time, then observe the patient calmly over a period of several minutes.

Do not put ideas into his or her mind as, in such circumstances, auto-suggestion is common and likely to confuse the diagnosis. Symptoms from a dangerous snake bite may appear in two classes:

(a) *Within half on hour of the bite:* severe and spreading pain at the site of the bite and substantial swelling; *within half an hour to one hour after a bite:* severe pain, swelling continues; *More than one hour after bite:* what appears to be severe bruising and discoloration about the bite; *for longer periods:* vomiting, diarrhoea, heamorrhaging, great pain, and more swelling. These symptoms indicate a viper bite which, though no less dangerous than the mamba and cobra nerve poisons, act more slowly and usually mean that you have up to five hours to get the patient to a doctor.

(b) *Within half on hour:* slight pain and a feeling of numbness about the bite — swelling slightly: *within half an hour to one hour:* sleepiness, difficulty in keeping eyes open, dizziness, double or blurred vivion, growing tightness in the chest; *more then one hour:* growing paralysis, difficulty in breathing, collapse — all without great swelling about the bite. These indicate a nerve poison such as that produced by mambas and cobras — and calls for immediate injection of serum.

A combination of both reactions also calls for the immediate injection of serum.

When the victim is (a) bitten by a mamba; (b) clearly developing difficulty in breathing; or (c) obviously very ill indeed from a viper bite — give serum intravenously, ten minutes to complete. In critical situations, up to 40 ml can be given. If breathing stops give artificial respiration for as long as the heart beats. In such extreme circumstances there have been recoveries.

The application of serum intravenously produces quick results with the neurotoxic snakes — mambas, cobras, etc. However, in the case of advanced viper bites, while it may prevent further deterioration, the inevitable tissue damage, with the risks of secondary infections, calls for urgent and extended medical care.

* The tight bandage placed around the bitten limb should not be left in position for more than twenty minutes: ample time for symptoms to have been assessed and the need for an immediate intravenous injection to have been made.

* If, from swellings and pain around the bite, it is clear that the patient has been bitten by a poisonous snake, but has not developed any difficulty in breathing or blurred vision, when the bandage is removed serum should be injected in the following manner. One ampoule of 10 ml should be injected intramuscularly at the base of the affected limb; and another 10 ml injected intramuscularly about the bite. The patient should then be kept quiet and under observation for the next four hours. If symptoms neither abate nor worsen, further serum should be given intravenously.

* In about one case in a thousand, snake bite serum causes anaphylactic shock in the injected patient. This is a severe condition that can be fatal. To avoid this, *all* patients should be routinely subjected to the Besredka desensitisation procedure: injecting 0.1 ml of the serum subcutaneously, followed fifteen minutes later by a further subcutaneous injection of 0.25 ml, the full curative dose then being injected after a further fifteen minutes. In cases where there is some certainty that the patient has definitely been bitten by a dangerous snake, the desensitization can be started even before the symptoms become acute. This means that once the need has been confirmed, the curative dose can be applied with a minimum of delay.

* If anaphylactic shock does develop — paleness, sweating, weak pulse, fainting — it can be cured rapidly by injecting adrenalin 1:1000 subcutaneously. The injection is made little by little (not more than 0.1 ml at a time) up to a maximum of one ml, until shock is relieved. Usually recovery is very rapid. Again, however, anyone venturing into the bush far beyond medical help would be well advised to seek advice on the administration of adrenalin as routine first aid knowledge.

* Other injectable aids that should be routinely applied whenever serum is injected in the treatment of snake bite are an antihistamine and hydrocortisone.

* Strong coffee is a suitable drink for the snake-bitten. Under no circumstances should alcohol be consumed. Nor should the snake bite be cut or bled.

The Flying Doctors' Society of Africa

The society was founded fifteen years ago with the aim of raising funds to help AMREF's Flying Doctor Service.

Based at Wilson Airport, Nairobi, and manned by five flight nurses, five pilots, and the medical staff of the Clinical Department, the service provides medical counselling and emergency evacuations by air to a medical centre — usually Nairobi.

At present the service operates air ambulance services in Kenya and Tanzania — evacuations from the surrounding countries can be undertaken from cities, once the immigration clearance and landing permits have been obtained from their end. This is a normal requirement for all unscheduled flights.

The request must come from the site of the emergency whenever possible.

Information

When you call AMREF, please give the following information:
Number of patients
Name, age, sex
Condition of patients:
    Conscious
    In pain
    Bleeding
    Breathing adequately
Nature and time, duration of illness/accident
Nearest airstrip, condition, and weather report.

Please mention if patient is a member of the Flying Doctors Society as members are entitled to one free emergency evacuation a year.

Contacts:

For Medical Emergencies

The Flying Doctors can be reached by telephone or by radio call. If no telephone is available, the radio room operates twenty-four hours a day and may be contacted through the radios in most police stations and national park lodges.
Telephone Nairobi 336886
                or 501280

For Membership

Flying Doctors Society
P.O. Box 30125
Nairobi, Kenya
Telephone: 501280/1/2/3
                   501341
                   500508
Telex: 23254 AMREF

Individual Membership Fees (rates for 1989)

Adults over 18 years Ksh. 250.00 per year

Juniors under 18 years Ksh. 100.00 per year

Special Trust Membership
Ksh. 90.00 per year

CAMP FIRST AID KIT

Must include a good general first aid manual.

Instruments:

Forceps	x	2
Scissors	x	1
Scalpel blades	x	3
Mounted needle and thread	x	3

Dressings:

Cotton wool roll
Gauze roll or sterile compresses

Bandages of different sizes	x	10
Triangular bandages	x	5

Disinfectant:

Lotion, e.g. Savlon
Mercurochrome
Surgical or methylated spirits
Calamine lotion

Analgesics:

Aspirin	x	100
Paracetamol	x	100

Anti-spasmodic, i.e. buscopan, for stomach cramps

Antihistamines:

e.g. Piriton, 4 mg tablets	x	100
10 mg/ml injection	x	10

(or the non-sedative variant Incidal)

Antibiotics:

Ampicillin, 500 mg	x	100
Bactrin or Septrin Tablets	x	100
Metronidazole (flagyl)	x	50

Antimalarials:

Prophylaxis in low humid areas, i.e. Paludrine, in 100 mg pills.
Treatment Chloroquine, 250 mg pills

Oralites for Rehydration:

Sachets	x	20

Anti-Diarrhoea:

Immodium
Lomotil
Intetrix

Anti-dysentery (amoebic):

Flagyl	x	50

Snake Bite Serum:

Pasteur Institute, 10 ampoules of 10 ml (is of long duration) and if kept away from direct sunlight, fairly durable under 25 °C.
Recommended:
Serum Pasteur 10 ampoules
Ipser Africa Serum of 10 ml
Anti Bitis — Echis — Naje — Dendrosapis venoms. Long lasting, heat resisting, reasonable prices (available from May and Baker agents). Need 10 ml syringes and needles.

Adrenalin:

1/1000

Hydrocortisone:

1/10 vials	x	10

Anti Rabies Vaccine:

Merieux diploid cell vaccine 1 ml	x	2
Syringes — disposable 10cc	x	2
Needles — disposable 2cc	x	4
Adrenalin injection 1/1000 1 ml	x	5
Antihistamine injection		

Chapter 21 Mountain Gorilla

Gorillas are special. So different from man, and yet in many ways so alike. Few animals have sparked the imagination to the same extent as the gorilla. But only in the last twenty-five years have scientists learned sufficient details about gorilla life in the wild to be able to dispel the many myths and misconceptions about them.

The gorilla is a member of the ape family, as are the **chimpanzee** and **pygmy chimpanzee** also found in Africa, and the **orang-utan** of Asia. Though the gorilla is the largest living primate, oddly it was the last to be known to science.

The species *Gorilla gorilla* is represented by three subspecies or races. **Lowland gorillas** account for two of the subspecies: the **western lowland gorilla** *(Gorilla gorilla gorilla)* is found in West Africa; and the **eastern lowland gorilla** *(Gorilla gorilla graueri)* lives in eastern Zaire. Physical barriers such as rivers apparently determine their distribution for gorillas do not swim and even hesitate to enter shallow water.

The third, and rarest, of the subspecies is the **mountain gorilla** *(Gorilla gorilla beringei)*. It is found only in the high Virunga Mountains where the borders of Rwanda, Zaire, and Uganda meet, and in the tiny Impenetrable Forest of Uganda. Anatomical differences between the three races are slight, but the mountain gorilla is larger and has longer, thicker black to blueish-black hair.

Concern for the rare mountain gorilla and its spectacularly beautiful montane rain forest habitat, led, in 1925, to the Virunga volcanoes' inclusion in Albert National Park — the first in Africa. However, poaching, disturbance and loss of habitat in the 1960s and 1970s brought mountain gorilla populations from 450 to an all-time low of about 250. The world was made aware of the mountain gorilla's plight and a determined conservation effort has hopefully brought it back from the brink of extinction. With more protection, populations have stabilized and now show slight increases. Individual groups are becoming larger, with a significant increase in the number of young gorillas.

The gorilla is shy and retiring, and not — as folklore would have you believe — a ferocious and treacherous blood-thirsty beast. It seeks no trouble unless threatened, but a male will valiantly defend its family group.

The basic group is composed of at least one mature breeding male, one or more females and a variable number of young and immatures. Occasionally old males become solitary, or a few males may stay together in loose bachelor groups for differing periods of time.

Gorillas have strong attachments to their own family group and when groups meet, mingle and then subsequently part, individual animals tend to remain with their respective groups. These stable family units are each led by a silverback male, so called for the conspicuous silvery-grey hair that develops on the back when he reaches maturity. The silverback in charge of his family is ever alert and ready to defend it from any perceived danger.

Occasional serious fights take place between gorillas, mainly between silverbacks from different groups who are competing for females, sometimes ending in death. For the most part the heirarchical organization avoids problems within a group. Ritualized behaviour and bluff charges against males of other groups usually serve to avoid contact. This ritualized behaviour consists of screaming (with the inflation of a throat sac), grabbing foliage and placing it in the mouth, standing erect on the hind legs, tearing up and throwing plants, drumming on the chest with hands or fists, stamping feet, lowering on to hands and galloping in a mock attack, and striking the ground with the flat of the hands.

When done by a six-foot-tall, 400-pound gorilla, all this can be quite intimidating. Should a person be confronted by this display manage to hold their ground, the gorilla will usually stop short of attacking, but should they turn and flee, they will be pursued and bitten.

The only known enemies of gorillas are leopard and man. In western Africa **lowland gorillas** are commonly hunted for meat or in retaliation for crop raiding. This is less the case

Opposite: The biggest living primate, the mountain gorilla, survives in small pockets on the peaks of the Virunga volcano chain where Zaire, Rwanda, and Uganda meet.

in eastern Africa where mountain gorillas fall victim to snares and traps set in the forests by poachers hunting antelope and other animals. But entire families have also been destroyed by poachers in their attempts to capture infants for zoos — no zoo in the world has a captive mountain gorilla — while others have been killed for their heads and hands, which are sold as gruesome trophies.

One of the most serious threats to their existence is the continued loss of habitat. The rich, volcanic soil of the Virungas is potentially valuable as farmland; and the gorilla's habitat is in one of the most heavily populated regions of Africa. Protection of the remaining forest reserves in the Virungas is of prime importance to the gorilla.

A fully adult male gorilla, at 1.3 to 1.75 metres (four and a half to six feet) tall, and from 140 to 275 kilos (300 to 600 pounds), is twice as large as a female. Animals of this size need lots of food and the vegetarian gorilla is no exception. Although it eats up to sixty plant species, wild celery, bamboo, thistles and stinging nettles, bedstraw and certain fruits are the favourites. Gorillas seem to derive the moisture they need from plants and do not drink water.

Continually wandering through a home range of ten to fifteen square miles, a mountain gorilla's day is spent feeding and resting. When resting at midday, it may or may not prepare a nest, but at dusk each gorilla over three years of age quickly prepares a sleeping nest. Younger gorillas still sleep with their mothers. The nest is a rough, circular structure, made of bent branches up in a tree, or from grasses on the ground. A new one is built each night. Gorillas commonly urinate and defecate in their nests, but as their copious dung is fibrous, with a consistency similar to that of horse manure, it does not stick to or foul their coats. A lining of dung in the nest may act as insulation in cold, wet habitat.

With its short, broad trunk and wide chest and shoulders, the mountain gorilla looks massive. The eyes and ears seem dwarfed by the large head with its short muzzle. Old males develop a high cranial crest, making their heads even longer. The face is bare and shiny black, and the arms are longer than the rather stubby legs.

Gorillas spend most of their time on the ground, and although they can stand erect and walk upright for some distance, the normal mode of locomotion is on all fours. They walk on the knuckles of the hands which rest on the ground, with the weight distributed between them and the soles of the feet.

Mountain gorillas have a slow rate of reproduction. The female is receptive for only about three days each month and gestation is about eight and a half months, after which a single young is born. Females give birth for the first time at about ten years of age and then will have other infants only once every four to five years. A male usually does not breed before he is between twelve and fifteen and has become a silverback in charge of his own group. The life span for a gorilla in the wild is probably about forty years.

Newborn gorillas are tiny, only weighing one to two kilos (two to four and a half pounds). They are unable to hold on to their mother's hair for more than a few seconds, and so are constantly carried. Just like those of human infants, their movements are disoriented.

The stages of a gorilla's development are as follows:

Infant (zero — three years): During the first six months, a gorilla infant is totally dependent on its mother. She suckles it and carries it everywhere, cradled in her arms, and sleeps with it, holding it close to her warm body. At about four months the infant starts to take its first awkward steps away from its mother and begins to eat plants, although the mother continues to suckle it for up to three more years. By the time it is a year old it can climb small trees and play with other young gorillas.

Juvenile (three — six years): By the age of three and a half, the young gorilla has been weaned and no longer sleeps with its mother. It builds its own sleeping nest near her but becomes increasingly more independent. Play is an important activity.

Young adult (six — eight years): At this stage of development, males and females are not easily distinguishable as they are about equal in size, weighing between seventy to eighty kilos (150 to 180 pounds). They continue to play and have close social contacts with other young gorillas. At maturity the young females transfer directly to other groups, while young males join up with other males or become solitary until they can attract females to join them.

Adult female (eight years and older): Females reach sexual maturity after eight years of age and regularly come into oestrus, remaining reproductive into their early 30s. Long spacings of four to five years between births are due to long lactation and infant care periods. Infants are not weaned until three years of age. Solitary births are generally the rule; the only recorded twin birth in the wild was in 1986, but neither infant survived. Infant mortality is high, usually about thirty-five per cent.

Adult male (eleven years and older): Even though considered adults at eight years, the **'black-backed'** male gorillas do not reach sexual maturity until they are eleven or twelve. At this time they become **'silver-backed'** and are easily recognized by the conspicuous saddle of silvery-white hair on their backs and their large cranial crests. As they mature, their body mass increases to almost double that of females.

Mountain gorillas are susceptible to various parasites and diseases, especially pneumonia during the long, cold, wet seasons in the mountains. The Virunga volcanoes rise to 14,000 feet and scientists do not know if these high mountains have always been the mountain gorilla's habitat, or if they have sought these high elevations as a last refuge.

The long-term survival of the mountain gorilla is still not guaranteed but hopefully the work done by the **Mountain Gorilla Project (MGP)** will prevent its extinction. MGP has often been called Africa's most successful conservation programme. MGP was founded in 1979 by the **African Wildlife Foundation (AWF)**, **Flora and Fauna Preservation Society (FFPS)** and **The People's Trust for Endangered Species (PTES)**. This conservation management consortium assists **Rwanda's l'Office Rwandais du Tourisme et des Parcs Nationaux (ORTPN)** in its efforts to protect the mountain gorillas and their habitat.

Over the past ten years MGP has provided, and continues to provide, personnel and funds for a programme of park protection, tourism development and conservation awareness. These three complementary, and mutually reinforcing, programmes are carried out simultaneously. Rwanda, with the highest population density on the continent and a high birth-rate, is one of Africa's poorest nations. With a ninety per cent rural agricultural society, almost all available land has been cleared and crops are planted to the very tops of Rwanda's innumerable hills. Setting aside land, even an area as small as the Parc des Volcans (30,000 acres) for the exclusive use of wildlife may seem hard to justify when there are such pressures.

In its conservation strategy, MGP has developed a tourist industry around the mountain gorilla. Now one of the largest earners of foreign currency for the country, this industry was developed with the express intention of making gorilla conservation the most profitable use to which the park land could be put. Four gorilla groups are accustomed to the close presence of visitors, providing a unique tourist experience. The visits are tightly controlled: each gorilla group is limited to one daily visit, of approximately one hour, by a group of visitors (maximum six people). All groups are accompanied by guides and guards, and strict rules to prevent disturbance of the gorillas are enforced.

The park also contains Rwanda's most important watershed. People were educated about the crucial role this undisturbed watershed plays in providing water supplies and controlling erosion of their farming land. The park has no buffer zone and cultivation goes right up to the borders, which sometimes causes problems with gorillas and other wildlife going onto farms, or people going into the park to gather wood or hunt.

Although there are still some intrusions into the park and illegal poaching of other wildlife, the increased protection that MGP has providing has decreased these activities and prevented direct poaching of the mountain gorillas.

MGP plans to continue to increase local participation and benefits from the gorillas and the park. More jobs, both directly and indirectly related to the gorillas, are being sought and alternative sources of income are being developed. Based on the success of MGP in mountain gorilla conservation in Rwanda, Zaire, and Uganda have initiated similar programmes.

Ultimately it is the people who compete with wildlife for the same land that will determine the success of any wildlife conservation project. Educating school children of the value of the mountain gorilla and other wildlife has been an important part of the MGP programme. However, for a programme to be truly successful, adults as well as children must support it, and given today's realities they must receive some benefit from it.

Therefore, effective gorilla conservation must include human development and aspirations.

PART FOUR: CONSERVATION & THE NATIONAL PARKS

Above: The old and new: Hot-air balloon drifts over topi and impala in a setting that will have changed little in the last million years.

Opposite: 'Mosi-oa-tunya' — the smoke that thunders — the apt vernacular name for the great Victoria Falls.

Chapter 22   Conservation in Eastern Africa

It is widely and incorrectly believed that conservation was introduced to Eastern Africa during the colonial era which began in 1885. But Africa has a longer history of conservation.

The traditional grave sites of the Chewa and Manganja of Malawi make a cogent point. Small copses of indigenous woodland are scattered across their country. Protected from fire, firewood collection or any form of disturbance, they are examples of what the general vegetation would be like in the absence of man and other large mammals — creating havens for many small mammals and birds.

The Chewa and Manganja believed that the spirits of the departed played an important role in the lives of the living. Society's welfare demanded that these spirits should be content. Grave sites were places of veneration — as is the case in Christianity, Islam, and many other religions. Vegetation was undisturbed to ensure peace for the spirits that resided there.

The Chewa and Manganja perceived a strong connection between tranquillity and undisturbed nature; a perception also central to western conservation. People visit national parks for peace and spiritual refreshment. The difference between this and the Malawi instance is that the Africans were catering for the departed, the westerners catering for the living.

Today the traditions of both Chewa and Manganja have wilted under the onslaught of new ideas and religious influences, but the connection between tranquillity and undisturbed nature would have been a much better base on which to build national parks, rather than alien ideas which local people have had to be 'educated' to accept.

There are many other examples: the Mwami (ruler) of Rwanda and Shaka Zulu both maintained royal preserves to ensure good sport for the rulers. Europe's feudal rulers did the same — Britain's William the Conqueror conserved the New Forest for hunting. Across Africa there were countless similar instances where, for aesthetic, religious, or material reasons, animals, plants, or places were conserved from despoliation.

Before colonial times, Africans exploited wildlife extensively. It was a source of food — and still is. Many items of everyday use derived from wildlife — hides and skins for clothing and adornment, sinews for sewing and making bowstrings, ivory for trade. Some, such as the pastoral Maasai and agricultural Agikuyu of Kenya, did not eat wild animals if they could avoid it. But the Maasai had many other uses for wildlife products: medicines from zebra, hare, rhinoceros, rock hyrax, eland, giraffe, elephant, mole rat, and porcupine; clothing from the skins of Thomson's gazelle, Grant's gazelle, impala, rock hyrax, duiker, bushbuck, spring hare, Syke's monkey, and colobus monkey; wildebeest hides made ropes, their tails fly whisks.

Waterbuck hides were favoured sleeping mats. Rhinoceros horns made excellent clubs. Eland hide also made rope and their sinews, bowstrings. Giraffe hair was used for fly whisk handles. Buffalo and giant forest hog hides made the best shields. Ornaments and talismans came from bush pig, wart hog, lion, leopard, aardvark, colobus monkey, and ostrich. Eland, buffalo and giraffe were readily eaten.

The onset of colonialism in Eastern Africa was sudden. At the 1885 Berlin Conference, Eastern Africa was carved into imperial estates. Ethiopia alone remained independent — indeed it joined the scramble for territory by claiming extensive lowlands about its central highland massifs not considered before as part of the Amhara realms. Somali lands were divided between the Italians, British, Ethiopians, and the French. The British also established rule over what are now Kenya, Uganda, Zanzibar, Zambia, and Malawi. The Germans took what are now Rwanda, Burundi, and Tanganyika.

Among the first laws enacted by the new rulers were decrees which gave the state a monopoly over ivory. Rulers' claims to ivory were nothing new in Africa. Throughout the continent chiefs had traditionally claimed a tusk from all elephant killed, usually that which touched the earth on the underside of a dead elephant. With the onset of colonial rule, however, no one could hunt elephant or own or trade tusks without official permission.

Above: Raising money for conservation, a Kenyan walks across Africa.
Overleaf: The Victoria Falls throw a plume of spray so high into the air that, from a distance, it looks like a great column of smoke.

These rules may have conserved elephants, but derived as much from strong commercial desires to perpetuate supplies of ivory as from concern for elephant welfare.

In the closing years of the last century, a strong conservation ethic prevailed in both Germany and Britain. Preserving wildlife for its own sake was in vogue and the early colonial laws included rules to ensure wildlife's survival. They stipulated what could or could not be shot, fees to be paid for the privilege of hunting, and designated certain areas as sanctuaries in which hunting was forbidden. Although the term 'national park' was not in vogue between 1895 and 1910, the principles they enshrine today were both widely perceived and accepted.

Some of the leading British explorer-administrators — Sir Harry Johnstone of Malawi and Uganda, and Sir Frederick Jackson of Kenya and Uganda are prime examples —

were ardent conservationists. So, too, was Hermann von Wissman, first Governor of what was then German East Africa. Indeed, he was a moving force behind the first 'International Conference for the Preservation of the Wild Animals, Birds, and Fishes of the African Continent' in London in the spring of 1900.

The conference resulted in a convention which was not, however, ratified by France, Belgium, Egypt, Portugal, Natal, Cape Colony, or Rhodesia (the Second Boer War was yet to be concluded, and South Africa as a single entity was, as yet, unborn).

The influence of colonial game law varied from country to country. In Ethiopia things continued as they had before 1885. In both British and Italian Somaliland, wildlife was not so prominent an aspect of the environment as elsewhere in Eastern Africa and, at best, conservation was a low-key issue.

This was not so in Kenya. From the outset

sport-hunting tourists flocked to the country and their licence fees, together with revenue from ivory, was the single largest source of income for the Government prior to 1910. As a colony, the interests of the white settlers carried considerable weight and, though the earliest game laws did allow the indigenous people to hunt for tradition and necessity — indeed Kenya's Boni were allowed to hunt elephant *ad libitum* providing they surrendered one tusk of each animal killed to the Government — it was not long before this was barred.

This came about from ignorance, not a wilful desire to deny them rights. No administrator fully understood the role that wildlife had played in African lives. But no Africans could afford the licence fees needed to hunt legally, nor were they allowed firearms. Thus Africans were barred from hunting in Kenya until after political independence.

In Uganda, where white settlers were not allowed to own land on any scale, some African hunting rights were preserved. The conflict between elephant and agriculture was so severe in the southern half of that country, that the Government actually issued firearms and ammunition to local farmers as an incentive to kill elephant — the tusks, of course, were to be Government property. Subsequently, the British Government in Uganda brought licence fees within the reach of wealthier Africans.

Similar conditions prevailed in Zambia and Malawi, though without the conflict between people and elephant, and they were not very different in German East Africa.

Game reserves were amongst the earliest conservation creations. In 1897 most of 'Kenia' District, incorporating all of what is now Laikipia (between Mount Kenya and the Aberdares, stretching northward) was designated Kenya's first game reserve. But this was revoked because it included land needed for white settlement.

Instead, in 1909 two new game reserves were gazetted, the northern and the southern. The former was a vast rectangular block whose northern edge ran from the southern end of Lake Turkana to Marsabit, and whose southern border ran from Lake Baringo along the northern Ewaso Ngiro River to Archer's Post.

The southern game reserve included all of Kenya's Maasailand, east of the southern Ewaso Ngiro River — the whole of modern Kajiado District.

No hunting at all was allowed in the reserves, but this did not effect the indigenous people who lived within them.

Not all game reserves were created for conservation. In some situations, where people were moved out of an area for administrative reasons, declaring it a game reserve denied them lawful re-entry. For example, this was applied to move people out of areas in which sleeping sickness was rampant. Murchison Falls National Park in Uganda, parts of the Selous Game Reserve in Tanzania, and the Luangwa Valley National Parks in Zambia, are three sanctuaries whose beginnings were connected, wholly or partly, to sleeping sickness control measures.

The First World War dispossessed Germany of Tanganyika and Britain took over under a League of Nations mandate. This led to a more relaxed attitude towards indigenous hunting. Licence fees were well within the reach of Africans: five shillings a year allowed a man to hunt many of the larger animals, but not elephant or rhinoceros.

The end of the First World War also saw Rwanda and Burundi — as Ruanda-Urundi — come under Belgium's suzerainty as its reward for helping defeat the Germans. And in 1934 the Belgians proclaimed Eastern Africa's first national park — Akagera, in what is now Rwanda. Even earlier, Rwanda's Virunga volcanoes' became part of Zaire's Albert National Park when it was created in 1925. The idea of national parks caught on during the 1920s and 1930s. Many game reserves were scheduled to acquire this status, but plans were delayed by the onset of the Second World War.

The region's second national park, in Tanganyika, was proclaimed in 1940 when the Serengeti Game Reserve was upgraded; the third — Nairobi National Park in Kenya — in 1946; followed by Tsavo in 1948; Mount Kenya in 1949; and the Aberdares in 1950. Uganda declared two national parks in 1952: Queen Elizabeth and Murchison Falls.

During the 1960s, all countries in the region, except Ethiopia which was already independent, gained political freedom. The event accelerated the process of establishing national parks, which are listed in the next chapter.

Illustrating a basic wish to conserve fauna and flora, these national parks form a far greater proportion of national estates than those in either Europe or the United States.

The stark exceptions have been Burundi and Somalia: in the former, there is little left to conserve. The tiny country (27,500 square kilometres) has more than 160 people to the square kilometre. And Burundi shares extreme poverty with Somalia, a severe condition that pushes conservation issues far to the back of government minds.

But the enthusiasm has not been matched by effectiveness in enforcing conservation laws. Through the 1970s and 1980s, with the exception of Malawi, the region has been swept by a tide of unprecedented and, seemingly, uncontrollable poaching.

Yet many factors have influenced Eastern Africa's loss of elephant and rhino. First, from colonial times, there was a legacy of public ill-will towards conservation. Independent governments have perpetuated this by pursuing similar policies and it is taking time to convince their people of the sense of general conservation; though, in some places — particularly Kenya — there are encouraging signs of public awareness. In some cases there has been war or civil chaos. Yet, even in Uganda, the parks still exist, and there is a glimmer of promise that they will persist when normality returns.

Obsolete policy lies at the root of many conservation failures. Many national parks originated far back in the colonial era when human populations were much smaller and there was far more space. Poaching was no problem because there were few people, and the majority of poaching met subsistence needs.

Then these conservation areas were not subject to any serious challenge — economic, demographic, or territorial. This was wrongly construed as conservation's success, as fauna and flora would have survived quite well in most areas anyway.

Now African populations are progressively more involved in interdependent, international economics, increasing demand for hard currency where little existed before. This has coincided with international economic chaos: the oil embargo, escalating industrial costs, and declining raw commodity prices have all added to the economic incentives to poach — and raised to an exceptional degree by exploding human populations. Small wonder that national parks and reserves are under intense challenge. Resisting that challenge costs money

that no Eastern African country has available.

From the beginning of the colonial era, Kenya has been the single most powerful conservation influence in Eastern Africa. Its systems have been copied throughout the region. Kenya spends more each year on conservation than any other African state, except South Africa and Zimbabwe. And it is here that new appreciations are being forged.

Painful though abandoning the very big parks will be to the traditionalists, Kenya has already taken the first steps toward a policy of quality rather than quantity. It appreciates that below certain critical thresholds money and effort will be wasted and that results will only be forthcoming through concentrated resources. The plight of the black rhino crystalizes this thinking. They could not be looked after in large parks. Remnants of once extensive populations are now being captured and redistributed into a series of small, defensible sanctuaries that can be effectively looked after within the means available.

But certain large areas will lose their entire *raison d'être* if they are drastically reduced in size. Pre-eminent among these is the Serengeti ecosystem that includes the Serengeti National Park, the contiguous short-grass plains in the Ngorongoro Conservation area — both in Tanzania — and the Maasai Mara Game Reserve in Kenya. Those parts of the ecosystem in Tanzania have already been declared a 'World Heritage Site'. The bit in Kenya could also be included within this category. However, unless the world is prepared to back it with the funding that so large a unit calls for — and which may be beyond the means of the host nation to provide — the term is a hollow title.

Conservation in Eastern Africa faces many severe problems in the coming century. Yet given the will that has been demonstrated, they are not insurmountable. Solutions may not accord with the precise formulas laid down by non-Africans in distant Switzerland, or elsewhere in the industrialized temperate zone.

In many ways, though well-meaning, they repeat the mistake of a hundred years ago — of assuming that Africa is without indigenous conservation initiatives. But Africa's successes in the past, with methods that suited local societies, are grounds for optimism in the future.

Chapter 23 The National Parks

Land committed to conservation comes under many legal categories in Eastern Africa. As well as forest and game reserves, some areas have been established as faunal, floral, or scenic sanctuaries by local, rather than national, authorities. The highest national conservation status is currently that of 'national park'. This chapter presents a list of conservation areas, country by country, and a thumbnail sketch of each national park and its features. The information is drawn mainly from the Directory of Afrotropical Protected Areas of the International Union for the Conservation of Nature and Natural Resources.

Conservation Areas List:

Ethiopia:
National Parks = 8
Wildlife Reserves = 11
Wildlife Sanctuaries = 3
Proposed new National Parks = 2

Somalia:
Proposed National Park = 1

Uganda:
National Parks = 4
Nature Reserves = 1
Game Reserves = 12
Sanctuaries = 1
Forest Reserves = 12
Controlled hunting areas = 14

Kenya:
National Parks = 23
National Reserves = 29

Rwanda:
National Parks = 2
Forest Reserve = 1
Hunting Reserve = 1

Burundi:
Proposed National Parks = 2
Proposed Managed Nature Reserves = 2
Proposed Natural Forest Reserves = 3
Proposed Natural Monuments = 2

Tanzania:
National Parks = 10
Game Reserves = 15
Conservation Area = 1
Forest Reserves = 5

Zambia:
National Parks = 19
Game Management Areas = 32

Malawi:
National Parks = 6
Game Reserves = 4

NATIONAL PARKS

ETHIOPIA

Conservation Authority:
The Wildlife Conservation Organization,
P.O. Box 386,
Addis Ababa, Ethiopia.

Abijatta-Shalla Lakes, 880 square kilometres. Lying in Ethiopia's central Rift Valley between 1,400 and 4,000 metres above sea level, the park protects lakes Abijatta and Shalla and part of their watersheds. Both are saline, and their waters comprise fifty per cent of the park area. The vegetation around the lakes is mainly *Acacia* and *Ficus* savanna. Large mammals are few but include some greater kudu and Swayne's hartebeest. Aquatic bird life is abundant. Accommodation: a hotel on the park boundary at nearby Lake Langano.

Awash, 720 square kilometres. Located in the northern Rift Valley between 840 and 2,005 metres above the sea, the park is mostly hot, dry, semi-arid *Acacia* savanna. Large mammals include oryx, Soemmering's gazelle, Grevy's zebra, and Swayne's hartebeest. More than 450 bird species occur. The wildlife is shy and unaccustomed to humans. Accommodation: a campsite and trailer lodge.

Bale Mountains, 2,200 square kilometres. East of the Ethiopian Rift, this mountain park lies between 1,500 and 4,317 metres above sea level. Rolling plateau land about the base of Mount Batu; its vegetation, which varies with altitude, is relict montane forest and moorland. Night temperatures drop to minus 15°C. Mammals include mountain nyala and the Simien jackal (or fox), both of which are tame, abundant, and endemic to Ethiopia. Bird life includes fourteen of Ethiopia's twenty-three endemic species. There is excellent trout fishing in the park's rivers. Accommodation: a modern hotel at Goba near the park and camping is allowed.

Mago, 1,500 square kilometres. Located in the distant south-west of Ethiopia between 500 and 1,000 metres above sea level, the park provides a sample of broad-leafed *Combretum* and *Terminalia* savannah interspersed with tall grasses and thicket. Large mammals include buffalo, elephant, zebra, waterbuck, greater kudu, hartebeest, giraffe, lion, and leopard. However, this area is undeveloped and still used by poachers and graziers. Visitors are not permitted.

Nechisar, 700 square kilometres. Situated between lakes Abbaya and Chamo in south-

central Ethiopia between 1,500 and 2,000 metres above sea level, Nechisar is mainly open grassland with some savannah woodland and a little highland forest. Thirty-eight large mammal species occur, including hippopotamus, common zebra, Swayne's hartebeest, buffalo, greater kudu, reedbuck, Grant's gazelle, lion, and leopard. Accommodation: a tourist hotel in nearby Arba Minch.

Omo, 3,450 square kilometres. This park is close to and basically similar to the Mago National Park, with the same fauna and flora. It, too, is undeveloped.

Simien Mountain, 225 square kilometres. Located west of the Rift in the north-west of Ethiopia, this park lies on the Simien massif between 3,500 and 4,624 metres above sea

level. The lower fringes have Afro-Alpine trees, but for the most part the vegetation is high-altitude heath and moorland. Ethiopia's highest peak, Ras Dashan, within the park, is high enough for snow to lie on it for long periods, though not permanently. It is the only national park in which the Walia ibex and gelada are found, along with that other Ethiopian endemic, the Simien jackal (or fox). Both ibex and gelada live on and in the spectacular cliffs and gorges where the Amhara plateau falls away to the lowlands below. Some cliffs exceed 1,500 metres in height and provide what may be Africa's grandest scenery. Accommodation: three simple camp sites; access to the park is poor.

Yangudi-Rassa, 2,000 square kilometres. Like the Awash National Park, this is in the arid northern Rift lowlands some 350 kilometres north-east of Addis Ababa. It is traversed by the Awash River, and among its unusual animals is the Somali wild ass — ancestor of the domestic donkey. Other mammals are typical of the arid Horn of Africa: Grevy's zebra, gerenuk, greater and lesser kudu, and cheetah among them. The park is not yet open to the public.

Gambella, 2,000 square kilometres. A proposed park, lying close to Ethiopia's western border on the lowland fringe (under 500 metres above sea level) that rings the highlands, Gambella is typically southern Sudan-like savannah. Its fauna, likewise, is more typical of the continent's savannah, containing the classic Big Five — lion, leopard, elephant, rhino, and buffalo. The white-eared kob also occurs in Gambella. As yet undeveloped, this park-to-be has no visitor facilities.

SOMALIA

Conservation Authority:
Department of Wildlife,
National Range Agency,
Ministry of Livestock,
Range & Forestry, BP 1759,
Mogadiscio, Somalia.

Somalia lags far behind other countries in Eastern Africa in establishing national parks. Only one has been proposed — Lag Badana — that will encompass the country's southernmost toe, against the Kenya border. For the moment, though, it is a paper project only.

UGANDA

Conservation Authority:
Uganda National Parks,
P.O.Box 3530,
Kampala, Uganda.

Kidepo Valley, 1,334 square kilometres. Lying along both banks of the seasonal Kidepo River, this park is fringed by tall hills — up to 2,750 metres — but is for the most part below 1,350 metres. Situated in north-eastern Uganda, the driest part of the country, both vegetation and fauna are typical of dry woodlands and savannahs. The fauna contained the Big Five, but rhino are probably now extinct through poaching. Accommodation: one lodge at Apoka.

Murchison Falls, 3,840 square kilometres. Astride the Victoria Nile at altitudes between 500 and 1,292 metres, this park contains the wildest water in the entire length of the White Nile. Eighty kilometres of cataracts and rapids culminate in the Murchison Falls, where the great river boils through a gap only six metres wide. Vegetation is open grassland and woodland with species of Africa's moister savan-

nahs. The Big Five occurred, but rhino have been poached to extinction. The park is famous for its riverine scenery and is the best place in Africa to see crocodiles at close quarters. Accommodation: three large hotels.

Queen Elizabeth, 1,978 square kilometres. Located on the Equator in south-west Uganda, the park has an extensive shoreline on Lake Edward and is bisected by the Kazinga channel that links Lakes Edward and George. The fauna includes elephant, buffalo, hippo, topi and Uganda kob in mainly open grassland dotted with Acacia or, in the south, with *Euphorbia*. The centre of the park contains a large section of tall forest that is home to

chimpanzee and giant forest hog. Accommodation: a single, well-equipped but rather run-down lodge at Mweya.

Lake Mburo, 536 square kilometres. Situated in the undulating open plains of southern Uganda near the town of Mbarara, this park contains the country's only protected impala population. Buffalo, zebra, hippo and roan antelope also occur and the vegetation is predominantly *Acacia*-dotted grassland. The scenery is enhanced by a series of small lakes and swamps, of which Lake Mburo is one. Accommodation: a small guest house and three campsites; access is easy as the park lies on the metalled main road west from Kampala.

KENYA

Conservation Authority:
Wildlife Conservation &
Management Department,
Ministry of Tourism & Wildlife,
P.O. Box 40241,
Nairobi, Kenya.

Aberdare, 766 square kilometres. The park constitutes all the ground above the 3,030-metre contour. In the north-east, a narrow tongue runs down to 1,820 metres — the 'Treetops salient'. For the most part the park is high-altitude moorland above the tree line, but the salient contains forest. Mammals include elephant, rhino, buffalo, bongo, and giant forest hog, as well as lion and leopard. Trout may be caught in the moorland streams. Accommodation: two lodges — Treetops and the Ark — in the park cater for nightly game watching, self-help bungalows for fishermen on the moorlands, several special campsites, and two hotels, one — the Aberdare Country Club — at the nearby village of Mweiga, the other — The Outspan — in the town of Nyeri.

Amboseli, 392 square kilometres. Located at an altitude of 1,100 metres in the rain shadow of Kilimanjaro, this park is mostly arid *Commiphora/Acacia* woodland. A series of large underground springs create luxuriant swamps as oases in an otherwise inhospitable situation. The swamps support fifty-six large mammal species including elephant, buffalo, rhino, lion, leopard, and cheetah as well as various plains herbivores. Accommodation: four large, modern lodges and several campsites.

Hell's Gate, sixty-eight square kilometres. Lying close to the southern end of Lake Naivasha, Hell's Gate is as much a scenic as faunal or floral park. Taking its name from a cleft in the local volcanic hills, its cliffs contain some interesting birds, including the lammergeier. Accommodation: none in the park, but several hotels and lodges on the shores of nearby Lake Naivasha are within easy reach.

Lake Nakuru, 188 square kilometres. Lying in Kenya's central highlands, Nakuru is an ephemeral Rift Valley lake whose name derives from the Maasai for swirling dust. At times it is a dry, flat salt-pan. At others it fills with saline waters that support large flamingo and other bird populations. It is best known as a bird sanctuary, but recently the *Acacia* woodlands about the lake have been selected as a special rhino sanctuary. The park also contains some Rothschild giraffe. Accommodation: one lodge and one 'luxury camp' in the park, with several campsites and other hotel accommodation available in nearby Nakuru town.

Ruma, 120 square kilometres. This thicket-filled valley floor is close to the shores of Lake Victoria at an altitude of 1,400 metres. The thickets harboured tsetse flies that carry fatal human sleeping sickness. As a result, the mammals — roan antelope, topi, and buffalo — survived despite a fairly dense surrounding human population. Recently zebra, giraffe, and ostrich have been introduced. Accommodation: none, but camping is allowed.

Meru, 870 square kilometres. On the lowest slopes of the Nyambeni Hills east of, and close to, Mount Kenya between 366 and 900 metres altitude and on the north bank of Kenya's largest river, the Tana, Meru is at an ecological crossroad. Here the dry Horn of Africa vegetation merges with the better-watered savannahs and woodlands associated with Mount Kenya. Blessed with numerous streams, it has the Big Five animals — though its rhino are in danger through poaching. Accommodation: one luxury lodge, another forty-bed facility with partial catering, and several camping grounds.

Mount Elgon, 169 square kilometres. Astride the Kenya-Uganda border, Mount Elgon takes its name from an indigenous people — the El Gony — who lived on its lower slopes. The park is a strip that runs from the lower edge of the montane forests through the complete range of vegetation up to the 4,200-metre mountain peak and its surrounding moorlands. The park is noted for its mining elephant who enter caves and go deep underground for minerals. Accommodation: three campsites and a small hotel on the park boundary.

Mount Kenya, 715 square kilometres. Located in central Kenya, the park contains Africa's second-highest mountain peak — Batian — at 5,199 metres. It comprises all the land above the 3,030-metre contour, all alpine moorland, and a salient to the west running down through the lower forest zones to settled land near Naro Moru hamlet. Though the park contains the same big game as the Aberdares, it is better known for mountaineering, attracting climbers from all over the world. Accommodation: campsites within the park, climbing huts below the main peaks, hotels in nearby Nanyuki and Nyeri, and a game lodge in the adjoining forest reserve.

Nairobi, 117 square kilometres. This unique national park is within the Nairobi city limits and offers the chance to watch lion or cheetah on a kill against the backdrop of a modern city. Elephant are the only members of the Big Five that do not occur. Accommodation: none in the park and no camping facilities, but all the city's hotels are within fifteen minutes of the park entrance.

Ol Doinyo Sabuk, eighteen square kilometres. Fifty kilometres north-east of, and readily visible from, Nairobi, Ol Doinyo Sabuk means the 'buffalo mountain'. Like an upturned pudding bowl in shape, the forested top of this small mountain comprises the park. Buffalo and bushbuck are resident, as well as many forest birds and the park has wide scenic vistas. Although not well known, it is easily accessible from both Nairobi and its nearer satellite town of Thika. Accommodation: none, but available in both towns.

Saiwa Swamp, two square kilometres. Near the town of Kitale in western Kenya, this park encompasses a small swamp on the Saiwa River that contains the only population of sitatunga, or swamp antelope, in Kenya.

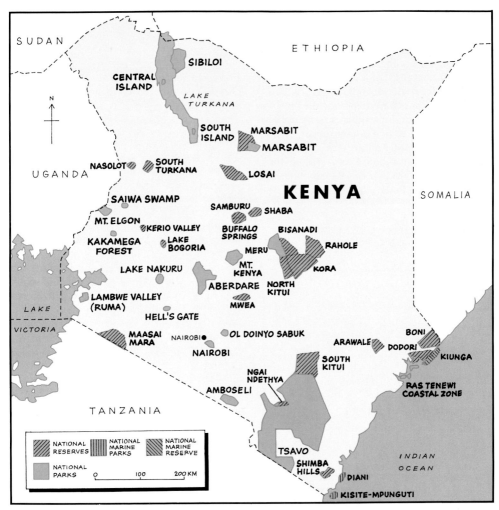

Accommodation: nil, open to day visitors only, hotel available in Kitale twenty kilometres away.

Sibiloi, 1,570 square kilometres. A strip of land along the eastern shore of Lake Turkana, together with the lake's **Central** and **South Islands,** Sibiloi is the most remote and rugged of Kenya's parks. Palaeontologically important — it has yielded some of the earliest human fossils — the Lake Turkana shoreline supports numerous grazers: Grevy's zebra, common zebra, topi, oryx, and gazelle among them. The shoreline is also prime crocodile habitat and has abundant bird life. Accommodation: camping is permitted and, by arrangement with the National Museums of Kenya, use can be made of self-help *bandas* at Koobi Fora. Visitors should not visit this park without consulting the authorities beforehand.

Tsavo (including the tops of the **Chyulu Hills**), 20,812 square kilometres. The largest national park in Kenya, Tsavo lies across the arid hinterland between the coast and the central highlands, and most of it is below 300 metres above sea level. Because of its aridity, mammal densities are low, but include the Big Five, many grazing antelope and representatives of the Horn of Africa such as gerenuk; and plants that produce both frankincense and myrrh. Accommodation: three luxury lodges, three partially serviced lodges, several camping sites, and four luxury lodges just outside the park borders.

Kisite/Mpunguti Marine Park, twenty-eight square kilometres. Located off Kenya's coast south of Mombasa, this marine park contains four small coral islands, but was established mainly to protect their fringing coral reefs and associated marine life. The fish and their surroundings are typical of the tropical Indo-Pacific, and offer excellent underwater viewing. Accommodation: none within the park, but many beach hotels are within easy reach.

Malindi and Watamu Marine National Parks, sixteen square kilometres. These contiguous national parks are north of Mombasa, one close to the ancient sea town of Malindi, the other off the more recent settlement of Watamu. Both were established to preserve examples of fringing coral reefs and offer first-class goggling and diving opportunities. Accommodation: readily available in the numerous beach hotels close to each park.

RWANDA

Conservation Authority:
Office Rwandais du tourisme
et des parcs nationaux,
BP 905, Kigali, Rwanda.

Akagera, 2,500 square kilometres. Comprising the north-eastern corner and just under ten per cent of Rwanda, the Akagera Park, established in 1934, is the oldest in Eastern Africa. Mainly about 1,250 metres above sea level along the banks of the Kagera River, often considered the true source of the Nile, and with a series of lakes, scenically the park is amongst Africa's most attractive. The vegetation is a mixture of West and East African influences with short-grass plains, tall grassland, and woodland interspersed with thicket. Over fifty mammals species include the Big Five together with sitatunga, roan, and eland. Accommodation: one central lodge at Ihema Lake, another on the western border at Gabiro.

Volcanoes, 125 square kilometres. This is a high-altitude park lying between 2,400 and 4,507 metres in the north-west of Rwanda. Taking in the forested peaks of the Virunga volcanoes, it was established specifically to conserve the mountain gorilla. It has succeeded and a number of habituated troops are now regularly visited by tourists. Accommodation: a guest house for visitors at the park offices.

BURUNDI

Conservation Authority:
Institut national pour
la conservation de la nature,
Presidence de la Republique,
BP 938, Bujumbura, Burundi.

Minute (27,731 square kilometres), impover-
ished, and densely settled — more than 300
people per square kilometre — Burundi has
been unable to develop national parks. Several are planned and have attained basic legis-
lative status but, for the moment, they remain
parks on paper only.

TANZANIA

Conservation Authority:
Tanzania National Parks (TANAPA),
P. O. Box 1994,
Dar es Salaam, Tanzania.

Arusha, 137 square kilometres. Located in
northern Tanzania near the town of Arusha,
the park takes in the peak of the 4,565-metre-
high volcanic Mount Meru and runs down its
south-eastern slopes through a broad swathe
of montane forest to its lower fringe at 1,525
metres. In the lower levels the park includes a
number of subsidiary craters, several with
grassy bottoms in which there are either
swamps or small lakes. Wildlife once included
elephant and black rhino, but both may now
have been poached to extinction, and a range
of species typical of the highland forests dotted throughout northern Tanzania and Kenya.
Accommodation: Momela Game Lodge at the
park and hotels in nearby Arusha.

Gombe, fifty-two square kilometres. A tiny
park on the north-eastern shores of Lake
Tanganyika, Gombe was proclaimed to protect relict chimpanzee populations that
inhabit the gallery forests along the Gombe
stream and other watercourses. Accommodation: crude camping facilities at the park's
research centre.

Katavi, 2,223 square kilometres. An undeveloped park in the miombo woodlands of south-
western Tanzania, it is dominated by a flood
plain around lakes Katavi and Chala. Vegetation is open grassland with scattered *Acacia*
and a fringe of miombo trees. The fauna is
typical of the region — elephant, buffalo, hippo,
lion, leopard, zebra, eland, roan, sable antelope, topi — but no rhino. Accommodation:
an unequipped rest camp which provides no
service other than a roof.

Kilimanjaro, 756 square kilometres. Containing the highest point in Africa — Kibo peak at
5,895 metres — the park was created to preserve the high-altitude moorlands and forests
of Mount Kilimanjaro. While its flora and
fauna are typical of the East African mountains, this scenic national park is visited mainly
by those who wish to walk up to its highest
point. Accommodation: three fully-equipped
huts at different levels to cater for visitors
making the four- to five-night round trip to get
up to the peak and back, with a modern hotel
at Marangu below the park.

Lake Manyara, 325 square kilometres. A
narrow strip of land between the scenic western Rift wall and alkaline Lake Manyara in
northern Tanzania, this small park is mainly
Acacia woodland of varying openness. It has a
wide range of animals typical of eastern
Africa's savannahs — including the Big Five
— but is perhaps best known for its elephant
and the research work that has been carried
out on them. Accommodation: a luxury hotel
overlooks the park from the Rift wall above,
campsites within the park.

Mikumi, 3,230 square kilometres. Located
in east-central Tanzania, not far from Dar es

Salaam, Mikumi contains the Mkata River flood plain with grassland and wooded *Combretum-Terminalia* savannah. To the east, south, and west of this flood plain there are extensive miombo woodlands. Its large mammals are species found widely in Eastern Africa's national parks, but also include sable antelope. Accommodation: a tented camp and luxury lodge.

Ruaha, 12,950 square kilometres. Taking its name from the Ruaha River, this big national park in southern Tanzania is primarily an example of deciduous miombo woodland, a broad swathe of which is the dominant vegetation from Angola, across Zambia, and the southern half of Tanzania. The fauna contains the Big Five and the area was very much an 'elephant' park. Severe poaching may have exterminated rhino and has greatly reduced elephant. Roan and sable antelope both occur in Ruaha. Accommodation: a camp of huts at Msembe, several authorized camping sites and a lodge fifty kilometres upstream from Msembe.

Rubondo, 457 square kilometres. This park is an island in south-west Lake Victoria. The vegetation is moist, evergreen forest and had a fauna that included hippo, sitatunga, and large numbers of bushbuck. At the instigation of the Frankfurt Zoological Society, elephant, rhino, giraffe, roan antelope, suni, chimpanzee, and black-and-white colobus monkeys were introduced onto the island. Accommodation: there are several huts for shelter.

Serengeti, 14,763 square kilometres. Arguably the best-known African national park, the

Serengeti of northern Tanzania is famous for its spectacular herds of plains grazers and their annual migrations. Accommodation: Two luxury lodges and four authorized camping sites.

Tarangire, 2,600 square kilometres. Tarangire, 114 kilometres south-west of Arusha, lies at the intergrade of the Maasai short-grass plains and the dry thickets and woodlands that separate them from the great miombo belt further to the south. Arid, undulating country, the park nonetheless supports a variety of big game that includes the Big Five (though rhino may have been poached out) but also contains some of the most southerly and westerly distributions of Somalian species like the lesser kudu. Accommodation: one lodge and several camping sites.

ZAMBIA

Conservation Authority:
National Parks & Wildlife Service,
Private Bag 1,
Chilanga, Zambia.

Blue Lagoon, 450 square kilometres. Lying on the north bank of the vast Kafue River flood plain, this is essentially a wetland park. The most prominent mammals are vast herds of red lechwe antelope, and the water birds are spectacular in both numbers and variety. Accommodation: none and in 1988 the park was closed to visitors for military reasons.

Isangano, 840 square kilometres. Lying on the north-eastern edge of Lake Bangweulu, Isangano is partly a wetland park, with swamp forest, open flood plain, as well as some drier woodland. The fauna includes black lechwe seasonally, with a few elephant, buffalo, hippo, reedbuck, and zebra. It is undeveloped and inaccessible. Accommodation: none.

Kafue, 22,400 square kilometres. The largest national park in all Eastern Africa, Kafue in western Zambia is also one of the least well known. The monotony of the miombo woodland is broken by the Kafue River and flood plains associated with major drainage lines. The fauna contains the Big Five and as wide a variety of other large mammals as may be found in any other large park in Eastern Africa. Accommodation: A lodge at Ngoma offers catering, one at La Fapa camp is self-catering, and there are camping sites.

Kasanka, 390 square kilometres. Lying in central Zambia, this undeveloped miombo park gains variety from the rivers and their associated wetlands that flow through it. The fauna includes the wetland sitatunga, puku, and lechwe, also elephant and other widely-distributed species. A bird of particular interest is the shoe-billed stork. Accomodation: none.

Lavushi Manda, 1,500 square kilometres. Another undeveloped miombo park, Lavushi Manda lies at the south-eastern edge of Lake Bangweulu. The wide variety of mammals typical of these woodlands occur, but mostly at very low densities. Accommodation: none.

Liuwa Plains, 3,660 square kilometres. A miombo park near the borders of Angola, with a wide variety of animals at low densities. Currently undeveloped and inaccessible to tourists.

Lochinvar, 410 square kilometres. On the opposite side of the Kafue flood plain to Blue Lagoon National Park, Lochinvar offers the same spectacular wetland assemblage of red lechwe and water birds. It also has a more extensive component of miombo woods. Accommodation: one small self-catering lodge.

Lower Zambezi, 4,140 square kilometres. A miombo park along the northern bank of the scenic Zambezi River, this area has a wide variety of animals, but is heavily poached and currently a park in name only. Accommodation: none.

Luambe, 254 square kilometres; **Lukusuzi,** 2,720 square kilometres; **North Luangwa,** 4,636 square kilometres; and **South Luangwa,** 9,050 square kilometres. These four national parks form part of a conservation complex in the Luangwa River valley in eastern Zambia. Luambe and Lukusuzi lie east of the river, and the two Luangwa parks lie on the west separated by a narrow corridor. Currently part of an ambitious development programme that seeks to integrate conservation with other land uses, this park cluster is the best known in Zambia. Though lying in the miombo belt, the scenic monotony is broken by a Rift Valley wall along the western edge of the Luangwa Valley and the Luangwa River itself. Its fertile flood plain supports high wildlife densities. Accommodation: two catering lodges and three non-catering lodges in South Luangwa Park and one non-catering lodge in Luambe Park.

Lusenga, 880 square kilometres. Located in northern Zambia near Lake Tanganyika, Lusenga National Park is a miombo park with a severely depleted fauna. It is undeveloped and has no visitor facilities.

Mosi-oa-Tunya, sixty-six square kilometres. Located on the north side of the Victoria Falls on the Zambezi River, this highly-developed park is primarily scenic, but has elephant, buffalo, hippo, waterbuck, and bushbuck among its larger mammals. Accommodation: a hotel, two restaurants, a non-catering camp, and a campsite, together with more facilities in the nearby town of Livingstone.

Mweru-Wantipa, 3,134 square kilometres. Lying in the extreme north of Zambia between Lake Tanganyika in the east and Lake Mweru in the west, this park has greater vegetational variety than most other miombo woodland parks. Its fauna and flora both reflect its closeness to the Zaire basin and the rain forest influences. It is undeveloped and access is poor. Accommodation: campsites outside the park.

Nsumbu, 2,020 square kilometres. Situated on the south-western shores of Lake Tanganyika, the park has a variety of wildlife, including elephant, but is dominated by its 100-kilometre lake front. The rocky shoreline

interspersed with small sandy beaches and the crystal-clear lake waters that offer good sport fishing make it exceptionally attractive. Accommodation: two luxury lodges and a self-catering facility.

Nyika, eighty square kilometres. This small national park on Zambia's eastern border with Malawi encompasses the Zambian portion of the Nyika plateau between 1,295 and 2,225 metres above sea level. On the higher ground the vegetation is upland grassland, interspersed with relict forest patches, while the lower slopes are miombo woodland. There are few large mammals, but the area is of ornithological and botanical interest. Accommodation: one ten-bed non-catering rest house.

Sioma Ngwezi, 5,276 square kilometres. On the extreme south-western border of Zambia, this national park presents a fauna and flora that is influenced, zoologically, by the Kalahari to the south. It is undeveloped and currently closed to visitors.

West Lunga, 1,684 square kilometres. Located in north-western Zambia, this is a miombo park, the woodland interspersed with dense thickets that contain some forest species such as yellow-backed duiker. The park is undeveloped. Accommodation: none.

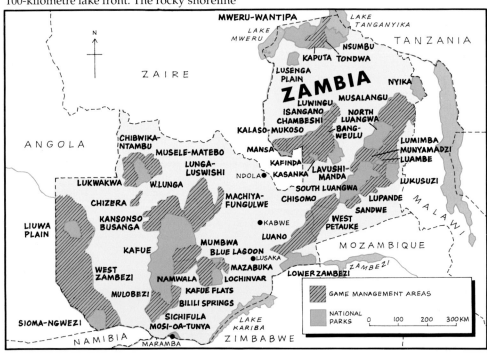

MALAWI
Conservation Authority:
Department of National Parks & Wildlife,
P. O. Box 30131,
Lilongwe 3, Malawi.

Kasungu, 2,316 square kilometres. Midway along Malawi's western border with Zambia, Kasungu is the country's best known and most highly-developed national park. The vegetation is typical miombo woodland in undulating country. The mammals and birds are also characteristic of this huge zone, but they are readily visible and fairly tame. Ac-

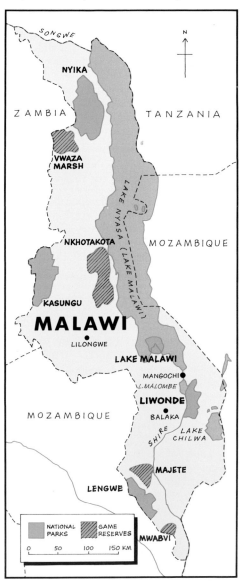

commodation: a luxury lodge at Lifupa and a tented campsite.

Lake Malawi, Ninety-four square kilometres. Unique in Africa, Lake Malawi Park offers underwater goggling that rivals the world's coral reefs. Over half of the lake's 500 fish species may occur in the park, many of them brightly coloured and endemic to Malawi. Although established primarily for its aquatic habitats, the Lake Malawi Park also has some large mammal species — hippo, zebra, greater kudu, impala, and bushbuck — though they are not readily seen. Accommodation: several small hotels are planned.

Lengwe, 887 square kilometres. Most southerly of Malawi's national parks, lying in the lower Shire Valley (altitude 130-393 metres), Lengwe was originally established to protect the northernmost population of the southern nyala. The species is perhaps more easily seen here than in any other part of its range. A large section of miombo woodland was added to the original Lengwe Park in 1975.

Liwonde, 548 square kilometres. An attractive park with some excellent stands of 'cathedral' mopane (Rhodesian ironwood) along the left bank of the Shire River, Liwonde has a range of large mammals that includes elephant, but it is noted for sable antelope. Accommodation: campsite outside the park near Makanga.

Nyika, 3,134 square kilometres. The largest park in Malawi, the Nyika encompasses most of the high Nyika plateau between altitudes of 600 and 2,606 metres above sea level. Being some 11° south of the Equator, this altitude produces the same climatic effect as an additional 600 metres on the Equator. The predominant vegetation is short, windswept grassland, with patches of relict forest tucked away in hollows and along valleys. The rivers are stocked with trout. The park's lower slopes are miombo woodland. Nyika contains fewer large mammal species than most parks its size, but it is the best place to watch roan antelope. The scenery is on the grand scale with vistas that take in hundreds of miles. Accommodation: a luxury lodge at Chilinda, the park headquarters.

Chapter 24 Major Theatres of the Wild

'Which is the best park?' The answer to this perennial question depends on individual interest. This chapter presents a general overview of the region's better-known parks and game reserves and comments on some of those with more specialized features.

Every country in the region wants to develop tourism. But only Kenya has a substantial business in this field. Today, Kenya's visitors approach one million a year, and the tourist industry caters for a wide range of tastes. The country can handle this number of tourists because its infrastructure of roads, air connections, and both internal and international communications, are sophisticated by international standards.

Burundi and Somalia have virtually no facilities for wildlife tourism. They have no readily-viewed concentrations of wild animals. What they have are wary and widely scattered. Somalia has several interesting species — such as the dibatag and the beira — but finding and seeing them is difficult.

In socialist Ethiopia and Tanzania, state bodies either run or oversee tourism closely and private entrepreneurs are discouraged or find it difficult to operate. Both countries have much to offer in the wildlife field and are well worth visiting, but tourism services are limited and somewhat inflexible.

In Rwanda and Malawi there is more choice. Private enterprise is encouraged and wildlife tourism is expanding. Zambia's tourism has made several starts, but is inhibited by the country's poor economic record. Uganda had a fast-growing tourist industry until Idi Amin.

For ease of entry, facilities and services available, and the range of options open to tourists, Kenya is far ahead of other states in Eastern Africa. Yet this does not mean that there are no rewarding wildlife experiences in the other countries. Providing allowance is made for the lesser levels of development, excepting Burundi and Somalia, there is much to see and enjoy in all.

'Big game' is still widespread in Eastern Africa. No less than forty-six parks and reserves have elephant, and nearly as many have the complete complement of the Big Five animals — elephant, rhino, buffalo, lion, and leopard. But wild animals are cautious by instinct. Irrespective of any other influences, they tend to run away from unfamiliar sights and sounds. Thus visitors to out-of-the-way parks or game reserves are often disappointed when they see little.

Constant exposure to people and vehicles without disturbance accustoms wild animals to close human presence. In open areas where the animals can see both approaching vehicles or people but cannot hide, this develops more rapidly. Frequently approached, unable to get away but suffering no harm, they rapidly accept human presence.

In dense vegetation — forest and thicket — where animals can hide and people cannot see them, the process takes longer. The outcome is that the most approachable wildlife is where tourist traffic is highest and the landscape most open.

Those with limited time, who wish to see large numbers of animals, quickly and at close quarters, should go to the open parks most heavily visited. In this respect, Kenya offers the best opportunities in three grassland sanctuaries: the **Maasai Mara Game Reserve, Nairobi**, and **Amboseli National Parks**. The animals are accustomed to vehicles and tolerate them at close quarters with little concern. All three sanctuaries are accessible and can accommodate large numbers of people either within their borders or close by.

Of the three, the 1,500-square-kilometre Maasai Mara Game Reserve offers the best value. Part of the Serengeti ecosystem, the Mara forms the dry weather grazing ground for the vast migratory herds of wildebeest that have made the region famous. Towards the end of July they return from their foraging far to the south. Grazing as they go, long before the van comes into sight, their approach can be heard. Grunting and bleating, their million and more voices blend into a dull murmur, like waves on a distant shore.

Accompanying them come zebra and ga-

Opposite: Sharp, unworn teeth and lack of scarring indicate this irascible individual is a youngster. Newly adult he will soon be seeking a place in a pride.

Above: Nature's ceaseless cycle: lionesss dispatching a wildebeest.

zelle in their hundreds of thousands. With the host of predators that live off them, it forms one of the greatest natural spectacles on earth. This vast throng live in and about the Mara until the rains break in October or November, when they move south. Even then, the Mara still has abundant resident herbivores and carnivores — more than enough to satisfy the average visitor.

There are at least seven luxury lodges and tented camps within its borders, and more outside. Each has an airstrip and is accessible by charter aircraft. Some are served by scheduled flights out of Nairobi's Wilson Airport. An all-weather road connects the reserve to Nairobi, and many all-weather and seasonal tracks give wide access to most of the reserve.

Amboseli, at 392 square kilometres, is much smaller than the Mara and does not have any spectacular migrations, though there are seasonal movements in and out of the park. The swamps which form the park's core provide year-round forage that keeps many animals within its borders.

The range of species is similar to the Mara's but, if anything, they are tamer and more approachable. This is particularly true of Amboseli's elephant, which have been closely studied for nearly twenty years. Indeed the population is probably the best known in Africa; research workers recognizing every individual.

The park lies at the north-western foot of Kilimanjaro, which provides a spectacular backdrop to the wildlife and swamp scenery. But there is one drawback here: traffic around the park's tracks raises clouds of fine, irritating, volcanic dust. Despite this, the number of visitors continues to grow, giving thousands memorable impressions of wildlife in a spectacular setting.

Amboseli, with several luxury lodges, is accessible by air and is well served with roads and tracks that are seldom subject to occasional wet weather closures. Indeed, for a visitor who comes to Kenya at the height of the rains, is limited to a few days, yet wishes to see a wide range of wild species at close quarters, Amboseli is a better bet than the Mara.

Because it is actually in the capital, Nairobi National Park cannot provide that ambience of wild, untamed Africa which is part of visits to the more distant sanctuaries. Yet its range of species is similar to those of both the Mara and Amboseli — only lacking elephants from the

Big Five. For the person without time to make a safari further afield, Nairobi Park can introduce African wildlife as satisfactorily as many larger wilderness areas.

Tanzania's **Serengeti National Park** and the contiguous **Ngorongoro Conservation Area** rival — and perhaps exceed — the spectacles provided by the Mara and Amboseli. Both are predominantly open, rather short grassland habitats, and offer excellent visibility. Both have abundant animals that have been sufficiently exposed to tourist traffic to be relatively tame.

When the rains break in November, the 1.4 million wildebeest, half a million gazelle, and 200,000 zebra that have spent the dry months in Kenya's Mara head into the Serengeti. Their destination is the short-grass plains that lie in the south of the park and in the Ngorongoro Conservation Area. There they will stay for as long as the water pans hold out. And there, in normal years, the wildebeest calve.

In a three-week birthing season the Serengeti plains are freckled with the bleating, dun-coloured offspring. The vistas, mile after mile, of seemingly endless wildebeest imparts an incomparable sense of nature's grandeur. The Serengeti's very size (14,763 square kilometres) and its lower density of visitors, together with the wide dispersal of animals, evokes a feeling of wilderness impossible to experience in the Mara where everything is more concentrated.

The Serengeti is accessible by air from Dar es Salaam, Arusha, and Nairobi and by road from Arusha. Two other wildlife sanctuaries lie on this route — Ngorongoro and **Manyara National Park** — so the journey can be broken into three pleasant stages by visiting them on the way to the Serengeti.

Internally the Serengeti Park is well served with rough tracks that are adequate for game viewing, though some are suitable for only four-wheel drive vehicles. Two lodges offer courteous, friendly service and adequate accommodation. There are four campsites at Seronera, the park's headquarters.

Ngorongoro Conservation Area (8,288 square kilometres) contains a spectacular assemblage of wildlife. However, because it is home to several thousand Maasai herdsmen and their stock, it is not a national park. Official policy seeks as far as possible to marry both human and wildlife interests. Currently this is successful, though predicted increases in Maasai numbers over the coming century will place the system under increasing strain.

The core of the conservation area is Ngorongoro Crater, a huge volcanic caldera with an average diameter of 18 kilometres. The 264-square-kilometre floor is open grassland, enhanced by a small alkaline lake and a patch of *Acacia* forest. Surrounded by the old volcano's steep 600-metre walls, the crater is a vast, self-contained amphitheatre.

Elephant do move between the forested crater rim and its floor, and the grazers do occasionally go out onto the nearby Serengeti plains. Yet, for the most part, the wildebeest, zebra, and gazelle herds stay in the crater, together with a variety of other antelope, rhino, buffalo, hippo, and a whole range of predators from lion, leopard and cheetah down to the smaller viverrids. Ngorongoro is an exceptionally beautiful setting.

Three lodges on the crater rim look down on the stage below. To reach the crater floor, visitors must hire vehicles and guides from the managing authority. Away from the crater there is another lodge at Ndutu, not far from one of the world's most famous palaeontological sites: Olduvai Gorge, where some of mankind's earliest remains have been found.

Two other national parks in Eastern Africa where there is open terrain and abundant, tame animals, are **Murchison Falls** and **Queen Elizabeth National Parks** — both in Uganda. Over the past two decades civil conflict has affected them, and elephant, in particular, have been severely reduced. But their basic potential as outstanding wildlife exhibits remains.

Both parks have predominantly open habitats with good visibility and tame, approachable wildlife. However, there is a major difference between these two Uganda parks and their rivals in Kenya and northern Tanzania. While the Mara, Amboseli, Serengeti and Ngorongoro have some elephant, rhino, hippo and buffalo, they are predominantly plains game sanctuaries. The most numerous animals are the medium-sized grazers. The two Uganda parks have a similar range of animals, but the most numerous species are the biggest — elephant, hippo, and buffalo. They are thus big game rather than plains game sanctuaries. This, together with the wetter, warmer Ugandan climate, gives them a strikingly different ambience to the Kenyan and Tanzanian parks.

Both Queen Elizabeth and Murchison Falls National Parks have a well-developed tourism infrastructure. These include game viewing tracks and roads and a welcome variation to the motorized game viewing that is normal in most African national parks.

Both contain major waterways: the Kazinga Channel in Queen Elizabeth Park and the Nile in Murchison Falls. Launch trips along them permits game viewing in cool, comfortable surroundings. Moreover, animals allow launches to approach far closer and in greater safety than would ever be the case on land. The Nile trip gives visitors access to a spectacular crocodile population and the great Murchison Falls.

Queen Elizabeth Park has a modern luxury lodge at Mweya, while Murchison Falls has two — one at Paraa and another at Chobe — and another planned. These, together with the tourist infrastructure generally, were due to be refurbished, and considerable international aid is being given to this end.

One park, as yet somewhat undeveloped, rivals both the Kenyan, Tanzanian and Ugandan open parks in potential — Rwanda's **Akagera National Park.** It has open grassland, numerous animals, visibility, and exceptionally attractive scenery. As tourism grows in that country and an infrastructure develops to carry it, the popularity of Akagera will rise, and its animals will become tamer and more viewable.

Seeing a variety of animals at close quarters is not the only reason to visit parks and game reserves. Many relish woodland for its own qualities. Lack of visibility may restrict the number of animals seen, but it creates a greater sense of expectation. Each bend in the track may produce a surprise; one is never sure of what lies around the next corner. And for those who relish a sense of 'getting away from it all', of being out of sight of other people, woodland provides welcome screening. Clusters of minibuses about a lion or cheetah — such a feature of the popular grassland parks — are uncommon.

In Eastern Africa, three woodland parks stand out: **Luangwa North** (4,636 square kilometres) and **Luangwa South** (9,050 square kilometres) in Zambia, and **Kasungu** in Malawi. All are in the basically monotonous miombo vegetation characteristic of the old infertile soils that dominate a great deal of Angola, Zambia, Malawi, southern Tanzania and Mozambique. This sense of endless monotony is enhanced by generally low mammal densities — the outcome of infertile soils.

Though North and South Luangwa are basically miombo parks, they are different. Both are on the Luangwa River, from which they get their names. Not only is the river scenically beautiful, but it has created a flood plain of rich alluvial soils. This fertility is reflected in the productivity of the plant life and both the variety and numbers of animals.

The Luangwa parks' hippo populations are reminiscent of the very high densities in Uganda. Crocodile, buffalo, waterbuck, and puku are common and greater kudu are seen around every other corner. Elephant were exceptionally abundant and caused extensive woodland damage until they and the parks' black rhino were severely reduced by poachers during the 1980s. Lion and leopard are numerous and the latter are frequently seen by spotlight during the night game drives arranged by the park authorities. Away from the river, the quietness and solitude of miombo becomes more apparent.

The Luangwa Parks are inaccessible during the Zambian rainy season from October to June. They are, however, open to visitors during the dry months between June and October. North Luangwa is undeveloped. South Luangwa is served with a network of tracks, accessible by air and road, and has two luxury lodges. In addition there are three more which provide accommodation only. Walking safaris are permitted in Luangwa and are popular with those tired of motorized game viewing.

An unadulterated miombo sanctuary, Kasungu National Park is not on any major tourist circuit and relatively unknown outside Malawi. Efficiently run, well served with tracks, and home to respectable densities of woodland species — many reasonably tame — Kasungu is attractive to the visitor who has got over the first-time compulsion to keep travelling and see everything. Uncrowded and quiet, it is rewarding for the person who wants to move slowly, and stop and watch in solitude.

Kasungu has a single, unpretentious lodge at its Lifupa headquarters, pleasantly situated overlooking a large dam. A non-catering tented campsite is also available and the park is accessible by road and light aircraft.

Another area in the miombo belt currently accessible only to those prepared to pay for a personalized, private safari, is the vast **Selous Game Reserve** in south-eastern Tanzania. Like the Luangwa parks, the Selous is endowed with large rivers that open the landscape and create zoological as well as scenic variety. If the necessary funding becomes available and Selous can be upgraded to national park status, it could outshine all other miombo sanctuaries.

Elsewhere, other miombo parks, which include most of those in Zambia, may be rewarding to those who enjoy camping and visiting new places, but they are short on both wildlife and scenery.

Only one forested area in Eastern Africa presents big game, close up, in any numbers — the 'Treetops Salient' of Kenya's **Aberdare National Park.** In 1932, long before the park was proclaimed, the late Eric Sherbrooke-

Below: This new born baby elephant will be dependent upon its family until its mid-teens.

What to See and Where

Legend:
- ● Resident species
- ■ Species likely to be seen
- ▲ Species most seen
- █ Endemic in this park only

COUNTRY / Parks or Reserves	Gorilla	Chimpanzee	Baboon	Gelada	Hamadryas	Aardwolf	Hyaena Striped	Hyaena Spotted	Jackal Simien	Jackal Black-Backed	Jackal Side-Striped	Cheetah	Leopard	Lion	Wild Dog	Elephant	Black Rhino	Hippo	Giant Forest Hog	Wart Hog	Bush Pig	Wild Ass	Common Zebra	Grevy's Zebra	Buffalo	Ibex	Giraffe	Grey Duiker
ETHIOPIA																												
Abijata-Shalla						●	●	●		●			●		●					■	●							●
Awash			●		█	●	●	●		■		●	●	●	●					●	■			▲			█	●
Bale Mts.						●	▲		●	●		●								●	●							
Gambella			●			●				●		●		●	●					■	●		●		●			
Mago			●			●	●	●		●		●	●	●	●					●	■		●		●			●
Nechisar			●			●	●	●		█		●	●	●						●	■							●
Omo			●			●	●	●												●	■				●			●
Simien				█					▲	●			●													█		
Yangudi Rassa			●	●		●				●			●	●	●					●		●	█		●			●
SOMALIA																												
Lake Badana			●			●	●	●		●			●	●	●	●				■			●		●		●	●
UGANDA																												
Kidepo		█				●	●	■		●	●	●	●	●	●	█				●			●		●		█	●
Lake Mburo			●					●		●	●		●	●			■	■		●	■		●		■			●
Murchison Falls		█						▲		●	■		■	■		▲		▲		▲	●		▲		▲		█	●
Queen Elizabeth	●	█						▲		■	■		■	■		▲		▲	■	▲	●				▲			●
KENYA																												
Aberdare		▲					▲			█	■	●	▲	■		▲	●		▲	▲	●				▲			●
Amboseli		▲			●	●	▲		▲	●	▲	■	▲	●	▲	●	●		■	■			▲		▲			●
Hell's Gate		●			●	●	●		●	●		●	●	●					●	■			●			█		█
Kakamega			●						●	●			●						●									
Nakuru		▲			●		█		▲	■		●	●	●			■	■		●			▲		▲			●
Lambwe		●			●			●		●	●		●	●						■			●		●			●
Mara		▲			●	●		▲	▲	▲	▲	▲	▲	●	▲	●	▲	●		▲			▲		▲		▲	●
Marsabit		●			●	●	●		█	●		●	●	●	●					●			●	●		█		●
Meru		█			●	●	■		▲	■	█	●	●	■	■	●		▲		●	■		●	▲	▲			●
Mt. Elgon		●			●			●		●	●		●			█			●	■	●				●			●
Mt. Kenya		●			●			●		●	●		●	●		●			█	■	●				█			●
Nairobi		▲			█	●			▲	▲	▲	▲	●	▲		●		▲		●			▲		▲		▲	●
Ol Doinyo Sabuk		█				●				●			●							●					█			●
Saiwa Swamp		●						●		●			●			●												
Samburu		▲			█	█	●			▲		█	█	█		█		●		●			■	▲	█		▲	●
Shimba Hills		█								●	●		●	●	█					●					█			●
Sibiloi		●	●			●	●			●		●	●	●						■			●		●		●	●
Tsavo		█			█	▲	■		▲	●	█	■	●	●		█	█		■			■	●	█		▲	●
RWANDA																												
Akagera		█				■		█		●			●		●	●	●	■		●			■		█			●
Volcans	█												●								●							

Gazelle Pelzeln's	Gazelle Grant's	Gazelle Thompson's	Gerenuk	Bushbuck	Eland	Sitatunga	Mountain Nyala	Southern Nyala	Bongo	Greater Kudu	Lesser Kudu	Roan Antelope	Sable Antelope	Oryx	Lechwe Red & Black	Puku	Kob	Waterbuck	Reedbuck Bohor	Reedbuck Southern	Reedbuck Mountain	Pigmy Antelope	Klipspringer	Dikdik	Oribi	Stei buck	Suni	Impala	Hartebeest	Topi	Tsessebe	Wildebeest	Hunters Hartebeest
										■									■														
		■								●	■			▲				●					●	■					■				
				■			■												■														
				■								●																					
				■	■					●								●	■										●				
				■	■					■								●	■										■				
				■	■					■	●							●											●	●			
		■								●	■			■									●	■									
●		■	■	●										●				●						■	●								
●		■		●						●	●			●				●					●	■				●				
				●													●	■	■					■				■	■				
				●													▲	▲	■							▲		■					
				●													▲	▲	■			■				▲					▲		
			▲	●					▲									■	▲	■						■							
▲	▲	■	●	■	●						■			■				■	●	●			■		●		■	■			▲	
●			■															●	●					■	■	●		■	■				
			■																		●												
			■															▲	■	●			●	■	●		▲						
			■	●														■	●				●		●		●	●					
▲	▲	■	●	▲					●				●					▲	●				●	■	●	●	▲	▲	▲		▲		
●	■	●								■	■							■	●				●	●				■					
■	■	●																■					■					■					
				●					●																●								
			■	■					■									●	■		■												
▲	▲		■	▲														▲	■				●	■		●	●	▲	▲			■	
			■															●	■				●				●	●					
			■		▲																		●										
■		▲	●	●						■			■					■	●				●	■		●		■					
			■									●	▲					■	■				●			●		■					
■		■							●	●	●			▲																			
■	●	▲	●	■						●				▲				■					●	■				●	■			●	
			■										●					■	■						■		■						
			■																														

What to See and Where

COUNTRY / Parks or Reserves	Gorilla	Chimpanzee	Baboon	Gelada	Hamadryas	Aardwolf	Hyaena Striped	Hyaena Spotted	Jackal Simien	Jackal Black-Backed	Jackal Side-Striped	Cheetah	Leopard	Lion	Wild Dog	Elephant	Black Rhino	Hippo	Giant Forest Hog	Wart Hog	Bush Pig	Wild Ass	Common Zebra	Grevy's Zebra	Buffalo	Ibex	Giraffe	Grey Duiker
TANZANIA																												
Arusha			■				●	■		■	■		●	●	●	●				■	●		■		■		■	■
Gombe		▲	■					●					●					●		●	●							■
Katavi			■					■					●	●	●	●		■		■	●		■		●		●	●
Kilimanjaro			■					●			■		●	●	●	●				●	●				●			
Lake Manyara		▲				●	●	■		■	■		■	■	●	▲				■	●		■		■		●	
Mikumi			■				●	●			■		●	■	●	■				■	●		■		●		■	■
Ruaha			■				●	●		■	■	●	●	●	●	●				●			●				●	
Rubondo		●																●			●				■			■
Selous			■					■		■	■	●	■	■	●	■	●	▲	●	●	■				■		■	
Serengeti / Ngorongoro			■				●	▲		■	▲	●	▲	▲	▲	■		●		▲	●		▲		▲		▲	
Tarangire			■				●	●		■	■	■	■	■	●	■				■	●		■		■		■	■
MALAWI																												
Kasungu			■								■		●	●	●	■		●		■	●		■		■			
Lake Malawi			■								■		■	●				●			●		●					
Lengwe			■								■		■	●	●	●		●			●				●			
Liwonde			■								■		■	●	●	■		●			●				●			
Nyika			■								■		■	●	●	●		●			●				▲		●	
ZAMBIA																												
Isangano											■		●		●	●		●							●		●	●
Kafue			■								■		●	●	●	■	●	●		●	●		■		●			●
Kasanka			■								■		●	●	●	●		●			●				●			●
Lavushi/Manda			■								■		●	●	●			●			●				●			●
Liuwa Plains											■		●		●			●			●				●			●
Lochinvar		■				●					■		●	●		●					●							●
Lower Zambezi			■								■		●	●	●	●		●		●	●				●			●
Luambe			■								●		●	●	●	■		●		■	●		●		●			●
Luangwa North			■								■	■	●	■	■	■	■	●	▲	●	■		●		■		■	●
Luangwa South		▲									■	■	●	■	▲	■	▲	■	▲	●	■		●		■		●	
Lukusizi			■								■		●	●	■	■	■	●							●			
Lusenga			■								■		●		●	●		●			●				●			●
Mosi-oa-Tunya			■								●		●			●		●			●		●					●
Mweru Wantipa			■								●		●		●	●		●			●							●
Nsumbu			■					●					●	●	●	●		●			●				●			●
Nyika			■					●					●	●	●	●					●							●
Sioma Newezi			■					◼					●	●		●		●			●		●					●
West Lunga			■					●					●	●	●	●		●			●				●			●
Blue Lagoon			◼					■					●		●			●			●							●

Gazelle Pelzeln's	Gazelle Grant's	Gazelle Thompson's	Gerenuk	Bushbuck	Eland	Sitatunga	Mountain Nyala	Southern Nyala	Bongo	Greater Kudu	Lesser Kudu	Roan Antelope	Sable Antelope	Oryx	Lechwe Red & Black	Puku	Kob	Waterbuck	Reedbuck Bohor	Reedbuck Southern	Reedbuck Mountain	Pigmy Antelope	Klispringer	Dikdik	Oribi	Steinbuck	Suni	Impala	Hartebeest	Topi	Tsessebe	Wildebeest	Hunters Hartebeest
				■														●		●						●	●	●	●				
				■																													
				●								●				●		●	●	●				●	●	●		●	●	●			
				●						●								●	●		●					●	●	●	●				
				●														■	●				●			●		●	●				
				●								●	●			●		●	●														
				●						■		●	■					■	●	●			●	●	●			●	■				
				▲		■						●														●							
				●						■		●	●			●		■	●				●	●	●	●		●	●			■	
				●														■	●	●	●		●	■	●	●		●	■	▲		▲	
				●							●			●				●	●		●							●					
				●						■			●			■		●	●				●	●				●	■				
				●						●								●	●				●	●									
				●				■		●			●					●	●					●	●								
				●						●		▲	▲					●	●					●	●								
				●						●		▲						●	●				●						●				
				●		●									●											●		●					
				●		●				■		●	■		●	●		●	●				●	●				●	■			●	
				●		●												●	●									●	●	●			
				●		●						●	●				●	●	●			●						●	●	●			
				●						●			●			●		●	●				●					●	●			●	
				●		●									▲			●	●				●	●				●	●				
				●						●		●	●					●	●			●						●	●			●	
				●						●		●	●					●	●				●					■	■			●	
				■						■		●	■		■			■	●			●						■	■			●	
				■						▲		●	■		▲			■	●			●						■	■			■	
				●						■		●	●		■			●	●									●					
				●								●	●			●		●	●		●							●					
				●																			●					●					
				●								●	●			●		●	●				●		●			●	●				
	●			●		●						●	●			●		●	●				●			●		●	●			●	
				●						■		●	●		■			●	●									●	●		▲	●	
	●			●		●						●	●			●		●	●			●			●			●	●				
				●											▲			●	●						●				●				

Above: Elephant sleep lying down. Adults normally recline in the early hours of the morning before dawn, while youngsters in the protection of a herd do so regardless of the time of day.

Walker built a lodge in a big tree overlooking a water-hole in the Aberdare forest. By placing salt — which the animals crave — near the water, it soon became exceptional for game viewing. The original Treetops has been replaced with a larger lodge on stilts and augmented, higher up the salient, with another similar facility — The Ark.

Still-watching, as developed by Treetops and The Ark and also a feature of Malawi's Lengwe Park — is particularly suited to forest, woodland and thicket environments where visibility is restricted. Bringing animals to the watchers, rather than the other way about, it is the best way to see shy animals such as bongo and the southern nyala. It is less tiring than driving hither and thither over rough roads, and it is gentle on the environment.

Although the Aberdare Park gained its initial popularity from Treetops, as visitors increased, the animals became accustomed to vehicles and the roads and tracks through the park's forested salient offer good game viewing. Elephant, buffalo, rhino, giant forest hog, and bushbuck are commonly seen in the grassy glades. On the high, open moorlands, visitors may leave their vehicles and fish for trout or just enjoy the spectacular scenery.

Access to the Aberdares is by road from both east and west. There are good hotels near the eastern entrance in Mweiga and Nyeri. Visitors are accommodated overnight at The Ark and Treetops, though advanced booking is essential, and there are several campsites both in the forested salient and on the moorlands.

Rwanda's **Volcanoes National Park** is unique for its mountain gorillas. Several troops have been conditioned to the close proximity of people, and the authorities now take visitors right up to these magnificent primates.

Without the protection of a vehicle, sitting within feet of these immensely powerful and potentially dangerous animals provides a memorable thrill. Just as memorable is meeting animals that, genetically, are so close to us. Few experiences can both emphasize how much an animal man is, yet how different he has become to all others. Visiting Rwanda's gorillas must rank as one of the most extraordinary wildlife experiences in the world.

Because the gorillas are few, the number of visitors is limited. Arrangements have to be made through Rwanda's tourism and national parks office in Kigali.

There are only two lowland rain forests within Eastern Africa's national parks and reserves system. One is the **Maramagambo** forest in Uganda's **Queen Elizabeth National Park.** It contains Bate's pygmy antelope — the smallest of all the antelope — and red colobus monkeys, as well as chimpanzees. This forest is, as yet, undeveloped relative to the savannahs around it. A track gives vehicles access, but the forest residents are shy and unaccustomed to people.

The second lowland forest is **Kakamega** in western Kenya. Only proclaimed a national reserve in May 1985, it is still somewhat undeveloped. Lying in densely-settled farmland, Kakamega has no Big Game other than a few secretive leopards and bushbuck. It is, however, still well-endowed with smaller representatives of western rain forest fauna. The birds, in particular, attract many bird watchers. But there are also forest guenon monkeys — red-tailed and de Brazza's — and, recently, the potamogale, a rare otter shrew, was discovered here.

The only residential facility is an ex-Forest Department rest-house that can be used on a self-help basis, or visitors can camp.

Outside of the national park systems, lowland forests are well represented and protected in Uganda's Forest Reserves, the best known of which is the 500-square-kilometre **Budongo Forest.** Relict lowland forest patches also occur in Kenya's **Shimba Hills National Reserve,** close to Mombasa. However, while these patches are well worth a visit from any ornithologist or botanist, the reserve is better known for its sable antelope.

Though the grassy glades and hill tops in Shimba are not normal sable habitat (miombo woodland is more characteristic), they are perhaps more easily seen here than anywhere else in their entire African range. Not far from the many luxury hotels in Mombasa and along the coast to the south of the port, the Shimba Hills Reserve is second only to Nairobi National Park in the quantity and variety of accommodation within easy reach. A new 'Treetops'-type lodge that opened in the Shimba Hills in 1987 provides enjoyable game watching.

At the other end of the vegetational spectrum from the forests are the arid zone parks and reserves. Low rainfall limits plant productivity and ensures that animal densities are generally low throughout the 'badlands' in the Horn of Africa. Game viewers will never see the numbers of animals that exist in the higher or moister climates.

In Kenya, two national parks — **Tsavo** and **Sibiloi** — and three reserves — **Samburu, Shaba,** and **Marsabit** — conserve samples of these habitats. All are atypical of arid country in that they contain supplies of permanent water. Tsavo, Samburu, and Shaba are bisected or lie on perennial rivers — Sibiloi runs along the shore of Lake Turkana, and Marsabit has the crown of Marsabit Mountain as a source of permanent water.

In Ethiopia the **Awash** and **Yangudi Rassa National Parks** conserve arid ecosystems. But they, too, lie on a permanent river — the Awash. Thus in both Kenya's and Ethiopia's dry land parks, animals attracted to water become visible in uncharacteristically high numbers for such low rainfall areas — a bonus for visitors.

Of Kenya's and Ethiopia's seven arid land parks and reserves referred to, and taking accessibility, accommodation, and easily-seen animals as criteria, Samburu (165 square kilometres) on the banks of Kenya's northern Ewaso Ngiro River offers the best value for money. The range of species contains the stalwarts — elephant, rhino (which may have been exterminated by poachers), buffalo, hippo, lion, leopard, and cheetah. It also contains gerenuk — or, as it is also known, the giraffe-necked gazelle — dik-dik, lesser kudu, Grevy's zebra, and vulturine guinea fowl, all of whom are very much Horn of Africa species.

Samburu is hot and dry. It is well served with tracks and offers good game viewing along the banks of the Ewaso Ngiro. Accessible by air and road, it has one 139-bed luxury lodge, another with 79 beds adjacent to the reserve and three campsites.

Tsavo, Kenya's largest park (20,821 square kilometres), has the same range of species as Samburu except Grevy's zebra. Small numbers of them have been introduced into the park along with another rare animal — Hunter's antelope — which occurs in no other park. Though both species now exist in small numbers, they may be too few to guarantee survival.

Tsavo is administered in two sections, Tsavo East and Tsavo West. Of the two, wetter and more productive Tsavo West offers better game viewing. It contains a section of the scenically beautiful Chyulu Hills — a geologically new volcanic range whose forested crowns rise to over 2,000 metres above sea level. It contains two luxury lodges, both of which have man-made water-holes to attract animals for night viewing. In addition, there are two self-service lodges and several camping sites in the park. Close by the park boundaries there are four more lodges. The park is particularly well served with roads.

Tsavo East is drier, flatter and altogether more barren than Tsavo West. Visitors may traverse the whole width of the park without seeing any large mammal. Yet for all this, it has a strange fascination, imparting the same sense of loneliness as the open ocean. The northern half of Tsavo East is closed to the public, but the southern section is well served with roads, has one luxury lodge and a self-help lodge, together with camping sites. Both Tsavo East and West are also accessible by air.

Sibiloi National Park, remote and inaccessible, is for the intrepid, self-sufficient traveller. Those of this ilk will be well rewarded by the wild, hostile environment, the numerous grazers, the crocodiles and bird life that live along the lake edge.

Ethiopia's Awash National Park is scenically rather similar to Kenya's Samburu, but there are fewer mammal species — no elephant, buffalo, or common zebra, for example. There are, however, Grevy's zebra and the hamadryas — the sacred baboon of ancient Egypt. With a low visitor volume the animals are shy compared to those in Samburu and Tsavo in Kenya. Like most of the dry land parks, the Awash is rich in birds. It is also accessible by air and a good tarmac road.

Further down the Awash River, deep in the Danakil dry lands is undeveloped **Yangudi Rassa National Park.** Inaccessible and not open to visitors, it is the only national park in Africa that has a population of the Somali ass, wild forebear of the domestic donkey.

Some of Eastern Africa's parks and reserves have spectacular scenery, and nowhere is this more true than in the mountain parks. The great altitudes produce panoramic vistas; vast distances to horizons rimmed with blue highlands hundreds of miles away. The great peaks may be snow-crowned, the lesser summits are capped with cold, brown moorlands, and nearly all wear capes of deep green forest. Here and there the more austere landscapes may be riven by stark gorges or skirted by cliffs.

However, all these grand highland scenes share a drawback — they are likely to be covered with cloud and mist for extended periods during the wet seasons. Prospective visitors to Eastern Africa's mountains should ensure that trips coincide with dry seasons.

There are three permanent snow fields in Eastern Africa: Ruwenzori, Kilimanjaro, and Kenya, all on or within three degrees of the Equator. Of them, the Ruwenzori snow field is the most extensive. Yet it is the least frequently seen as, lying in a very high rainfall zone, the Ruwenzori peaks are in dense cloud for ten months of the year. They are only visible with reasonable certainty in January and February.

Kilimanjaro's snow field is the most accessible of the three and — despite the effects of altitude, which can be severe — is within walking reach of most healthy adults. Mount Kenya is a climbers' mountain and, like all which offer a worthy challenge, takes an annual toll of lives from those who are careless or unfortunate. It and the neighbouring Aberdare Mountains have long offered fine fly fishing for trout.

Perhaps the most rugged and impressive scenery in Eastern Africa is in the **Simien Mountain National Park** of Ethiopia. The lofty Amhara plateau falls thousands of metres in a series of spectacular cliffs and gorges to lowlands far below. The visitor's bonus in the Simien is that the strange, leonine gelada baboon will almost certainly be seen and, with luck, so will Walia ibex and Simien jackal.

More gentle, but equally lofty, the **Bale Mountains National Park** across the Rift Valley offers different, but no less impressive scenery. Instead of the Walia ibex, there is another readily-seen wildlife bonus that is found nowhere else — the mountain nyala, a shaggy, regal, high-altitude look-alike of the greater kudu.

The Bale Mountains are also becoming known for excellent trout fishing and are a regular venue for anglers from other countries. They may well become an international fly-fishermen's Mecca, for there can be few more attractive or exotic environments in which to practise this sport. The Bale Mountains are readily accessible through arrangement with the National Tourist Organization.

Another highland park deserving mention

is Malawi's **Nyika National Park.** Like the case of sable antelope in Kenya's Shimba Hills, roan antelope are found in Nyika, an atypical roan habitat. In their normal woodland environments they are not easy to see. Yet, in Nyika they are out in open grassland — both visible and tame.

Other wildlife includes zebra, eland, reedbuck, duiker, hartebeest, lion, leopard, cheetah, and wild dog. They are not numerous, however, and apart from the roan, the Nyika would rank low on any list of parks to visit to see wildlife. Yet a temperate climate and rolling scenery — wide vistas eastward across the great Lake Malawi to the Livingstone Mountains in Tanzania, or westward across the endless Zambian plateau — combined with the prospect of trout fishing in several of the icy streams that cross the park, make it an attractive holiday resort.

Aside from the great wildlife and scenic parks, several other sanctuaries offer unique attractions. Perhaps the most unusual potential is **Lake Malawi National Park.** Underwater photography, brilliantly-coloured fish, and crystal-clear, warm water usually conjure up images of coral gardens, Jacques Cousteau and the Great Barrier Reef. Yet, deep in Africa, Lake Malawi offers similar opportunities in its fresh waters.

Isolated from competitors, the lake's cichlid fish have radiated out into more than 400 hundred species. Of them, the rock-loving 'mbuna' haplochromids have become as diverse and colourful as any coral reef community.

For those who enjoy diving and water sports, Lake Malawi is an attractive venue. Combined with a visit to see big game in Kasungu and a few days' trout fishing in Nyika, it offers a pleasant holiday.

Bird watchers are of many minds as to which of Eastern Africa's conservation areas is the best. Birds are abundant everywhere — both the drab miombo woodlands and the harsh arid lands have many interesting and colourful species. Indeed, where such environments include rivers with associated gallery forests, there are more bird species than there are in the grasslands that support the more spectacular mammal assemblages.

Two habitats seem to catch the ornithologists' interest more than other areas. The first is the lowland rain forest of Uganda and western Kenya. Uganda's **Budongo Forest** is the best example — not only does it contain many western forest forms, but it is exceptionally well served with motorable tracks that give access to all the various vegetation types. Kenya's small **Kakamega Forest National Park** is a second best, not for a particularly large number of forest bird species, but for its accessibility.

The shallow lakes in the eastern Rift Valley are the second of the habitats of particular interest to bird watchers. And of these, two stand out — **Lakes Nakuru** and **Naivasha** — both of which are in Kenya. The abundant water birds are easily seen — there are many resident species — and these are augmented between October and April every year by a host of migrant waders from Eurasia.

The ornithological spectacle of the entire region is the flamingo host that moves up and down the Rift Valley's saline lakes. Often this population of millions concentrates on Lake Natron in Tanzania. At other times it may be further north in Ethiopia. Yet, when the water levels are right, Lake Nakuru National Park seems to be their base of choice. Several million birds massed along the shore line is magnificent and quite as spectacular, in its own way, as the Serengeti wildebeest migration.

The region also has several marine national parks to conserve coral reefs and gardens. Of them, one in the Red Sea about Ethiopia's Dhalac archipelago, is the best zoologically. However, it is not easy to get to. The most accessible are Kenya's three marine parks. The tourist industry along the coast is highly developed and can provide everything from training and equipment for beginners to equipping the most experienced divers. And, together with these facilities, there is a range of accommodation that will suit millionaires down to the most simple bed and breakfast services.

Overleaf: Sunset — that golden no-man's hour when diurnal life is settling down and the animals of the shadows stir and stretch in preparation for the night.

Above: Leopard. Overleaf: The highest point of Bale Mountain National Park, Ethiopia – 4,377 metres (14,360 feet). Following pages: The colourful world beneath Africa's Indian Ocean.

Opposite: Red-fronted barbet, *Lybius diadematus*. Above: Red-headed weaver, *Anaplectes rubriceps*. Overleaf: Verreaux's eagle owl, *Bubo lacteus*.

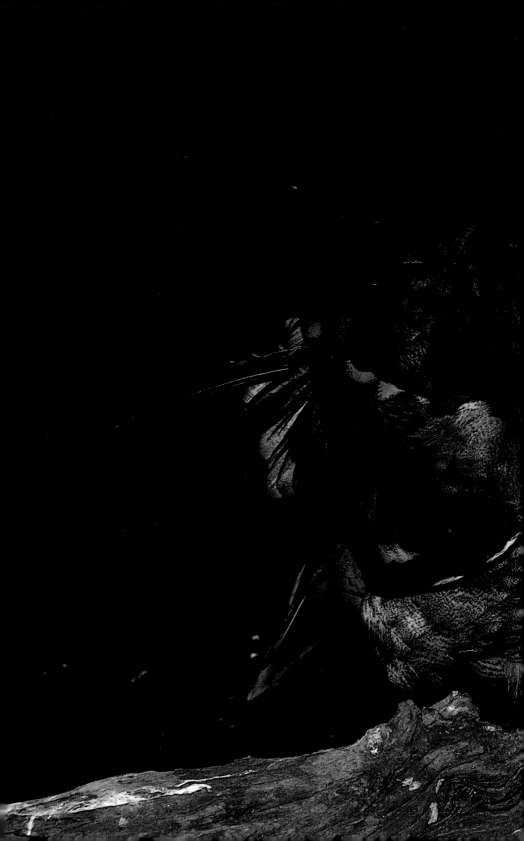

Above: Highland gorilla of East Africa. Opposite: Mountain elephant. Overleaf: Wilde-beeste migrating from the Serengeti. Following pages: African sunrise and sundown.

PART FIVE: APPENDICES

APPENDIX I Tour Agencies and Operators in Eastern Africa

KENYA

Aardvark Safaris Ltd
PO Box 69496
Nairobi, Kenya
Tel. 331718, 334863

Abercrombie & Kent Ltd
PO Box 59749
Nairobi, Kenya
Tel. 334955/6/7

Across Africa Safaris Ltd
PO Box 49420
Nairobi, Kenya
Tel. 332744

African Tours & Hotels Ltd
PO Box 30471
Nairobi, Kenya
Tel. 336858, 336165/6

Airland Tours & Travel Ltd
PO Box 70509
Nairobi, Kenya
Tel. 338869, 339411

Afro Aviation Services Ltd
PO Box 39422
Nairobi, Kenya
Tel. 26944, 336139

Alfaraj Ltd
PO Box 44444
Nairobi, Kenya
Tel. 27989

Alick Roberts Safaris Ltd
PO Box 24405
Nairobi, Kenya
Tel. 891338

Andrew James Ltd
PO Box 24874
Nairobi, Kenya
Tel. 882147, 882625

Archer's Mombasa Ltd
PO Box 84618
Mombasa, Kenya
Tel. 25362, 311884

Archer's Tours & Travel Ltd
PO Box 40097
Nairobi, Kenya
Tel. 331825

Arrows Cars Ltd
PO Box 46808
Nairobi, Kenya
Tel. 24668, 25673

Avenue Motors Ltd
PO Box 83697
Mombasa, Kenya
Tel. 315111, 25162

Balloon Safaris Ltd
PO Box 43747
Nairobi, Kenya
Tel. 338041

Bankco Tours Travel
& Car Hire
PO Box 11536
Nairobi, Kenya
Tel. 26736, 336144

Baringo Bird & Game Safaris
PO Box 1375
Nakuru, Kenya
Tel. Molo 51Y4

Bashir Safaris Ltd
PO Box 42562
Nairobi, Kenya
Tel. 29600

Bateleur Safaris Ltd
PO Box 40627
Nairobi, Kenya
Tel. 27048

Best Camping Tours
PO Box 40223
Nairobi, Kenya
Tel. 28091, 27203

Big Five Tours
& Safaris Ltd
PO Box 10367
Nairobi, Kenya
Tel. 29803, 28352, 25167

Bill Winter Safaris Ltd
PO Box 24871
Nairobi, Kenya
Tel. 882526

Bookings Ltd
PO Box 56707
Nairobi, Kenya
Tel. 25255, 21845, 336570

Bruce Safaris Ltd
PO Box 40662
Nairobi, Kenya
Tel. 27311

Bushbuck Adventures Ltd
PO Box 67449
Nairobi, Kenya
Tel. 60437, 728737

Car Hire Services Ltd
PO Box 42304
Nairobi, Kenya
Tel. 22813, 25165, 28799

Central Rent a Car
PO Box 49439
Nairobi, Kenya
Tel. 22888, 332296

Centrex Tours & Travels Ltd
PO Box 41830
Nairobi, Kenya
Tel. 332267, 337296

Cheli & Peacock Ltd
PO Box 39806
Nairobi, Kenya
Tel. (0154) 22170

Coast Car Hire & Tours Ltd
PO Box 90789
Mombasa, Kenya
Tel. 311752/225, 24891

Coast Car Hire (Nbi) Ltd
PO Box 56707
Nairobi, Kenya
Tel. 20365, 21845, 25255

Concorde Car Hire
PO Box 25053
Nairobi, Kenya
Tel. 747216, 48027

Crossway Car Hire & Tours
PO Box 10228
Nairobi, Kenya
Tel. 23949, 20848

David Read Safaris Ltd
PO Box 183
Kitale, Kenya

Desojin Ltd
PO Box 74612
Nairobi, Kenya
Tel. 339780

E A Ornithological
Safaris Ltd
PO Box 48019
Nairobi, Kenya
Tel. 48772

E A Wildlife Safaris Ltd
PO Box 43747
Nairobi, Kenya
Tel. 27217, 331228

El Tome Safaris Ltd
PO Box 10243
Nairobi, Kenya
Tel. 23133

EMM International Ltd
PO Box 48017
Nairobi, Kenya
Tel. 331801, 27883

Eric Risley Tours & Safaris
PO Box 24751
Nairobi, Kenya
Tel. 891370

Flame Tree Safaris Ltd
PO Box 9
Nanyuki, Kenya
Tel. Nanyuki 2053

Flamingo Tours Ltd
PO Box 44899
Nairobi, Kenya
Tel. 28961/2/3, 331360

Flamingo Tours (Coast) Ltd
PO Box 83321
Mombasa, Kenya
Tel. 331978/9

Four by Four (4x4) Safaris Ltd
PO Box 24397
Nairobi, Kenya
Tel. 21065, 332323

Franz Lang Safaris Ltd
PO Box 42026
Nairobi, Kenya
Tel. 62670, 891745

Funga Safaris Ltd
PO Box 41558
Nairobi, Kenya
Tel. 337751, 337422

Furaha Travel
PO Box 41641
Nairobi, Kenya
Tel. 336686, 26593

Galana Game & Ranching Ltd
PO Box 76
Malindi, Kenya
Tel. 25853

Galu Safaris
PO Box 99456
Mombasa, Kenya
Tel. 314226

Gametrackers (K) Ltd
PO Box 62042
Nairobi, Kenya
Tel. 335825

General Tours & Safaris Ltd
PO Box 30585
Nairobi, Kenya
Tel. 22303

Glen Cottar Safaris Ltd
PO Box 44626
Nairobi, Kenya
Tel. 558331, 558122

Glory Car Hire Tours Ltd
PO Box 66969
Nairobi, Kenya
Tel. 25024, 24428

Grand Africa Safaris
PO Box 33189
Nairobi, Kenya
Tel. 724217

Gupta Sea Tours Ltd
PO Box 83451
Mombasa, Kenya
Tel. 311477, 25734

Gyro Travel Agency Ltd
PO Box 53364
Nairobi, Kenya
Tel. 335903

Habib's Cars Ltd
PO Box 48095
Nairobi, Kenya
Tel. 20463, 23816

H.A.T. Ltd
PO Box 55182
Nairobi, Kenya
Tel. 24079, 728002

Haya Safaris Africa Ltd
PO Box 73
Malindi, Kenya
Tel. 20374

Highways Car Hire
Safaris Ltd
PO Box 84787
Mombasa, Kenya
Tel. 316490/3

Highways Car Hire
Safaris Ltd
PO Box 30984
Nairobi, Kenya
Tel. 340684

Homeland Travel and
Tours Ltd
PO Box 57571
Nairobi, Kenya
Tel. 339151, 22125

Inside Africa Safaris Ltd
PO Box 59767
Nairobi, Kenya
Tel. 337154, 23304

Intasun Holidays
PO Box 42977
Nairobi, Kenya
Tel. 340161

Intercontinental Tours
& Travels Ltd
PO Box 49473
Nairobi, Kenya
Tel. 339518

Intra Safaris Ltd
PO Box 50096
Nairobi, Kenya
Tel. 29961

Intra Safaris Ltd
PO Box 71
Ukunda, Kenya
Tel. Diani 2118

Ivory Safaris (1976) Ltd
PO Box 74609
Nairobi, Kenya
Tel. 26623, 26808

Jet Travel Ltd
PO Box 58805
Nairobi, Kenya
Tel. 332544, 330144

J.H. Safaris Ltd.
PO Box 42238
Nairobi, Kenya
Tel. 28168, 334112/77

Kenebco Tours & Travel Ltd
PO Box 20640
Nairobi, Kenya
Tel. 27203, 337679

Kenya Photographic
Safaris Ltd.
PO Box 25253
Nairobi, Kenya
Tel. 569870, 566223

Kenya Rent a Car (AVIS)
PO Box 49795
Nairobi, Kenya
Tel. 336794, 334317/8

Kenya Mystery Tours Ltd
PO Box 30442
Nairobi, Kenya
Tel. 336876, 21808, 27101

Kenya Wildlife Trails Ltd
PO Box 44687
Nairobi, Kenya
Tel. 28960

Ker & Downey Safaris Ltd
PO Box 41822
Nairobi, Kenya
Tel. 556466, 556373

Kimbla Kenya Ltd
PO Box 40089
Nairobi, Kenya
Tel. 337892

Kuldip's Touring Co Ltd
PO Box 82662
Mombasa, Kenya
Tel. 25928, 24067, 26407

Leisure Car Hire Tours
& Safaris
PO Box 84902
Mombasa, Kenya
Tel. 24704, 314846

Let's Go Travel
PO Box 60342
Nairobi, Kenya
Tel. 29539/40, 340332

Lofty Safaris Ltd
PO Box 80629
Mombasa, Kenya
Tel. 314397, 20241

Marajani Tours Ltd
PO Box 86103
Mombasa, Kenya
Tel. 314935, 312703

Mashariki Tour & Hire Co.
Ltd
PO Box 30179
Nairobi, Kenya
Tel. 558144, 554366

Mathews & Roberts Safaris
PO Box 47448
Nairobi, Kenya
Tel. 882559

Menno Travel Service
PO Box 40444
Nairobi, Kenya
Tel. 333051, 334927

Michaelides Safaris Ltd
PO Box 48010
Nairobi, Kenya
Tel. 340196

Mini Cabs & Tours Ltd
PO Box 43374
Nairobi, Kenya
Tel. 336138, 20743

Mongoose Tours & Safaris
PO Box 70192
Nairobi, Kenya
Tel. 20048, 336803

Mumbiastros Safaris Ltd
PO Box 11366
Nairobi, Kenya
Tel. 21171

New Horizon Travel
Agency Ltd
PO Box 40193
Nairobi, Kenya
Tel. 338837, 22416

Nilestar Tours (Int) Ltd
PO Box 42291
Nairobi, Kenya
Tel. 28941

Njambi Tours Ltd
PO Box 30618
Nairobi, Kenya
Tel. 331762, 335550

Oak Tours & Travel
PO Box 32846
Nairobi, Kenya
Tel. 21399, 21981

Olechugu Safaris Ltd
PO Box 295
Nanyuki, Kenya
Tel. Timau 24

Orbit Travel Ltd
PO Box 18509
Nairobi, Kenya
Tel. 21498

Pan African Travel
Organization
PO Box 4420
Nairobi, Kenya
Tel. 333281

A Pelizzoli Safaris
PO Box 48287
Nairobi, Kenya
Tel. 331231

Percival Tours Ltd
PO Box 43987
Nairobi, Kenya
Tel. 331667, 27977, 23594

Perry Mason Safaris Ltd
PO Box 49655
Nairobi, Kenya
Tel. 882249, 564107

Pollman's Tours &
Safaris Ltd
PO Box 84198
Mombasa, Kenya
Tel. 20703, 312565/6/7

Pollman's Tours &
Safaris Ltd
PO Box 45895
Nairobi, Kenya
Tel. 27250, 29792

Private Safaris (EA) Ltd.
PO Box 45205
Nairobi, Kenya
Tel. 337104

Resident's Travel Den Ltd
PO Box 1496
Nairobi, Kenya
Tel. 743415/4

Rhino Safaris Ltd
PO Box 48023
Nairobi, Kenya
Tel. 28102, 25419, 332372

Richard Bonham Safaris
PO Box 24133
Nairobi, Kenya
Tel. 882521

Robin Hurt Safaris Ltd
PO Box 24988
Nairobi, Kenya
Tel. 882826/2026/2086

Ross and Young Safaris
PO Box 57046
Nairobi, Kenya
Tel. 338041

Safari Camp Services Ltd
PO Box 48023
Nairobi, Kenya
Tel. 28936

Safaris Unlimited (A) Ltd
PO Box 20138
Nairobi, Kenya
Tel. 332132

Safari Travel Kenya Ltd
PO Box 31120
Nairobi, Kenya
Tel. 22290/1, 23141

Safariworld Kenya Ltd
PO Box 56803
Nairobi, Kenya
Tel. 20940

Sapieha Tours & Safaris
PO Box 48582
Nairobi, Kenya
Tel. 512283

Scenic Safaris Ltd
PO Box 49188
Nairobi, Kenya
Tel. 26526, 20830

Sea Sports & Safaris (K) Ltd
PO Box 24959
Nairobi, Kenya
Tel. 882594

Senator Travel Service
PO Box 46654
Nairobi, Kenya
Tel. 2410, 22855

Shimba Tourist Service Ltd
PO Box 41942
Nairobi, Kenya
Tel. 501366, 501488

Silverspear Tours Ltd
PO Box 40500
Nairobi, Kenya
Tel. 334722, 556688

Somak Travel Ltd
PO Box 48495
Nairobi, Kenya
Tel. 332346, 20557

Southerncross Safaris Ltd
PO Box 48362
Nairobi, Kenya
Tel. 26069, 21030

Special Camping Safaris Ltd
PO Box 51512
Nairobi, Kenya
Tel. 338325

Star Travel and Tours Ltd
PO Box 48225
Nairobi, Kenya
Tel. 26996, 20165

Sunny Safaris Ltd
PO Box 74495
Nairobi, Kenya
Tel. 27659

Supersonic Travel &
Tours Ltd
PO Box 22839
Nairobi, Kenya
Tel. 334131, 27956

Swanair Travel &
Safaris Ltd
PO Box 43502
Nairobi, Kenya
Tel. 21314, 22379

Texcal House
Service Station Ltd
PO Box 49473
Nairobi, Kenya
Tel. 331327, 330787

Thorn Tree Safaris Ltd
PO Box 42475
Nairobi, Kenya
Tel. 26529

Tippett's Safaris (K) Ltd.
PO Box 43806
Nairobi, Kenya
Tel. 332132

Tor Allan Safaris
PO Box 41959
Nairobi, Kenya
Tel. 891190

Trade & Travel Ltd
PO Box 14365
Nairobi, Kenya
Tel. 335039

Trans-African Guides Ltd
PO Box 49583
Nairobi, Kenya
Tel. 891172

Transworld Safaris (K) Ltd
PO Box 44690
Nairobi, Kenya
Tel. 333129, 29579/70

The Travel Mart Ltd
PO Box 46085
Nairobi, Kenya
Tel. 22508, 27637

Travel Promoters Ltd
PO Box 14365
Nairobi, Kenya
Tel. 749473/5/7

Tropical Ice Ltd
PO Box 57341
Nairobi, Kenya
Tel. 23649

Tropical Land Tours
and Safaris
PO Box 14874
Nairobi, Kenya
Tel. 749259

Turkana Safaris Kenya Ltd
PO Box 99300
Mombasa, Kenya
Tel. 21065, 21937

Twiga Car Hire & Tours
PO Box 14365
Nairobi, Kenya
Tel. 337330, 337338

Ulf Aschan
PO Box 44715
Nairobi, Kenya
Tel. 337312, 330590

United Touring Company
Ltd
PO Box 42196
Nairobi, Kenya
Tel. 331960

Universal Safari Tours Ltd
PO Box 49312
Nairobi, Kenya
Tel. 21446, 339818

Vacational Tours & Travel
Ltd
PO Box 44401
Nairobi, Kenya
Tel. 338655, 29470

Visit Africa Ltd
PO Box 59565
Nairobi, Kenya
Tel. 23257, 20838

Waku Waku Safaris Ltd
PO Box 58989
Nairobi, Kenya
Tel. 729116

Westminster Safaris Ltd
PO Box 57046
Nairobi, Kenya
Tel. 338041/45

Wheels Car Hire Ltd
PO Box 47173
Nairobi, Kenya
Tel. 336038, 25103

Yare Safaris Ltd
PO Box 63006
Nairobi, Kenya
Tel. 337392

Zirkuli Expeditions Ltd
PO Box 34548
Nairobi, Kenya
Tel. 23949, 20848

Zodiac Travel Ltd
PO Box 46851
Nairobi, Kenya
Tel. 23148, 22789

TANZANIA
Bushtrekker Safaris
Box 3173
Arusha, Tanzania
Tel. 3241/3727
Telex: 42125

Bobby Tours
Box 716
Arusha, Tanzania
Tel. 3490

Executive Travel
Box 6162
Arusha, Tanzania
Tel. 7199
Telex: 42058

Kearsley's Tanzania
Tanzania
Telex: 41014

Laitolya Tours & Safaris

Lions Safari-International
Box 999
Arusha, Tanzania
Tel. 3181/6422
Telex: 42219

Range Safaris
Box 9
Arusha, Tanzania
Tel. 3074/3023
Telex: 42107

Sable Safari & Tours Ltd
Box 7145
Arusha, Tanzania
Tel. 3181
Telex: 42121

Savannah Tours
Box 2033
Dar es Salaam, Tanzania
Tel. 25753
Telex: 41652

Sean Travel Tours
Box 1054
Arusha, Tanzania
Tel. 6978
Telex: 42006

Sengo Safaris
Box 207
Arusha, Tanzania
Tel. 3181
Telex: 42006

Shah Tours & Travel
Box 1821
Moshi, Tanzania
Tel. 2370

Simba Safaris
Box 1207
Arusha, Tanzania
Tel. 3509/3600
Telex: 42095

State Travel Service
Box 1369
Arusha, Tanzania
Tel. 3113/3300
Telex: 42138

State Travel Service
Box 5023
Dar es Salaam, Tanzania
Tel. 29291
Telex: 41061

Takims Holidays
Box 2035
Dar es Salaam, Tanzania
Tel. 25691-3
Telex: 42351

Tanzania Game Trackers Ltd
Box 2782
Arusha, Tanzania
Tel. 7700/6986

Tracks Travel
Box 142
Arusha, Tanzania
Tel. 142

Wildersun Safaris
Box 93
Arusha, Tanzania
Tel. 3880
Telex: 42021

Zanzibar Tourist Corporation
Box 216 Zanzibar, Tanzania
Tel. 32344
Telex: 57144

UGANDA

Uganda Tours & Travel Ltd,
Uganda Tourist
Development Corporation,
Hotel Equatoria,
84-86 Bombo Road,
PO Box 7211,
Kampala, Uganda
Tel. 259596/259598
Telex: 61150

Air Associates Travel
Bureau Ltd.

Concorde Tours &
Travel Safari Ltd.

Entebbe Tours & Travel
Co-op Soc. Ltd.

Hippo Tours & Travel Ltd.
International Tours
& Travel Ltd.

Leisure Tours Ltd.
Mbale News and Travel
Agency

Orbital Tours & Travel

Quick Tours & Travel

Shining Star Tours

S.M. Tours & Travel

Spear Touring Safaris

Tropical Tours Ltd.

Uganda Touring Co. Ltd.

V.I.P. Tours & Travel Ltd.

ETHIOPIA

Ethiopian Tourism
Commission
PO Box 2183
Addis Ababa, Ethiopia
Tel. 15-98-79, 44-74-70
Telex: 21067 ETC

National Tour Operation
(NTO)
PO Box 5709
Addis Ababa, Ethiopia
Tel. 15-29-55, 15-91-86
Telex: 21370

Ethiopian Tourism and
Trading Corporation (ETTC)
PO Box 5640
Addis Ababa, Ethiopia
Tel. 18-06-41
Telex: 21411

Ethiopian Hotels
Corporation (EHC)
PO Box 1263
Addis Ababa, Ethiopia
Tel. 15-27-00
Telex: 21067

Ethiopia Wildlife
Conservation Organization
(EWCO)
PO Box 386
Addis Ababa, Ethiopia
Tel. 44-59-70, 15-44-36
Telegram: 'WILDGAME'

Ethiopian Airlines (EAL)
PO Box 1755
Addis Ababa, Ethiopia
Tel. 18-22-22
Telex: 21012 ETHAIR

Ethiopian Airlines
85-87 Jermyn Street
London SW1Y 6JD, England
Tel. 01-839-1663

Ethiopian Airlines
Kaiserstrasse 33
D-6000 Frankfurt/Main
West Germany
Tel. 069-250077

Ethiopian Airlines
405 Lexington Avenue
New York, NY 10174, USA
Tel. 212-869-0095

ZAMBIA

Africa Bound Holidays
Farmers House, Cairo Road
PO Box 31567
Lusaka, Zambia
Tel. 216509/218080
Ext. 22/38/42

Anderson Travel
PO Box 31753
Lusaka, Zambia
Tel. 215234
Telex: ZA 43880

Andrews Travel and Safaris
1st Floor Chester House
Cairo Road
PO Box 31993
Lusaka, Zambia
Tel. 216409
Telex: ZA 40104/40450

Big Five Travel and Tours
Cairo Road
PO Box 33246
Lusaka, Zambia
Tel. 216118/216052
Telex: ZA 40091

Big Game Safaris Ltd.
PO Box 35813
Lusaka, Zambia
Tel. 214584

Bonar Travel
Provident House
Obote Avenue
PO Box 21211
Kitwe, Zambia
Tel. 215789

Bonar Travel
Electra House
Cairo Road
PO Box 33876
Lusaka, Zambia
Tel. 214008/44216
Telex: ZA 45370

Bonar Travel
Buteko House, Buteko
Avenue
PO Box 70631
Ndola, Zambia
Tel. 4211
Telex: ZA 3440

Busanga Travel & Tours
Chester House, Cairo Rd
PO Box 31322/30984
Lusaka, Zambia
Tel. 217817/21199
Telex: ZA 40009

Chinzombo Safari Lodge
C/O Save the Rhino Trust
Woodlands, T.G. Travel Ltd,
& Andrews Travel & Safaris
Lusaka, Zambia

Chunga Safaris and Tours
Lusaka Hotel Building
(First Floor)
PO Box 31010
Lusaka, Zambia
Tel. 212028
Telex: ZA 44230

Eagle Travel
PO Box 10808
Chililabombwe, Zambia
Tel. 313948
Telex: ZA 54120

Eagle Travel
PO Box 267
Chipata, Zambia
Tel. 21394

Eagle Travel and Tours
Bwafwano House
PO Box 10808
Kitwe, Zambia
Tel. 21948/313094
Telex: ZA 50200

Eagle Travel
PO Box 60451
Livingstone, Zambia
Tel. 510090/511162
Telex: ZA 24180

Eagle Travel
PO Box 90393
Luanshya, Zambia
Tel. 510090/511162
Telex: ZA 56

Eagle Travel & Tours
Head Office
Findeco House, Cairo Road
PO Box 33530
Lusaka, Zambia
Tel. 214916/212797
Telex: ZA 42670

Eagle Travel & Tours
Permanent House
Cairo Road
PO Box 35530
Lusaka, Zambia
Tel. 216857/217540
Telex: ZA 40420

Eagle Travel
PO Box 1094
Mufulira, Zambia
Tel. 4114421/412618

Eagle Travel and Tours
Broadway/Buteko Avenue
PO Box 76050
Ndola, Zambia
Tel. 3395/4602
Telex: ZA 34621

Embassy Travel Agency
PO Box 30986
Lusaka, Zambia
Tel. 211622

Island Safaris
PO Box 35943
Lusaka, Zambia
Tel. 218162/214955
Telex: ZA 44740

Jasat Travel Agency
PO Box 40
Chipata, Zambia
Tel. 21471

Jasat Travel Agency
PO Box 40
Kasama, Zambia
Tel. 21471
Telex: 6322

Kafue Boat Tours
PO Box 30813
Kafue, Zambia
Tel. 214926

Kafue Marina
PO Box 30813
Kafue, Zambia
Tel. 214926

Kapani Safari Lodge
C/O Norman Corr's Safaris
PO Box 100
Mfuwe, South Luangwa,
Zambia
Telex: ZA 40172 LUSAKA

Leopold Walford Travel
Independence Way
PO Box 80379
Kabwe, Zambia
Tel. 222336
Telex: ZA 81260

Leopold Walford Travel
Provident House
Obote Avenue
PO Box 20326
Kitwe, Zambia
Tel. 213255
Telex: ZA 52120

Leopold Walford Travel
Sapele Road
PO Box 34050
Lusaka, Zambia
Tel. 217217/216868
Telex: ZA

Luangwa Crocodile Safaris
PO Box 31701
Lusaka, Zambia
Tel. 253848
Telex: Baltic ZA 41330

Lubi Travel and Tours
PO Box 50657
Lusaka, Zambia
Tel. 215650

Lubungu Wildlife Safaris Ltd
PO Box 31701
Lusaka, Zambia
Tel. 253848
Telex: ZA 41530

Makora Quest
PO Box 60420
Livingstone, Zambia
Tel. 321679/321329/321320
(Res. 320401)
Telex: ZA 24230

Mercury Tours &
Travel Agency
Findeco House
Cairo Road
PO Box 32074
Lusaka, Zambia

Musungwa Safaris
PO Box 31808
Mearco, Zambia
Tel. 215493/21
Telex: MEARCOM ZA, 45530

Norman Corr Tours
C/O Eagle Travel Ltd
PO Box 341170
Lusaka, Zambia
Tel. 216465
Telex: ZA 45440

Omani Safaris
PO Box 31619
Lusaka, Zambia

Royal Travel and Tours
PO Box 71853
Ndola, Zambia
Tel. 4496/2336
Telex: ZA 33320

Savannah Trails
PO Box 30983
Lusaka, Zambia
Tel. 216848
Telex: ZA 45210

Shiwa Safaris
PO Box 80680
Kabwe, Zambia
Tel. 224665
Telex: ZA 81350

Sobek Expedition (Z) Ltd.
Zambia Limited
PO Box 60957
Livingstone, Zambia
Tel. 21432
Telex: ZA 24018

Southend Travel
Kent House
Mosi-Oa-Tunya Road
PO Box 60225
Livingstone, Zambia
Tel. 2536/2433

Stamul Tours Limited
PO Box 31541
Lusaka, Zambia
Tel. 217073

Steve Blagus
President Avenue
PO Box 71474
Ndola, Zambia
Tel. 3636/4504

Steve Blagus
Nkwazi Rd.
PO Box 31530
Lusaka, Zambia
Tel. 211498/218305
Telex: ZA 43320

Summit Safaris
PO Box 33419
Lusaka, Zambia
Tel. 216689/216318

Tan Tours
PO Box 36147
Lusaka, Zambia
Tel. 219120/1/2

T. G. Travel
(Head Office)
AFCOM House
PO Box 20104
Kitwe, Zambia
Tel. 215188
Telex: ZA 51390

T. G. Travel
Luangwa House
Cairo Road
PO Box 32591
Lusaka, Zambia
Tel. 211811
Telex: ZA

T. G. Travel
Gestetner House
Broadway
PO Box 71698
Ndola, Zambia
Tel. 4713
Telex: ZA 34721

Ticco Travel and Tours Ltd.
Kwacha Relax Hotel
PO Box 410707
Kasama, Zambia

Travel Care Ltd
Woodgate House
Nairobi Place
PO Box 31683
Lusaka, Zambia
Tel. 216544

Travel International
President House, Shop No. 1
PO Box 20290
Kitwe, Zambia
Telex: ZA 51480

Wilderness Trails
Lusaka, Zambia
Tel. 214008

Zam Travel & Tours
Luangwa House
PO Box 30056
Lusaka, Zambia
Tel: 212711/214369
Telex: ZA 45121

Zambezi Travel Bureau
Katendo Road
Lusaka Hotel Building
PO Box 31010
Lusaka, Zambia
Tel. 211627

APPENDIX II Some general reading on subjects covered in this Book:

CHAPTERS 1 & 2

The Bird Faunas of Africa and its Islands (1966), by R. E. Moreau, published by Academic Press, London.

African Islands (1989), by J. Kingdon, published by Collins, London.

CHAPTERS 5, 6, 7, & 8

The Encyclopedia of Mammals (1984), edited by Dr. David Macdonald, published by Facts On File, Inc., New York.

East African Mammals (Vol 1, 1971; Vol 2A & 2B, 1974; Vol 3A, 1977; Vol 3B, 1979; Vol 3C & 3D, 1982), by J. Kingdon, published by Academic Press, London.

A Field Guide to the Larger Mammals of Africa (1970), by J. Dorst and P. Dandelot, published by Collins, London.

The Mammals of Zambia (1978), by W. F. H. Ansell, published by the National Parks & Wildlife Service, Lusaka, Zambia.

CHAPTER 9

The Encyclopedia of Birds (1985), edited by Christopher M. Perrins and Dr. Alex L.A. Middleton, published by Facts On File, Inc., New York.

The Birds of Eastern and North Eastern Africa (Vol 1, 1957; Vol 2, 1960), by C. W. Mackworth-Praed & C. H. B. Grant, published by Longmans, Green & Co., London.

Birds of East Africa (1980), edited by P. L. Britton, published by the East African Natural History Society, Nairobi.

A Field Guide to the Birds of East & Central Africa (1963), by J. G. Williams, published by Collins, London.

The Birds of Zambia, by C. W. Benson, R. K. Brooke, R. J. Dowsett & M P. S. Irwin, published by Collins, London.

The Birds of British Somaliland & the Gulf of Aden (Vols 1 & 2, 1937; Vols 3 & 4, 1961), by G. Archer & E. M. Godman, Vols 1 & 2 published by Gurney & Jackson, London; Vols 3 & 4 published by Oliver & Boyd, Edinburgh.

The Birds of Africa (1982), Vol. 1, by L. H. Brown, E. K. Urban, & K. Newman, published by the Academic Press, London.

The Birds of Africa (1986), Vol. 2, by E. K. Urban, C. H. Fry, & S. Keith, published by the Academic Press, London.

CHAPTER 10

The Fishes of the Seychelles (1963), by J. L. B. & M. M. Smith, published by Rhodes University, Grahamstown.

Coral Fishes of the Indian and West Pacific Oceans (1977), by R. H. Carcasson, published by Collins, U.K.

CHAPTER 11

A Guide to the Snakes of Uganda (Revised Edition 1974), by C. R. S. Pitman, published by Wheldon & Wesley, U.K.

Poisonous Snakes of Eastern Africa (1985), by A. & J. MacKay, published by A. & J. MacKay, Nairobi.

CHAPTER 20

The African Safari: The Ultimate Wildlife and Photographic Adventure (1987), by P. Jay Fetner, published by St. Martin's Press, New York.

The SAS Survival Handbook (1986), by J. Wiseman, published by Collins, U.K.

The Wilderness Guardian (1984), by T. Corfield, published by Nairobi Space Publications, Kenya.

A Guide to Kenya and Northern Tanzania (1971), by David F. Horrobin, published by East African Publishing House, Nairobi, Kenya.

APPENDIX III National Park List

COUNTRY		PARK NAME	COUNTRY		PARK NAME
ETHIOPIA	1	Abijatta-Shalla Lakes	**RWANDA**	37	Akagera
	2	Awash		38	Volcanoes
	3	Bale Mountains	**SOMALIA**	39	Lag Badana (proposed)
	4	Gambella (proposed)			
	5	Mago	**TANZANIA**	40	Arusha
	6	Nechisar		41	Gombe
	7	Omo		42	Katavi
	8	Simien Mountain		43	Kilimanjaro
	9	Yangudi Rassa		44	Lake Manyara
				45	Mikumi
KENYA	10	Aberdares		46	Ruaha
	11	Amboseli		47	Rubondo
	12	Central Island (Lake		48	Selous Reserve
		Turkana)		49	Serengeti
	13	Chyulu		50	Tarangire
	14	Hell's Gate			
	15	Kisite/Mpunguti	**UGANDA**	51	Kidepo
		Marine		52	Lake Mburo
	16	Lake Nakuru		53	Murchison Falls
	17	Longonot		54	Queen Elizabeth
	18	Malindi Marine			
	19	Meru	**ZAMBIA**	55	Blue Lagoon
	20	Mombasa Marine		56	Isangano
	21	Mount Elgon		57	Kafue
	22	Mount Kenya		58	Kasanka
	23	Nairobi		59	Lavushi Manda
	24	Ndere Island (Lake		60	Liuwa Plains
		Victoria)		61	Lochinvar
	25	Ol Doinyo Sabuk		62	Lower Zambezi
	26	Ruma		63	Luambe
	27	Saiwa Swamp		64	Luangwa North
	28	Sibiloi		65	Luangwa South
	29	South Island (Lake		66	Lukusuzi
		Turkana)		67	Lusenga
	30	Tsavo East		68	Mosi-oa-Tunya
	31	Tsavo West		69	Mweru Wantipa
	32	Watamu Marine		70	Nsumbu
				71	Nyika
MALAWI	33	Kasungu		72	Sioma Ngwezi
	34	Lake Malawi		73	West Lunga
	35	Lengwe			
	36	Nyika			

APPENDIX IV Mammal List

PRIMATES		KILOS
1	Gorilla	275
2	Chimpanzee	80
3	Hamadryas	25
4	Gelada	25
5	Baboon	50
6	Mangabey, Black	11
7	Mangabey, Crested	10
8	Guenon, Red-tailed	6
9	Guenon, L'Hoest's	14
10	Guenon, Syke's	12
11	Guenon, Mona	6
12	Guenon, de Brazza's	8
13	Guenon, Vervet	9
14	Patas or Hussar Monkey	25
15	Colobus, Red	12
16	Colobus, Abyssinian	23
17	Colobus, Western	23
18	Potto	2
19	Galago, Greater	1
20	Galago, Lesser	0.3
21	Galago, Pigmy	0.1
22	Galago, Zanzibar	0.1
23	Galago, Needle-clawed	0.2

HYRAXES		
24	Hyrax, Rock	4
25	Hyrax, Yellow-spotted	2
26	Hyrax, Tree	3

PANGOLINS		KILOS
27	Pangolin, Giant	33
28	Pangolin, Ground	18
29	Pangolin, Tree	3

AARDVARK		
30	Aardvark	82

SIRENIANS		
31	Dugong	1,016

CARNIVORES		
32	Jackal, Golden or Common	15
33	Jackal, Side-striped	14
34	Jackal, Black-backed	14
35	Wild Dog	36
36	Fox, Bat-eared	5
37	Fox, Simien (jackal)	20
38	Fox, Ruppell's	3
39	Hyaena, Spotted	86
40	Hyaena, Striped	55
41	Aardwolf	14
42	Wild cat	7
43	Serval	18
44	Caracal	19
45	Golden Cat	16
46	Leopard	90
47	Lion	238
49	Cheetah	65

HERBIVORES		KILOS	HERBIVORES		KILOS
50	Elephant	6,000	85	Duiker, Bay	24
51	Rhino, Black	1,362	86	Duiker, Black-fronted	18
52	Rhino, White	3,600	87	Duiker, Blue	89
53	Zebra, Common	322	88	Duiker, Nata	114
54	Zebra, Grevy's	450	89	Duiker, Grey	25
55	Wild Ass	250	90	Duiker, Harvey's	16
56	Bushpig	115	91	Duiker, Peter's	21
57	Giant Forest Hog	275	92	Duiker, Red-flanked	14
58	Wart Hog	143	93	Duiker, Ruwenzori	17
59	Hippo	3,200	94	Duiker, White-bellied	18
60	Chevrotain	12	95	Duiker, Yellow-backed	80
61	Giraffe	1,930	96	Reedbuck, Mountain	38
62	Okapi	250	97	Reedbuck, Bohor	55
63	Buffalo	850	98	Reedbuck, Southern	80
64	Sitatunga	125	99	Kob	121
65	Bushbuck	77	100	Puku	91
66	Kudu, Lesser	108	101	Waterbuck	300
67	Kudu, Greater	315	102	Lechwe, Red (& Black)	100
68	Nyala, Mountain	230	103	Lechwe, Nile	86
69	Nyala, Southern	127	104	Gazelle, Thomson's	29
70	Eland, Giant	907	105	Gazelle, Grant's	82
71	Eland, Common	942	106	Gazelle, Soemmering's	46
72	Bongo	405	107	Gazelle, Pelzeln's	20
73	Ibex, Walia	18	108	Gazelle, Speke's	20
74	Pigmy Antelope, Bate's	3	109	Gerenuk	52
75	Suni	9	110	Dibatag	32
76	Steinbok, Sharpe's	12	111	Impala	76
77	Steinbok, Common	16	112	Hartebeest, Hunter's	80
78	Oribi	21	113	Hartebeest, Common	204
79	Klipspringer	18	114	Topi & Tsessebe	155
80	Dik-dik, Salt's	4	115	Wildebeest	270
81	Dik-dik, Kirk's	7	116	Sable Antelope	263
82	Dik-dik, Guenther's	6	117	Roan Antelope	300
83	Duiker, Abbott's	60	118	Oryx	209
84	Duiker, Ader's	12			

INDEX

(Illustrations are indicated in bold.)

318

All pictures taken by **Mohamed Amin** and **Duncan Willetts** except the following:

Peter Davey: Pages: 66, 67, 75, 80, 82, 84 , 85, 294, 295, 296 and 298.

Dr Jesse C and **Mrs Sheila M Hillman**: Pages: 226, 227, 228, and 291.

Tor Allan: Page 184.

Karl Ammann: Page 86 (bottom)

M.R. Stanley Price: Page 251.